ANIMALS
I WANT
TO SEE

ANIMALS

I WANT

TO SEE

*A Memoir of Growing Up
in the Projects and Defying the Odds*

TOM SEEMAN

Post Hill
PRESS

A POST HILL PRESS BOOK
ISBN: 979-8-88845-356-8
ISBN (eBook): 979-8-88845-357-5

Animals I Want To See:
A Memoir of Growing Up in the Projects and Defying the Odds
© 2024 by Tom Seeman
All Rights Reserved

Cover design by Jim Villaflores

Post Hill Press
New York • Nashville
posthillpress.com

Published in the United States of America
2 3 4 5 6 7 8 9 10

A MOMENT

Toledo, Ohio

'm thirteen years old, and I could kill someone. I don't mean hypothetically. I mean there's a reasonable chance that I could cause someone to die. But this possibility doesn't occur to me as I heave pumpkins off a bridge and into traffic with my friends. The four of us call ourselves The Halfs, because two of us are Black and two of us are white. It's 1972, just past dusk, days after Halloween, and the jack-o'-lanterns we've swiped from strangers' yards now explode onto the highway, igniting a ruckus of swerving and honking while we reign above, practically vibrating from an eruption of chemicals—adrenaline, endorphins, testosterone—that are telling us a story: even kids from the projects can be powerful.

I don't realize then that the bridge we're standing on is a metaphor. On one side of it looms prison, despair, hunger of all sorts. On the other, freedom, pleasure, and the untold treasures that come from living a purposeful life. Which way will I go? Statistics say I will not choose wisely.

For now, I run home to Bronson Street.

ONE

We were moving to paradise. As a family of twelve packed into a tenement house built for a family half our size, we weren't used to space. We were used to tripping over feet, knocking elbows, hearing each other's quietest breaths and swallows. But now, that was all going to change.

Our favorite uncles, Uncle Dick and Harold, showed up to help with the move, and as the house emptied, we flung our arms wide and spun in the sudden space until we were too dizzy to walk a straight line. "Maybe we'll have this much room in the new place even with our furniture in it," said Ernie, who at eight was a year older than I. Susie was four years younger. "Maybe it'll be a castle," she said, leaping across the newly bare concrete floor. "I bet it'll have smooth walls," said Marji, the second-to-oldest of the ten of us. She didn't like our cinderblock walls, but I was going to miss running my finger along the smooth, painted mortar lines between the blocks each night as I fell asleep at the foot of the bed, inches from Ernie's and Daniel's feet.

We'd been imagining what our new house would be like since Mom had told us about it three days earlier. I knew it must be something special, because she was usually too busy cleaning and cooking and tending the babies and doing the laundry to stop and gather us together outside of dinnertime. Only a special day like Christmas or Easter brought Mom to a halt in the middle of the day. "I have something to tell everyone," she said after calling us into the living room, where Dad sat in his corner of the couch, engulfed in a cloud of cigar smoke. This was the place where he spent most of his time at home, holding a beer or a cigar in one hand and a worn paperback, usually with a cowboy on the cover, in the other. Mom was smiling as she looked around at each of us. "I've found us a new house, and it's got—"

"I thought someone told you about it," Dad interrupted. "So, technically, you didn't find it, did you?"

Mom's hands fell in slow motion to her sides. "Technically, yes, Harry, that's true," she said, matter-of-factly, which is how she said most things, good and bad. "But I did apply for it." She turned back toward us kids. "Anyway, it's got four bedrooms upstairs and another bedroom downstairs, and we won't have anyone living on the other side of the wall like we do now. We'll have the whole house to ourselves!"

Several of my siblings and I broke into cheers and squeals at the news. I even started clapping, mostly because Mom seemed so happy. Meanwhile, Dad stubbed his cigar out in the ashtray as if he were angry at it. "Oh yes," he said, having to shout over us to be heard. "It'll be a real paradise!"

"What's paradise?" I asked Mary Jo, our eldest sibling.

"It's kind of like Heaven," she said, "but with palm trees."

"Uncle Dick and Harold"—that's how we referred to them, as a unit, even though they were both Mom's brothers. Uncle Dick was a tall, slender, fine-featured man with a prominent widow's peak and a calm manner of speaking. His fingers were long and graceful, and his lips were so pigmented that he always appeared to be wearing raspberry lipstick. He and Uncle Harold owned an elevator parts company, which they operated out of a workshop in the woods behind the house they lived in with Grandma. They inherited the business from their father, but according to Mom, it never made much money. Mom had grown up in the spacious wood-frame house with Uncle Dick, Uncle Harold, and seven other siblings—ten in all. When my little brother Rich was born, I heard Grandma say that Mom now had the same number of kids as she did.

Even in his work-stained overalls, Uncle Dick reminded me of a sophisticated movie star, often smoking a briar pipe he filled with sweet tobacco. Though he made elevator parts during the day, his true passion was music, and at night he sometimes played saxophone in a twelve-man band. I once watched him play at a relative's wedding, and the only thing I remember from that day was Uncle Dick's face during his solo—rapt and happy. It was the first time I'd ever seen a person transform into someone else.

Uncle Harold, on the other hand, had only one version of himself. He always seemed to be happy, even doing the simplest things, like spending hours following behind us on the tricycle he and Uncle Dick found at a junkyard and refurbished for us, or playing silly games to make us giggle, like tapping the backs of our knees with the sides of his hands until our legs buckled. He had a booming laugh that erupted easily from a cavernous mouth of crooked, cigar-stained teeth and a big hump at the top of his back that pushed his head forward. A kid in the neighborhood once called him a monster, but Mom said that Uncle Harold was the one who needed protection because he was too kind for his own good. I wondered if that was why Uncle Dick looked after him and had never started a family of his own.

Uncle Dick lined up the seven of us who were old enough to help, from oldest to youngest—Mary Jo, Marji, Beth, Ernie, me, Dan, and Susie, who, at almost four, wanted to be doing whatever the rest of us were doing—and he showed us the proper way to lift a box. "It's all about bending at the knees and not at the waist," he explained. "You want to keep your spine straight and let your legs do the work." He demonstrated by holding his arms out and sinking into a squat. "Your turn," he said, looking at us.

The seven of us descended into enthusiastic knee-bends, each of us trying to outdo the other, some going for speed, others for depth of the bend. "Yes," he said, as we popped up and down with invisible boxes in our outstretched arms. "You've got the hang of it!" We became a conveyer belt of squatting box-movers, a job I took seriously.

"Hercules!" Uncle Harold bellowed at me, giving me a wink as he and Uncle Dick lifted our large gray sofa onto the truck. I flexed my seven-year-old biceps back at him, setting off a new boom of laughter.

The house was almost empty when I found Mom cleaning the kitchen floor with a wet rag that she was swiping back and forth under her shoe like a windshield wiper. Both of Mom's arms were occupied by the twins—Jane and Judy—who were latched onto her hips like koala bears. For days, she'd been furiously scrubbing the back wall, trying to rid it of the black mold that grew on it. "I've been so worried the woman at the Housing Authority might change her mind about letting us have the new house on account of the mold," Mom told Grandma. "She said they don't want dirty people moving into the bigger houses." She gave the rag an exaggerated sweep with her foot.

In one arm, Grandma cradled my newborn brother Rich, who was tucked like a football against her chest, while she wiped down shelves with the other. Mom and Grandma could have probably swung on a trapeze while clutching multiple babies. "I bet you have the cleanest house in this neighborhood," Grandma said.

A quiet woman who wore oversized shift dresses and kept her hair wound into two tight coils, one on each side of her head, Grandma often came over to help Mom, the two of them regularly sitting together at the kitchen table, their voices rising and falling, their paring knives going round and round, peeling paper-thin apple skins into single spirals that rose into two hills between them. I liked picking the longest strips from the heap and holding them over my head as I chomped them down.

The sofa was one of the last things Uncle Dick and Harold carried onto the truck, and when it was gone, Dad ambled by, mumbling that he had nowhere to sit. I went back outside and sized up the craggy pile of our stuff towering in the sun. Somehow, it was only then that it really sunk in: *We're leaving this place.* Even though some people called Ravine Park Village "the ghetto" as if it were a curse word, I knew I'd miss etching snowmen onto the frost that sugared the insides of our windows in the winter and splashing in the rainwater that collected in the slabs of sunken-in concrete outside our house in the summer. The older kids in the neighborhood had a different use for the concrete slabs: after the sun went down, they threw their empty beer bottles onto them and cheered each time one shattered.

Mom had spent many mornings sweeping the glass up, buoyant as a person watering a flower garden. "I guess they've got nothing better to do," she once remarked as she loaded her dustpan with shards. She was always like that—unflappable, a seemingly endless well of calm. Even when I jumped into one of the rain puddles and cut my foot to the bone on the bottom edge of one of those bottles, she placidly poured soapy water onto my foot and then sopped up the blood while I peered into the gash. We didn't have the money to go to doctors for things like stitches, so one of Mom's many talents was administering first aid. "You'll be all right," she said, attempting to rejoin the two sides of the wound over the white part I knew I shouldn't be seeing inside my foot. She wrapped my foot with one of the old scraps of clothing she kept in a box and secured it in place with pieces of string from another box. She had boxes for lots of things other people threw away.

I wouldn't miss the broken glass, I decided, or Bobo Bennett, who was two years older than I was and liked reminding me that he was bigger and stronger. My most recent run-in with him had happened at the playground. Mom had just surprised us with a rare treat—popsicles from the "seconds" store, a place that stocked things that regular stores wouldn't sell, like dented cans, ripped bags of flour and sugar, and all manner of expired food—and I'd carried mine down to the playground so that I could enjoy it on the swing. I had just taken my first lick when Bobo appeared. With every other step, he whacked a stick onto the ground, until he came to a stop two feet in front of me. "Watchu lookin' at?" he asked. He always asked that, and I knew there was no good answer. I looked down and told him I was looking at my popsicle.

With his stick, he whacked the popsicle out of my hand and ground it into the dirt with his foot. "Keep on looking then," he said, turning around. While he strutted off to the beat of his stick, I cried on the swing. "One day I'm going to become the heavyweight champion of the world like Muhammad Ali," I whispered. "Then I can always protect my popsicles." I wiped at my eyes with my fists and swung on the swing a few last times before I would never see it again. "Or else the richest man in the world," I added, a little louder now. "Then I can buy all the popsicles in Ohio."

"The question is whether we can get everyone over to the new house in one trip." Uncle Dick's voice pulled me from my thoughts, and I turned to find him standing behind me with Uncle Harold at his side.

Uncle Harold smiled. "If we let some of the kids ride in the back of the truck, I think we can do it."

"I call first!" I practically shouted, not wanting to miss an opportunity to do something I'd never done before. Calling dibs was how matters were often decided in our family; it was the only peaceful way we'd found to designate who got what. If, for instance, one of us happened to spot the rare bag of M&M's that Mom brought home from a shopping trip, the claiming started. "I call first!" one of us would exclaim, followed by "I call second," "I call third," and so on. Then one of us—though it couldn't be the one who called first—would sort the M&M's into tiny piles, taking care to make sure they were as even as possible. This was an important job, and it was customary for everyone else to hover and inspect the pile-maker's groupings.

Though I was the fifth child, I always wanted to be first, and on moving day I got my wish. I climbed up into the back of the truck and wedged myself into the back right corner, and Ernie and Marji climbed up behind me. Ernie chose the opposite corner, and Marji knelt down in between us. Uncle Dick started the truck, and the rumble of the engine heralded our farewell to Ravine Park Village.

As we turned the corner and picked up speed, I imagined I was on one of those county fair rides we occasionally drove past. Ernie looked at me and smiled, but none of us spoke, perhaps out of that child-wisdom that knows sometimes words can bog things down. When we merged onto the highway and the air came at us as if from a hose turned on high, I closed my eyes and pretended I was at the helm of a ship and the ruffling sounds of the wind were the sails. I tilted my head back and breathed in the wind, and in those miles, anything seemed possible—even paradise.

I wanted the ride to go on forever, or at least for longer than the fifteen minutes it took to get from East Toledo to North Toledo. "This doesn't look that different from the old neighborhood," observed Marji when we pulled onto D Street, which was crumbling and pocked with potholes that bounced us up and down in the back of the truck. Older kids leered from the corners as if, as Mom would say, they had nothing better to do, and bits of trash scurried out from under our truck as if they were alive. When we turned onto our street—Bronson Street—I noticed that it was paved with concrete and was smoother and tidier than the others, with rounded concrete curbs on each side. A group of kids playing catch parted to let us pass, then resumed their positions in the road. Many of the houses on the street looked alike: boxy two-stories with brick below and white or yellow aluminum siding on the second floor.

"This must be it," said Marji, after Uncle Dick parked the truck in front of one of those houses.

"It has trees," I pointed out, sizing up the full, rounded branches and mottled bark of a tree in front of the house, which Grandma would later call a London plane, the spindly branches of another, "and a slanted roof." This seemed like a notable distinction, given the flat roofs of our previous neighborhood.

"Maybe this roof won't leak like the old one," said Ernie.

We climbed out of the truck, and everyone gathered at the door. Though Dad had been uninvolved in the harried three-day preparations to get us here, including Mom's many trips on foot to local stores to carry home stacks of empty brown boxes, he made a show of pulling the key out of his front pocket and dangling it in the air while we huddled around him. "Open it!" urged Dan. "Yeah, Dad, open it!" Susie echoed.

Dad opened the door and stepped inside, and we all followed in behind him. Immediately I felt something crunch under my shoe. The shades were pulled down, so someone turned on a light, and scores of roaches skittered in every direction—so many that you couldn't take a step without squashing one. Though we were no strangers to roaches, we'd never seen so many at one time. "It's okay," said Mom, handing the baby to Uncle Dick and walking into the kitchen, which was so infested that it appeared to be breathing. "We'll get this place cleaned right up. And look," she added, pointing next to the sink in the kitchen, "it has counters!"

"I knew they'd be smooth!" exclaimed Marji, darting across the room to plant a kiss on one of the walls.

The sound of the roaches crunching under Marji's feet must have struck Uncle Harold as funny because he broke into a roll of laughter. "Like potato chips," he said, hopping from one foot to the other to squash some anew. And while Uncle Harold launched into a roach-smacking tap dance in the middle of our new living room, I gave myself a challenge to not step on any. Though I wanted to run with abandon through our new house like my siblings, I treaded over the scattering roaches as if the floor were a hopscotch grid. Meanwhile, the older sisters had already darted upstairs to claim their bedroom. Soon everyone but Mom and Grandma was upstairs, milling from room to room. "The bathroom has a big tub!" one of the girls exclaimed. "But no shower like before," said another. "And the doors are made of wood!" I announced from the hallway, noticing how they made a pleasing hollow sound when I knocked on them.

Dad stood in the doorway of the room closest to the bathroom. "This'll be our room," he said to Uncle Dick, "and the bed can go right there on that wall." Dad pointed at the middle of the room without moving to let Uncle Dick step inside.

"Sounds good, Chief," said Uncle Dick, giving him a nod. I rarely saw them speak to each other, but whenever they did, Uncle Dick agreed with whatever Dad said.

"Can you believe we're going to have our own room now?" Ernie asked me. At seven, I had never slept in a big bed, but now Ernie and I would be sleeping downstairs all by ourselves in a double bed donated to us by one of Mom's sisters. "It's truly unbelievable," I said in what I thought was a grown-up voice, all the while checking the floor every time I took a step.

"Why don't you kids go outside and play," Mom called to us, "and let us sweep up these roaches and get the furniture in the house."

Mary Jo, Marji, and Beth stayed behind to help with the boxes and the babies, while Ernie, Dan, and I went out the back door. "Wait up!" called Susie, rushing out behind us onto the single concrete step, which was the only adornment in our overgrown yard. It was easy to tell where our yard ended because the grasses and weeds in the field behind our house were even taller than the ones in our yard, and four bent and rusty trashcans marked the boundary, standing in a row beneath the sole tree in our backyard—a crabapple—and linked together by a chain that ran through the handles of the cans and lids so no one could steal them, just like at our old house.

A lone oak tree stood wide-armed in the middle of the field, and we started into the deeper brush toward it. Some of the weeds were taller than Susie, but she didn't seem to mind. "Flowers!" she exclaimed, jumping like a bunny toward a patch of clover. But when she landed, something squealed at her feet. We all froze, and a rat scampered through the underbrush, away from us. "That's a big mouse," she said.

"Yeah," Ernie and I agreed, giving each other a knowing look. "A very big mouse."

We had to be careful about where we stepped, not only because of the rats but also because of the saw briars and stinging nettles and discarded beer bottles that lay hidden in the bindweed. But the gnarly field was not without its wild beauty. Butterflies landed on Queen Anne's lace, and purple burrs sprung up in clusters. Grasshoppers leapt into the air as if they were performing circus acts. Every few steps, we found something new—a car tire with roly-polies beneath it, a piece of decaying plywood sheltering slugs and spiders, a heap of bricks, a broken mirror, two hubcaps, and an empty glass bottle with a picture of a turkey on the label—so that by the time Mom called us, we hadn't even made it to the oak tree. *I'll be back here tomorrow*, I thought, wondering, as we pulled off all the burrs that stuck to our clothes, what other treasures were waiting to be discovered.

It seemed like we'd been gone only a short time, but when we came back inside, our furniture was already in place, and the remaining roaches had gone into hiding. Mom surprised us by pulling an enormous watermelon from the fridge. "I call first!" Ernie announced, followed by the rapid-fire calls of the rest of us. Then we all looked on, chirping to each other like frenetic birds about our new house's most exciting features—especially the red and white linoleum tiles that looked like a checkerboard and the closet under the stairs with a sloped ceiling—while Mom and Grandma cut the fruit into triangles and divvied them up onto fifteen plates. We kids selected first, according to our numbers, and the adults grabbed the last five plates. Then we said our first grace in the new house before digging in with gusto. "Bless us O Lord, and these Thy gifts...."

As we ate the triangles, not one of us stopped to wipe the crimson juice that dripped down our chins and in between our fingers. For a time, we spoke only in ravenous bites and slurps, and when we were finished, we cycled through our pieces again, eating the lighter pink parts, and then eventually the white rinds, until the table was strewn with striped green skin.

"That was the best watermelon I ever had," declared Uncle Harold, leaning back in his chair and patting his belly. Several of us agreed and patted our own bellies, while Dad got up from the table and left without saying a word.

"Paradise," he'd called our new house. And maybe he was right, because there was no other place I wanted to be than right there at our table on Bronson Street.

TWO

In our first week on Bronson Street, Mom somehow found the time—in between rolling hundreds of meatballs and baking trays upon trays of cookies and chain-washing never-ending loads of laundry and hanging it all in the backyard to dry and darning what needed to be darned and changing the diapers that needed to be changed and doing the grocery shopping, which entailed walking many blocks to the grocery store and back in the heat and periodically having to stop and rest the heavy brown-paper bags on a fire hydrant (while I forced myself to hold mine without any rest, in preparation for my future heavyweight boxing career)—to unpack our boxes and hang the three pieces of art we owned: an oil painting of the cabin Abraham Lincoln grew up in, a pastel of a pair of ducks lifting off from a marsh, and a pastel of a sunrise over a pond. Mom had painted them in high school, and when I asked her why she didn't paint anymore, she said, "I don't have the time. Now I put my art into sewing and baking." I thought of how my siblings and I devoured the dozens of her delicate black-and-white pinwheel cookies as soon as they came out of the oven, and I felt glad she'd once done a different kind of art that could last.

Summer unfurled in our new neighborhood, and my siblings and I spent our days treasure-hunting in the field behind our house. We captured bumble bees in old jars. We flipped over every piece of plywood, every tire, every brick, and anything else we could find that had been dumped into the field's deep reaches. Each time was no less exciting than the last because we never knew what might present itself. On one bright day, Ernie, Dan, and I came across a garter snake with a huge lump in it, but it didn't whip away from us like all the others. Ernie and I reached for it at the same time, and it darted toward us, ready to strike. "Maybe it's pregnant," I said.

"And it's protecting its babies," Ernie added.

"It's not pregnant, dimwit," a voice said from behind us. We turned to find two older boys, one with long blond hair and the other with a short butch haircut, both wearing frayed cut-off shorts. The younger of the two was a paler and more fidgety version of the older one. "Probably just ate a rat. Swallowed it whole."

"That's how they eat you know," the younger one said, leaning in to get a closer look.

"I know," Dan said, puffing his chest out like a robin.

"Sure you do," said the older one. "Just like you knew we were behind you."

Ernie folded his arms across his chest. "At least we don't go creeping up on people."

"We're practicing to be spies," the younger boy informed us, hopping from one foot to the other for no apparent reason. He looked toward our house. "We saw you moving in. How many of you live in that house anyway?"

"Twelve," I said. After my first-grade teacher once asked me to name everyone in my family, I made it a point be able to name them from oldest to youngest in a single breath: "DadMomMaryJoMargeBethErnTomDanSusieJaneJudyRich." I wondered how long the name-string would become, since it seemed like Mom was always pregnant with another baby.

"Someone's gettin' busy over there," said the older one. The two of them laughed, and I thought about how Mom was probably doing something busy right that very moment. The boys turned and left the field then, guffawing and joke-punching each other's arms in a very un-spy-like way. Their names were Fred and Jim Peal, and they lived next door.

That day I scooped up another garter snake, this one almost as long as my arm, and we brought it home. Mom was holding a measuring cup in her hand, and when she saw the snake, she jumped and sent a puff of flour into the air. "What are you going to do with that?" she asked.

"It's a snake," Dan proudly informed her.

"I can see that," she said. "But why is it in our house?"

I gently stroked the top of the snake's head so that she could see how docile it was. "We want to keep him," I said.

"No," she said, shaking her head for emphasis.

"Please, Mom?" I urged. "We'll only keep it for a little while, and I promise not to let it loose in the house. Look how cute he is with his little flicky tongue."

Mom put her hand on her hip and regarded us, and I took her faint smile as a sign she was about to relent. "Well, you'll need to find something to keep him in," she said, dumping the flour into a bowl. "And make sure you give him some water to drink and some—"

But we'd already run back outside to collect things we thought he might like—leaves, grass, a couple of beetles. I let Ern and Dan scavenge while I let the snake drape over my hands and slip, cool and slick, between my fingers. "His name is Stripey," I announced. And once we had Stripey in his new home—a cardboard box left over from our move—we watched him not eat anything and not drink from the small bowl of water until Ern and Dan got bored and left.

I pulled him back out and looked at him, face-to-face. His forked tongue flicked in the air, bright red with a black tip, and I wondered what it would feel like against my nose. "Hi, Stripey," I said, leaning close. But instead of touching my nose with his tongue, he bit it. "Ouch," I said, quickly putting Stripey back inside his box and folding the four flaps of his ceiling. His small, sharp teeth left little cuts in my nose, but my feeling of betrayal was the real hurt.

In the living room, Dad was seated in his usual corner of the sofa, polishing off a beer. I always knew when he was home from his job—dispatching taxis across Toledo—because his musty scent traveled quickly through our small house. "Hey, Tom," he said, which surprised me because he rarely spoke to any of us. "Want my drops?"

He was referring to the dregs of beer left in the bottom of his bottle, an offering he occasionally made when he was in particularly good cheer. I always accepted his gift, even though the taste was foreign and bitter. "Thanks, Dad," I said, gulping them down and fighting off a shudder.

"Why's your nose all red?" He squinted his droopy eyes at me.

"I...um...bumped it."

"On what?"

I wanted to lie, but I worried that Mother Mary or my Guardian Angel might be watching, and I didn't want to get in trouble with God. "A snake."

"You kids sure are strange," he said, picking up his latest paperback Western and receding behind another cowboy.

The next day, Dad came home with some animals of his own—a large container packed with live crayfish, which he dumped into our bathtub. "I got them free at work," he told us, filling the tub with water. "Mom can make us a crayfish stew!"

"That's lovely, Harry," said Mom, as several of us stood over the tub and watched creatures that looked nothing like fish scuttle through the water on spindly legs. They seemed hungry, reaching forward at nothing and everything with their large pincers.

"They stink," Marji observed.

"Ew," said Susie. "They look like giant bugs."

Fascinated, I plunged my hand into the water to pick one up, but it darted backwards before I could catch it. I tried again, and this time one latched on. I yanked my hand away, but the crayfish came with me, dangling from my finger. "Ow!" I cried, while everyone else laughed. But as soon as I liberated my finger, I tried again. Ernie and Dan started fishing their hands through the water, too, and soon the bathtub was a storm of clutching fingers and scurrying shellfish.

Eventually we realized that if we picked them up right behind their heads, they couldn't pinch or bite while we stroked their backs. "He likes it," I said, noticing how the one I was holding seemed to relax and curl its tail as I rubbed my fingertip from his head to his tail.

"Mom," said Ernie, petting his crayfish between the eyes. "Can we keep them in the tub as pets?"

"Yeah, Dad," I said. "We can't eat them! They trust us now."

Dad scowled. "Fine," he said. "You can have them for tonight, but we're cooking them tomorrow."

When tomorrow came, Dad went to a bar after work, Mom made meatloaf, the crayfish spent another night in our bathtub, and I started a list titled Wild Animals I Have Seen, to which I added rats, garter snakes, milk snakes, and crayfish.

We didn't know what to feed the crayfish, so we gathered some beetles, ants, and grasshoppers from the field. But the crayfish weren't interested in insects and instead began eating each other. Ernie, Dan, and I became the tub referees, pulling the combatants apart whenever one started in on another. For several days no one bathed, the crayfish kept dying, and Dad, who by now had given up on eating them, sat in his corner with his beer, book, and cigar, while our house took on a stench so strong you could smell it from downstairs. Then Mom said she was putting her foot down, and the crayfish disappeared.

They weren't the only things to disappear. Stripey, whom I'd last seen curled up in the corner of his box, had let himself out of his enclosure and was loose somewhere in our house. I tried to be nonchalant as I peered under the sofa, rummaged through the closet under the steps, searched every corner, and when I heard Mom scream, I knew who had found him. I ran into the kitchen just in time to see her sweeping him out the back door. I ran out after him, but just like that, all our pets were gone.

THREE

The Sunday services at the stucco church on the corner across the street from our house ran later than the services at our church, St. Vincent de Paul, and on one Sunday, I sat outside on our front step and listened to the gospel singers' rendition of "People Get Ready" pour from the church with such power that it was hard to believe there were walls around it. The singing sounded as if it were rising up from the roots of the earth, so unlike the hymns we sang at our church, where most people didn't even sing.

That evening while Mom was feeding Rich a bottle, I asked her if we could go to that church instead of ours.

She looked up, surprised. "Why would you want to do that?"

"They have good music, and most people don't even sing at our church."

"I think we sing lovely hymns in church."

"Still, can we?"

Mom adjusted Rich's bottle. "No."

"Why not?"

"Because we're Catholic."

"What are they?"

"Protestant, I think."

"What's the difference?" I asked, sitting down beside her. Rich was squirming, kicking his chubby legs.

"They still believe in Jesus, but they don't believe in all the details we believe in."

"What kind of details?"

Mom looked toward the window in the direction of the church. "Well, they have a different service. And they don't believe in the pope." Rich started making tiny lip-smacking sounds, and Mom adjusted his bottle again with a sigh. Whenever she sighed like that, I knew I'd asked too many questions and the conversation was over.

When Mom informed us that she'd gotten Mary Jo, Marji, Beth, Ernie, me, and Daniel into the private school at our church for free, she explained that instead of paying the tuition with money, some of us would have to work at the school. "A small price to pay," she told us, "for a good education."

St. Vincent's was located in a Polish neighborhood only three quarters of a mile from our house, but it felt much farther. When my new teacher, Sister Mary, a tall and severe nun who seemed to be incapable of smiling, told us to hold the hand of the boy next to us as we walked to the church next door for what would be our daily mass, I reached for the hand of the kid standing beside me, a pale-haired boy named Paul, but he looked me up and down and moved his hand away. Though my feelings were hurt, I wasn't about to let him stop me from obeying Sister Mary's instructions, and I also really wanted to make a friend, so I grabbed his hand anyway. At first, his hand went rigid, but eventually he returned my grip, and I felt as happy as if I'd won a game of checkers.

Once we were inside the church, we all filed into the same pews we sat in with our families on Sundays, and Father Schmelzer—a rotund man with a ring of white hair encircling his otherwise bald head—entered from behind and walked down the aisle toward the altar while the organ began to play and we began to sing: "O God, our help in ages past, our hope for years to come. Our shelter from the stormy blast, and our eternal home."

On our first days of school, the six of us set off on the path, which we cleverly called "The Path." It cut through the field behind our house and ended on D Street, right next to a little cinderblock corner store that sold mostly candy, booze, cigarettes, and magazines. We walked to school and back home together, but after a few days, Mary Jo, Marji, and Beth lagged way behind while Ern, Dan, and I powered ahead. We were walking down Brigham Street, getting close to home, when a group of four older kids, slick with fury, stepped in front of us and blocked our way. We tried to go around them, but they matched our steps in whichever direction we moved until finally we stopped. "Where do you think you're going?" one of them asked.

"Home," said Ernie, looking down.

"I think these honkies must be lost," said another.

"We live on Bronson Street," I said, taking a step forward.

"You think you're tough?" asked the tallest of the bunch. They must have been in fourth or fifth grade.

"I know I am," I said, not knowing.

The kid replied by thumping my chest with the flats of his hands and pushing me backwards onto the street.

"Hey!" said Ernie, "Leave him alone."

The boys cheered and slapped each other's hands. "Shit, you knocked his ass *down*, didn't you?" said one of them, laughing. The tall one faced me again as I stood back up. "You still think you're tough?"

My elbows burned where bits of gravel had bitten into my skin, but this time I didn't answer.

Even at the age of seven, I understood that tension and separation existed between Black people and white people. I'd noticed that the four white families in the projects lived clustered next to each other on our block, even if I didn't understand why. When I asked Mom about it, she simply shrugged and said, "I just took the house they gave us without asking any questions." But on the day we moved in, it was the Nobles, a Black family who lived in another project house across the street, who knocked on our door and welcomed us to the neighborhood.

The day after our confrontation in the street, my brothers and I took a different way home from school by avoiding Brigham Street and cutting through a parallel alley that ran behind the houses. We quickly named it "Dog Alley." At first, I wasn't convinced we'd made a good decision, since I was sure we would be attacked by one of the many barking, lunging, teeth-baring dogs who were caged or chained up along the way. But the three of us huddled close together as we scurried down the center of the alley and made it safely to the end. At the last house on the alley, I noticed a smaller dog, white with brown spots, attached to a chain that was bolted into the ground. He was snarling at me, but he also had floppy ears and a liver-colored nose, which made him seem a little less ferocious. "Are you tough?" I asked him, and for a moment he stopped barking and looked at me with his head cocked to one side, as if no one had ever asked him a question before. The fur around his collar was rubbed off, leaving a necklace of raw, pink skin. Feeling sorry for him, I edged a little closer until Dan said, "Don't." So I got back in step with my brothers and walked the rest of the way home.

The one place I didn't expect to be physically harmed was in my classroom at school. But when I made the mistake of talking to Paul in the next seat over, Sister Mary looked directly at me. "Why are you talking in class?"

"I'm sorry, Sister Mary," I said.

"Come up to the front of the class right now," she said.

As I came timidly to the front of the room, I wondered if she would make me sit still in a chair like Mom sometimes did when we misbehaved. Instead, she pulled a ruler off her desk. "Hold your hands out next to each other, palms up. And don't you dare move them."

I did what I was told, and she whacked my palms with the ruler five times. I could feel the tears welling up in my eyes, but I knew my entire class was watching, including my new friend Paul, so I swallowed them back and returned to my seat.

When I came home that day, I announced to Mom that I wanted to move back to Ravine Park. She was standing at the kitchen table folding laundry, and she looked at me with wide-eyed surprise. "But why?" she asked. "This house is bigger."

"Because my teacher is mean and the kids in the neighborhood are mean and the dogs are mean." I looked down at my bright red palms and started to cry.

"You just need time to adjust," she said. "You'll be fine."

One Saturday morning, Uncle Dick and Harold unexpectedly arrived to announce that they were taking us to a special place. Mary Jo, Marji, Beth, Ernie, Dan, Susie, and I piled into the two cars, and we drove for a long time. As the city gave way to grassier neighborhoods and then to sprawling fields, we speculated out loud about where we might be going. To a farm? To the beach on

Lake Erie that Uncle Harold was always talking about? Uncle Dick laughed and refused to spoil the surprise. He turned onto a narrow two-lane road shaded by huge trees and then onto an even smaller road. Dappled sunlight fell on the car windows, while squirrels scampered in every direction. I peered into the spaces between tree trunks, searching for wild animals I could add to my list. Several times I thought I caught a glimpse of one—the tail of a bobcat, the paw of a bear, the quick blur of a reindeer's antlers. Compared to the field behind our house, which now seemed small, this place felt like true wilderness.

I had never seen so many trees in one place before, and I liked the feeling of being cocooned by them. After passing a wooden sign that read Pearson Park, Uncle Dick parked, and Uncle Harold pulled in right beside us. As we got out of the cars in a rush of excitement, I noticed that pine needles carpeted the parking lot pavement and made it feel soft underfoot. "I love this place," I decided on the spot. Uncle Dick pulled a tied plastic bag from his trunk, and we set off on a path through the woods. Eventually, we arrived at a pond filled with ducks that, upon the sight of us, came marching out of the water directly toward us. Making a mental note to add ducks to my list of wild animals, I wondered how it was that these wild creatures could be so bold and unafraid. As Uncle Dick started untying the plastic bag, the ducks came faster, as if they knew something I didn't. "It's a swarm of them!" I said, which made Uncle Dick start laughing, which made Uncle Harold start laughing, and soon all of us were laughing in the fractured sunshine.

Uncle Dick reached into the bag and took out a handful of bits of old bread, placing some in each of our hands. The ducks broke into a frenzy, quacking as if they were calling "first" and "second," just like we did when we got treats from Mom. Then the most amazing thing happened: one brazen, orange beak was suddenly nibbling from my palm. "Look, Uncle Dick," I exclaimed, "he's eating out of my hand!" I watched in awe as the duck took every crumb and then waddled off on his orange webbed feet looking for more, his white feathers aglow in the sun.

"Ouch," said Daniel when one duck became a bit too aggressive. "They're scary!"

Uncle Dick rushed over to shoo the ducks away from Daniel and Susie. "They must be very hungry," said Uncle Harold with his usual toothy laugh.

Everything about Pearson Park felt mysterious and new to me—the paths that seemed to wind forever through the woods, the sweet and resinous scent of pine, the patches of blue sky between canopies of branches, the boulders big enough to climb on, the small stones that felt cool in my hands, and the joy of having Uncle Dick and Harold there, making life feel safe and wondrous. I selected a smooth stone from the three I'd been holding in my hand and put it in my pocket so that I could bring that magic home.

FOUR

My list of Wild Animals I Have Seen now included a yellow-spotted salamander, a bullfrog, and a groundhog. And if I'd had a list of friends, I would have added two new ones to it—Jeffrey Huxley and Eddie Gonzalez. They also went to St. Vincent's school, which was north of our house, and because Jeffrey lived on St. John Street, which was one street south of Bronson Street, and Eddie lived on Paxton, which was one street south of that, we started walking home from school together. The three of us took to calling the neighborhood around St. Vincent's—where most of the other kids in my class lived—the White House, because only white people lived there.

Jeffrey was smart, funny, and a little bit pudgy, and he wore a short afro on what Eddie called "a kidney-bean-shaped head." Eddie was a year older than we were because he'd repeated a grade. He had an athletic body and spiky black hair that was coarser than my blond hair, which was cut short in a "butch," as my mother called it.

After another neighborhood run-in that landed me in the same position as the first—on the ground—I was grateful to have my new friends to walk home with as we teased each other and tried out curse words and kicked rocks and cans. Eventually the bullies began to recognize me as someone who lived in their neighborhood, and they mostly left me alone. Somehow, being from the neighborhood got you a pass. But we still avoided that section of Brigham Street because we preferred to take Dog Alley. There was something exhilarating about the barking dogs lunging and baring their teeth at us that gave us an air of toughness, as if we were walking home not down an alleyway but through a dangerous wilderness where a starving predator could attack at any moment.

I was still intrigued by the beagle-like dog that lived on a chain at the end of Dog Alley closest to our house. I'd taken to calling him My Dog and had slowly inched my way into his good graces. Both Jeffrey and Eddie, however, refused to get within petting distance. "Good luck playing basketball when you have no hands," said Jeffrey. "Or peeing!" added Eddie, while I showed off my heightened skills of animal communication and courage.

"Hey there, My Dog," I said, slowly extending my open palm and letting him sniff it before I dared to give him a quick scratch under his chin. I spoke in a soothing voice and was careful to avoid the part of his neck that his collar had rubbed raw.

"You're crazy, Seeman," they chanted in unison.

While I enjoyed my fleeting moments of seven-year-old bravado, I also visited My Dog when I was alone, and soon he began to perk up his ears and wag his tail when he saw me coming. I'd never seen anyone else interact with him, and it made me feel special to earn his trust, though I was also sad to see him living such a small radius of an existence. "I found a praying mantis," I told him. "Jeffrey, Eddie, and I raced halfway home from school today, and I won." "I'm going to be a hobo for Halloween." I talked to him a lot, as if I could broaden his world by sharing my adventures with him.

As a family who separated a single bag of M&M's into tiny, carefully arranged piles, we counted the days until Halloween, and when it came, Mary Jo, Marji, Beth, Ern, Dan, and I headed out into the crisp darkness with our temporary identities and the pillowcases we'd exuberantly yanked off our pillows. Ern, Dan, and I all wanted to be hobos, so Mom burned a cork on the stovetop and rubbed the black ashes onto our chins to produce our stubble. For Marji's bunny costume, Mom used the furry lining of an old coat from her pile of saved fabrics to make fuzzy ears and a small round tail, and she curled Beth's hair with big pink rollers and fashioned a large, swirled lollipop out of cardboard that she colored with crayons in an attempt to transform her into Shirley Temple. Beth, who always liked to look cute, kept bouncing her curls with the flats of her hands.

As we headed out toward the White House, which the kids at school said was where everyone trick-or-treated, Bronson Street was unusually dark and quieter than normal, with nary a jack-o'-lantern or other kid in sight. "We'll trick-or-treat on our block when we get home," Mary Jo said. D Street and Brigham Street were equally deserted, but as we crossed Ketchum, the streets came alive with clusters of monsters and heroes, bunnies and cats, angels and devils, hobos, witches, mummies, and hordes of unidentifiable kids behind store-bought plastic masks. I searched the throngs of children to see if I might recognize any of my classmates in their costumes, but I saw no one familiar.

I was noticing the shapes of things—the bent angles of skeletons, the triangles carved into jack-o'-lanterns and jutting up on pointy witch hats, the blobs of white-sheeted ghosts, the rounded corners on the bandits' masks, and the sphere of the moon, whose golden face appeared to be watching the festivities and following us as we walked.

"Let's go all night!" I said. At a house covered with enormous cobwebs, a ghoul popped out from behind a tree, and Marji jumped so high I thought the tips of her rabbit ears might touch the moon's edge. A scarecrow gave us each a Hershey's bar, and the pleasing weight of it dropping into my pillowcase was one of the night's highlights.

Eventually people started turning their porch lights off, and the streets began to clear. I stifled a yawn or two, and our bags were plenty heavy so we turned back toward home. The moon seemed farther away by then, higher in the sky and more silver than gold. We talked about some of our most prized scores along with the things we knew Mom wouldn't let us eat, like apples because they could have razorblades hidden inside them, or anything unwrapped because it could be poisoned. There was something thrilling in the thought of my lumpy pillowcase housing both delight and danger.

By the time we crossed Ketchum Street and got back into our neighborhood on Brigham Street, we'd quieted into our own private reveries about the night. But even in the quiet, I didn't hear them coming up behind us. It was Mary Jo who whispered, "Let's all huddle together now and hurry home." Only then did I peek over my shoulder and see them. They had no shape. They were four older boys dressed in black and trailing us. We quickened our pace, and they quickened theirs. The six of us drew into an even tighter bud and hustled forward just shy of running. But then the boys weren't quiet. They were footsteps pounding the ground. They rushed at us and knocked us down and ripped our pillowcases from our hands, then dispersed into the darkness without saying a word. I lay on the street crying. Dan and Beth were crying, too, and somehow seeing Beth cry in her Shirley Temple costume with her cardboard lollipop in her hand only made me cry harder.

"It's okay," said Marji, helping me up. "They didn't get my bag or Dan's. They didn't get it all."

When we got home, we told the story together, six voices climbing over each other at the really scary parts. Ern pointed at where they'd stepped on his hand to get his bag. Mom stopped doing dishes to come into the living room, and Dad glugged down the rest of a beer. I started to cry again just hearing everyone telling the story. Mom wiped her hands on her apron and said, "It's okay. You'll just divide up the candy you have left, and there will still be plenty for everyone."

"No, Ginny. It's not okay," Dad said, spitting a piece of cigar tobacco that was stuck on his tongue. "You're the one who had to move us here, to this shithole, with all these darkies."

Though my siblings and I didn't talk about our fear of our father, I could see on their faces that they were scared. In my mind, I was telling him how I really felt, kind of singing it to myself the way I imagined Muhammad Ali might say it. *My new friend Jeffrey is Black, and I like him better than I like you, and you don't know anything about anything, and Mom picked a good house, and Mom married a dope.*

"Oh, Harry," said Mom, in that lullaby voice she used whenever he was mean to her. "This is a much better place than Ravine Park. We have more room, and the house is newer, and there were just as many Blacks there, and—"

"Aw balls, Ginny, aren't you just Miss Perfect?"

Every time Dad said that, I wondered what kind of balls he meant. Basketballs? Baseballs? The walnut-sized bouncy balls I sometimes ogled in the grocery store dime-machines?

Mom retreated into the kitchen, and my sisters and brothers and I divided the candy into six piles on the living room floor. Mom came back in and told us to make a seventh, smaller pile for the "little kids," which is what we always called everyone from

Susie on down. I think it was hard for all of us to let go of any of the candy we had left, but we obliged with a smaller pile of softer candies that the little kids could more easily chew. Once all the piles were arranged, I called third and was still able to score a Hershey's bar—a buoy in my deluge of seven-year-old grief.

My Hershey's bar barely survived the few steps it took to get to our bedroom, and by the time Ern slipped under the covers, all that was left of my chocolate was the wrapper. Before I got into bed, I looked down at my naked pillow and wondered where my pillowcase was. Did the thieves keep it, or was it lying somewhere in the street? Were cars running over it? Had it blown into a gutter? I turned out the light and tried not to think about it. I shifted from side to side and eventually lay on my back, and when I still couldn't stop thinking about it, I started quickly rocking my head from side to side, a dizzying habit I sometimes found strangely comforting. I could tell Ern was also still awake. "Are you thinking about what happened?" I asked.

He cleared his throat. "Not really."

"Are you thinking about candy?"

"Nah."

"Then what are you thinking about?"

"Cars."

"Cars?"

"Yeah. One day I'm going to get one that's shiny and red."

"I bet you'll drive far away from here. Like back to that park Uncle Dick and Harold took us to."

"That's not so far. I'll probably drive all the way to Canada."

As I contemplated Canada by repeating it in my mind over and over until it made no sense, a scream ripped through the night somewhere outside our window. "What was that?" I asked, and before Ern could answer, it came again. And then it seemed like the screaming would never end—a primal yowl that sounded like a desperate mix of pain and rage. It was the worst sound I'd ever heard in my life, and I started to shiver, though I wasn't cold.

"It's probably some silly Halloween prank," said Ern, but I knew in my gut it was something worse and that he knew it too.

"I wonder if the others can hear it upstairs," I said, hoping that Mom would come down and tell us everything was all right.

"That's why I think of cars," he eventually said, after the screams finally came to a stop. "When something bad happens, I just think about things I like."

So I lay in bed and thought about elephants and tigers and all the animals I wanted to see in the wild one day. And Ernie's trick worked because before I knew it, it was morning.

The six of us had just headed out the back door and down The Path to D Street on our way to school when I noticed something in the field. I didn't understand what it was at first. From a short distance, it looked like a piece of black leather in the shape of an animal. As I got closer, I saw that its face was like that of a small saber-toothed tiger because its fangs looked so prominent compared to its small head. "What *is* that?" I said, walking ever closer. I heard one of my sisters say, "C'mon, leave that alone," which only prompted Ern and Dan to follow me. And soon the three of us boys were standing directly over it. Its face was bare of all detail: no lips, no nose, no eyes. "Is that a cat?" asked Dan as he knelt down to get a closer look. Its fur and skin were completely gone, leaving only shiny black muscles and bone. "Ew, it is. It's a cat!" I picked up a stick to turn it over. The sisters were calling us, but we hovered over the charred body, transfixed. "Someone must have set it on fire," said Ern. We had heard rumors about kids who would catch a cat, pour gasoline all over it, and set it on fire, but I hadn't believed it was true. My breakfast toast sloshed around in my stomach as I realized that this cat was what we'd heard the night before.

I tried to imagine the last minutes of the cat's life—not only the excruciating physical pain it must have felt but also the deeper pain of knowing someone had caused it for no other reason than to be cruel. I thought about evil and innocence—two words I heard a lot in church—and wondered why a "just God" would let such evil exist.

That day, through math problems and grammar facts, through recess and my walk home with Jeffrey and Eddie, the cat's body appeared in my mind—stiff, black, dead. As we neared Ketcham Street on our walk home, I told Jeffrey and Eddie I wanted to take Brigham instead of cutting through Dog Alley. What I didn't say was that I didn't want to walk past My Dog with them because I was planning to come back later and see him alone. I hadn't told them about the burned cat either, or about our stolen Halloween candy, not even when Jeffrey said he'd grown new muscles from carrying his heavy bag home.

"What? Are you afraid all of a sudden?" teased Eddie.

"I actually wouldn't mind some peace and quiet," I said.

"That's what my mama always says," said Jeffrey. He put the back of his hand against his forehead in an exaggerated imitation of his mother. "You just hush up now, Jeffrey, and do your home-work. Let me have some peace and quiet." He fluttered his eyelids dramatically. "What's a woman gotta do to get some peace and quiet around here?"

Eddie and I laughed, and soon the three of us were walking down Brigham Street saying, "Give us some peace and quiet. We need peace and quiet. Peace and quiet and peace and quiet." It was the happiest I'd felt all day.

After I got home, gulped down two large glasses of milk, and said "hi" and "bye" to Mom, who was tending to the twins in their wooden playpen, I went into the field to bury the cat, which was now covered with flies. I'd never been to a funeral, so I stood still for a moment, not knowing what to do. "Mother Mary, please send this cat to Heaven," I finally said. "Amen." Then I dug a hole with a stick and used the stick to push him in. After I smoothed the dirt over him, I marked his grave with a cross on the ground made out of rocks.

Then I ran over to Dog Alley. "Hi, My Dog!" I called. My Dog lifted his head from the ground. Even though he now allowed me to pet him, he still seemed tentative and sad, and given his lot in life, I understood. I heard him snarl a little as I approached, but I'd heard it all before. I knew he secretly loved me.

Maybe he didn't like that I was running. Maybe I squatted down to pet him in a slightly different way than I had before. Maybe the cat's screams had burrowed into everyone. Who can say for sure why the dog I visited every day suddenly jumped on me and bit my arm? "Ow!" I said, shocked. He bit my arm again and knocked me down. I struggled to roll away from him, while his teeth sank into my leg, then my torso. "Stop!" I yelled, trying to push him off me, but he was in a frenzy of growling and biting. Eventually I managed to roll out of the reach of his chain, and then I ran home crying.

"Let's get a look at these," said Mom, lifting up my shirt to assess my wounds. "I'll have to sew your pants and shirt," she concluded. Then she pulled my shirt back down and took a step back. "You'll be fine. Just go get in the tub and wash with soap and water."

I felt the sudden desire to lie down and rest my head in her lap, but we never did things like that—no one in our family even hugged or said I love you, not even Uncle Dick and Harold, not even on special occasions—so instead, I dutifully went upstairs and washed the blood off the places that hurt.

A few days later, I heard another scream. This one belonged to Mom, and it came with a thud and the sound of falling rocks. I immediately looked up from where I was sitting in the living room and saw Mom's leg dangling through the ceiling in the downstairs hallway, the shoe still on her foot. By the time I ran upstairs to help her, Ernie was already in the process of extracting her. "I had only taken the vent cover off for a minute just to clean," she explained breathlessly as I came around and grabbed her other arm, "and I must have looked away for a second when I misstepped." As she pulled her leg out, more of the ceiling fell to the floor below.

"You'll be fine, Mom," I said.

"Yes, you're right," she said, pressing the vent grate back down. "The question is, will the ceiling?"

And the answer, at least for the short term, was no. Mom swept up the drywall that had landed on the floor below, but her leg hole would last. It would last as the rest of the autumn leaves came down and scuttled and scratched along the streets, swirling around our feet as we walked back and forth to school. It would last through all the nights Dad sat slumped in his corner of the couch, hiding behind his books and cigars. It would last as the season cooled to cold and drew into winter and the first snowflakes fell, fat and wet. It would last because the "Housing Authority people," as Mom called them, would not come to fix it. We would come to laugh about it, though—particularly Susie, who loved when I described Mom's leg dangling in the hallway.

"You mean her whole leg, not just her foot?" she'd ask.

"Her whole leg," I'd say, pointing. "Right through the ceiling."

Even Dad couldn't stifle a laugh about it, though he also didn't neglect to mention that we lived in a piece-of-shit house. I wondered why he didn't find us a better one if he disliked it so much.

What I never laughed about was my experience with My Dog, whom I'd stopped thinking of as My Dog. I never petted him again, though I still watched him at times, lying with his face on the ground. I felt bad for him, and I couldn't help but wonder if he regretted what he'd done and if he missed our interactions as much as I did.

When pushed by Jeffrey and Eddie, who had noticed that I no longer got within reach of the dog, I had to admit that the dog had attacked me. "At least you still have your hands," said Jeffrey with real concern, and that reminded me why he was my friend.

Soon my thoughts of the burned cat and My Dog dimmed in the muted hues of winter, while the promise of Santa loomed. Songs about sleigh bells and silver bells, Rudolph and Frosty, poured in from the small plastic radio in the kitchen, while Mom baked triple batches of cookies. One night, while a soft, powdery snow was falling, Dad flung the front door open. He was slurring, back from another night at the bar. "He's gottallllitup."

Mom emerged from the kitchen. "What's that, Harry?"

Dad shifted on his feet. "I *said*..." He paused, as if he needed to summon all of his concentration in order to make the words cooperate. "He's got it...all...lit up."

"Who's got what all lit up?"

Dad pointed. "Up the street. For Christmas."

Dad rarely called our attention to anything, so we excitedly put on our coats and started up the street, with Mary Jo's and Marji's footprints leading the way in the snow. After walking a block, Marji stopped, so the rest of us stopped too. "Maybe Dad was just making it up," she said.

"Let's go a little farther," said Mary Jo, so we walked another block, and then we saw the twinkle of lights in the distance. "Wow," we all kept saying as we approached, but when we came upon the small yard, we all went silent for a moment. Festooned with lights and alive in a flurry of Christmas motion, a cast of handmade, animated papier-mâché characters were busy at work. Painted in vibrant shades of red, green, and gold, shiny shellacked elves hammered toys and lifted gifts; reindeer with white, wagging tails grazed on snowy grass; angels opened and closed their golden wings like butterflies; a green train filled with candy canes chugged forward and then back; and Santa ho-ho-hoed on repeat. Snow frosted the tops of their heads and ours as we watched, gobsmacked by the magic.

"I wonder how long it took them to make all that," said Mary Jo.

It occurred to me then that it's often the destruction of a thing that happens fast—a boy named Bobo knocking a popsicle out of my hand, a gang of boys stealing our Halloween candy, the match-strike that set a cat on fire—while good things take time to construct, like Mom's black-and-white pinwheel cookies, or the jungle scene that took me days to draw because I wanted to get the animals just right, or the wonderland here on our very own street, free for anyone who wanted to enjoy it.

"It's a miracle!" exclaimed Susie.

Only later would we learn the name of the man who made the wonderland—Mr. Chapman—and how right Susie was: in a neighborhood where you couldn't leave so much as a marble outside for fear of it being stolen, in all the years Mr. Chapman would display his illuminated creations, it was said that no one ever took a single thing from his yard.

FIVE

t's still dark on Christmas morning. Mom's rule is that every sibling must be up before we wake her. Whispers trail through our bedrooms as we shuffle back and forth, hissing a little more loudly beside the beds of those who are still asleep, "It looks like maybe Susie's waking up." "Yes, see, she moved!" "Your breath smells," she says as she blinks her eyes open. We try to be respectful, but we can't resist brushing against a shoulder or tapping a foot—until everyone has been roused.

We line up from youngest to oldest in the upstairs hallway, peering down the dark, narrow tunnel of the stairway, and Mary Jo slips into Mom and Dad's room. The rest of us are practically vibrating in this liminal space, this pause that is the perfect mix of known and unknown. We know that goodness awaits us, even if we don't know the specific nature of that goodness. We are still too young to know that this is the best part.

Mary Jo comes back out of the room, followed by Mom, who is as bright as the scent of peppermint. Dad trails out last, hacking up whatever has accumulated in his windpipe during the night—our cue to patter down the stairs and scurry toward our tree, which glows with candy-colored lights and thin mirrors of tinsel icicles. Someone exclaims that Santa has left behind a cookie with a bite taken out of it, and suddenly the room is alive with Santa's presence. Even the angel, perched on top of the tree in her illuminated robes, has the rapturous look of someone who has just seen the kindest man on earth.

There isn't enough room under the tree for all of our presents, so some of us find our piles in the surrounding territory of the living room. Some of us are neat about it, slow and deliberate, while others shred the wrapping paper. Mom collects all the paper, smoothing it as flat as she can. I receive a toy car, the fender of which I will later reshape by heating a knife at the stove to melt the plastic. Mom opens a Whitman's Sampler box of chocolates, and in a flurry of reaching hands, the box is reduced to only empty wrappers that remind me of insect shells.

Uncle Dick and Harold come over in the afternoon, and we show them what Santa has brought: building blocks, a painted wagon, a stuffed turtle, crayons. "Wonderful," they say. "Wonderful." I am not exactly sure what *good tidings* means, except that our uncles bring it. They smile it upon us. They cover us in it when we come in mittenless from the snow; they rub their calloused hands back and forth over our hands, and the quick friction warms us.

It will be many years before Mom will reveal the truth of our Santa Claus: in addition to the gifts Mom scrimped and saved to afford every year (starting on the day after Christmas when everything went on sale), Uncle Dick brought over bags filled with presents late on Christmas Eve, some of which he and Uncle Harold built and painted with their own hands and some of which they purchased with the small earnings from their elevator shop. And while Dad snored, Uncle Dick helped Mom wrap them all—quiet as a mouse.

SIX

I had always been captivated by Muhammad Ali—for at least four years anyway—starting with my starry-eyed discovery of him on the covers of magazines, back when he was still Cassius Clay and I was forming some of my earliest lasting memories. I was captivated by him the way children are captivated by heroes, maybe the way my sisters were captivated by Diana Ross. But I'd never really listened to him speak, mainly because we rarely had a television that worked. That spring of 1967, however, I spent a lot of time listening. I listened to gospel music from across the street. I listened for the quick clicks of flying grasshoppers and the whispers of snakes slipping through grass. I listened to Ernie's breathing deepen when he fell asleep next to me. I listened to the older kids in our neighborhood talking about the cool Buick Electra 225 they called "Deuce and a Quarter," which they decorated with curb-feelers, fuzzy dice, and imitation leopard fur coverings on the dashboard. And I listened to them talking about Muhammad Ali, whose refusal to join the army to fight in Vietnam cost him his heavyweight championship title. The older kids in our neighborhood said he was a hero and that the white man better wake up, and I wondered which white man they were talking about.

The kids at school also talked about Muhammad Ali, but unlike the kids on Bronson Street, they didn't seem to think Ali was a hero at all. They called him a coward and a criminal and said he deserved to go to jail. I wondered how some people could think a man is a hero and others could see the same man as a coward.

Then I saw Muhammad Ali on TV, and I started listening to him too: "I'm not going to help nobody get something my Negroes don't have. If I'm gonna die, I'm gonna die right here, fightin' you.... My enemy is the white people.... You're my opposer when I want freedom." Me, his enemy? Suddenly I felt as if my hero had jabbed me in the heart.

Because our old black-and-white television was, as Mom put it, "on the fritz," the screen rolled constantly no matter how you adjusted the bunny ears on top, so that a single Muhammad Ali became hundreds, each rolling into the next. Though my feelings were hurt and the screen was hard to watch, I didn't want to look away. I had never heard anyone speak like that before. He was almost singing, bold and fearless as if he were fighting another one of his famous fights. Though I was too young to grasp the meaning of his words, I could feel that they were important and incendiary.

"He doesn't deserve to be the champion if he won't even fight for our country," Dad said, puffing out a cloud of cigar smoke. "Someone needs to put that Black bastard in his place." He was holding the butt of his cigar with a straight pin stuck into the side, his solution for when it was too small to hold with his fingers.

I stopped watching Muhammad Ali and studied my father—his grimace, his over-sized nose, his oily skin that was always reddened by thick patches of acne, as if all the anger inside him was bubbling to the surface. I wanted to ask Dad why he was so angry at Muhammad Ali and why Muhammad Ali was so angry at white people, but some part of me already suspected my father was wrong.

Though I thought Dad was wrong a lot, there was something he almost never got wrong: the questions to the answers on *Jeopardy*. Whenever the show came on, we watched our slouching father rise like a marionette being pulled up by an invisible hand, obscure answers floating from his mouth as smoothly as Ali floated around the ring. In that half hour, from his corner of the couch, he would not only toss out a "Who is Polonius?" or "What is tungsten?" at just the right moment, but he would also do it with an aplomb and straightness of spine we weren't accustomed to seeing in him. We were Dad's own private audience, and he seemed to actually appreciate our presence then, occasionally even addressing us directly: "Can you believe that buffoon didn't know *Bonnie and Clyde*, for Pete's sake?"

SEVEN

By the time I was in third grade, I'd made some important decisions about my life. Though I'd been planning on being either the heavyweight champion of the world (or the richest man in the world) since the day Bobo Bennett knocked my orange popsicle out of my hand, I'd added one more option—president—because that seemed like the best thing anyone could be. I'd also been paging through the animal books at school and was already making travel plans for places I would visit: Africa, where cheetahs run as fast as cars; South America, where anteaters scoop up insects with two-foot-long tongues; Thailand, where Malayan tapirs whistle and wave their flexible proboscises; and oceans where killer whales breach under the sun.

But first, there was kickball.

Day after day, after school and into the dusk, we gathered in our backyard and got down to the serious business of bases. I learned that the trick to pitching wasn't only varying the speed of the pitch, especially opting for slower rolls, since a faster momentum often helped the kicker launch the ball that much farther. Getting to know the players was essential: some always tried to kick it as deep into the field as possible, while the smaller kids didn't have the power. Others varied their kicks just as I varied my pitches, so you had to learn their habits—slight changes in position or expression that gave away the kick before it came. Mary Jo, for instance, often tried to look nonchalant when she was going for a big kick, whereas Ern's expression intensified when he had a homerun attempt up his sleeve. Marji tended to look way out into the field when she was going to attempt a short kick, while Beth was inscrutable. My siblings and I were intensely competitive, and our games were the main thing we fought about.

During one game, I noticed that Fred and Jim Peal from next door were doing something with the tree in the middle of the field. Because they were older, they were rarely interested in joining our kickball games, but on this day, they traipsed back and forth through the field behind us, carrying pieces of wood, plywood, rubber, even a window—some of which appeared to come from the field itself. They were so focused on the tree that they barely looked in our direction, which made me focus on the tree, too, in between pitches and kicks. After lots of trips back and forth, the Peals eventually stayed put at the tree, and the sounds of hammer blows resounded into the field, punctuating our foul ball calls, our heroic declarations of "safe" when we arrived on bases, and our shouts of victory and disappointment. And soon, amid the branches of the field's lone oak, the beginnings of a tree house began to take shape.

The Peals worked on their tree house from morning to night for days, and I watched their progress with wonder. I'd never seen anyone build something before, and I was fascinated by the process—the installation of the ladder steps up the tree, the framing of the tiny house and its peaked roof, the open spaces for the windows and door. When they were finished, I was surprised by how professional it looked and amazed that they'd pulled it off without any apparent help from adults. If they could do that, I wondered, what kinds of things might I be able to do?

Soon after the house was finished, I meandered over to the tree. I knew Fred and Jim were in the tree house because I'd seen them climb up, so I poked nonchalantly through the field, busying myself with the field's usual inhabitants and arriving at the base of the tree as if by sheer happenstance. Nailed between the steps leading up to the tree house was a small wooden sign inked in black: "KEEP OUT." I looked for some way to announce myself, but the Peals had neglected to add a knocker or doorbell to their new digs. "Hello?" I called up.

A voice called down. "What's the magic word?"

"I, um—"

"Nope, that's not it."

I looked up at the door, which was closed and adorned with a second "KEEP OUT" sign. "It's Tom from next door."

"That's not the magic word, either."

As my frustration mounted, so did my desire to climb up the rungs and look inside the house. "I saw you building this, and you did a great job. I was hoping I could come up and see it."

This time Fred came to the door. He was shirtless and smoking a cigarette, from which he took a long draw as he looked down on me as if I were a peddler who'd just called him away from an important meeting. "We don't let little kids up here," he said, making the smoke come out of his mouth in little rings.

"I'm not a little kid," I informed him. "I even wear husky pants." I had grown a lot that year, and husky was the only size Mom found that could fit my thick legs and behind.

Fred started laughing. "Hey Jim," he called to his brother, "come over here."

Jim appeared in the doorway behind Fred. "What does *he* want?" he asked, flicking his chin in my direction.

"Get this," Fred said, smirking. "He thinks he should be allowed up here because he wears husky pants."

Suddenly embarrassed, I tried to backpedal. "That's not what I meant. It's just, you called me little, and—"

But their hyena-like guffaws rolled over my voice, and I saw it was no use, so I turned around and went home with the shrill sound of their amusement trailing behind me.

That summer, Jane and Judy, now three, were chasing after Susie, who, at five, already liked to be in charge, and Rich, now two, was toddling after Jane and Judy. Born in February, Joe was the newest member of the family, bringing the number of kids in our family to eleven, and he was already laughing and crawling from one end of the living room to the other before I could even get one pin closed on Rich's diaper. Though Mom did the majority of the diaper changes, it never bothered me to do it, no matter how wet or smelly the cloth got or how full the diaper pail became, except for when I accidentally stuck Jane with one of the pins. It happened to all of us, even Mom, because you had to forcefully push the large pin through thick cotton layers before you could close it, and occasionally it didn't go exactly where you wanted it to. The babies always cried bloody murder when it happened, a sound even worse than the Peals laughing at me.

Meanwhile, the older sisters were wearing out their little hand-me-down record player by accompanying countless hours of our lives with "Hey Jude," which topped the charts that summer and which they played on repeat—much to the delight of Judy, who was convinced the song was about her—while Mom was a perpetual story of motion and Dad was either gone or home and still gone. I noticed that he seemed to be coming home late more often, often staggering to his corner of the sofa, and though his family was growing, he seemed to be shrinking behind his slurred words. Then there were the things he said often enough that we recognized the words, like when he called us "cocksuckers" or threatened us with "a knuckle sandwich." It was as if our very existence grated against any potential happiness he might have.

The evenings were particularly trying, when it was too late to go outside and the thirteen of us were all piled up on top of each other in a constant racket of chatter and rattles and babbling babies. Each night there would come a time when Dad would peer over the top of his book and make a quick, sharp *psssst* sound, which meant it was time for us to go to bed. If we didn't hustle to bed fast enough, he'd slam his book down next to his ashtray on the end table, which immediately sent any stragglers running. One night I stood and looked at him after he'd given the final warning. I wanted to connect with him in some way, to say something that would unhinge a secret door of joy or warmth I believed was hidden in him, but I couldn't think of anything to say, so I simply stared at him, dumbstruck. "What the hell are you waiting for?" he asked.

I did not say, *for you to say one nice thing.* But then I lay in bed thinking, *I may not have a tree house, but I have a perfect family,* as if thinking it could make it true.

It was 1968—the year Martin Luther King Jr. and Bobby Kennedy were assassinated; the year when riots erupted all over the country; the year the Viet Cong launched the bloody Tet Offensive; the year two Black athletes raised their fists in silent demonstration against racial injustice while receiving their Olympic medals. Our country was rife with change and upheaval, but at nine, I was too young to grasp the depth of the snippets I heard on the news, and none of these current events was on the curriculum at

St. Vincent's. Dad's view was that "women and Negroes need to know their place," which he muttered to no one in particular while Walter Cronkite spoke from the rolling television screen, but that was the extent to which my family discussed the state of the world beyond Bronson Street.

When I asked Mom why people were being so violent, she told me they were angry. "About what?" I asked.

She was hanging laundry on the clotheslines that ran from the back of our house to a metal T-bar in the yard—white fraying diapers waving like flags in the breeze. "It's complicated," she said.

"Complicated how?"

"Oh Tom," she said, giving a pair of Dad's white boxers an extra good shake before pinning them to the line, "just complicated."

"You're Black," I said to Jeffrey not long after my conversation with Mom.

"Thanks for telling me," he said. "I never would have guessed."

"You didn't let me finish," I said, laughing. We were casually tossing a football in front of his house on St. John Street. "I was going to ask if you know why Black people and white people don't get along."

He put an extra spin on the ball. "*We* get along."

"I know, but I mean, all the stuff on the news. Fighting and riots and stuff."

"Because they killed Martin Luther King, the one man who was actually fighting for our rights."

"I know," I said. "It's terrible. But do you think that makes the riots right?"

"My mom says Black people can't get listened to any other way." He threw the ball high. "Think about it. White people came and stole us from Africa. They brought us here and made us slaves and killed a bunch of us. And once we were freed, we weren't allowed in half the places white people were. How would you feel if someone brought you somewhere and then told you they didn't want you there? Wouldn't that make you angry?"

I could still hear the Peals laughing at me when they wouldn't let me into their tree house. "Yes," I said.

"And wouldn't you want to fight for things to be fair?"

I thought about how mad I got when one of my siblings made what I believed was an unjust ruling in a game of kickball. And suddenly I began to understand why Mom used the word *complicated*. "Yes," I admitted. "But I still don't think it's right to burn down buildings because then you're only hurting more people."

"Whatever you say, Tom," said Jeffrey, putting the ball down and going to take a drink from his garden hose. "You're always right."

He was doing the thing he often did when we were discussing a potentially heated topic, such as which was the best superpower to have or which was the most perfect piece of candy: he was shutting me down. I enjoyed talking to Jeffrey more than anyone because he was smart and funny, but if I pressed him on something, it often invited the "You're right, you're always right, you're right about everything, Tom" game, which I always lost.

"I'm just saying," I tried to explain, following him, "that ruining the stores and buildings hurts everyone. Them too."

Jeffrey threw his hands up in the air. "You know everything, Seeman."

Once he started calling me by my last name, I knew it was over. And yet still I tried. "If you'd just listen—"

"Lalalaaaaa! I can't hear you!"

"I'm just—"

"I already said you're right, Seeman."

"But you don't mean it." I could hear my voice rising in frustration as I folded my arms across my chest. "Anyway, I'm actually planning to visit Africa one day to see the cheetahs, so then I can make Black friends there who will listen to me." Fearing I might have hurt his feelings, I softened my tone. "I'm going to travel all over the world one day."

Jeffrey laughed. "In case you haven't noticed, you live in the projects."

"So?"

"So, you need money to travel all over the world."

"I'll make money then."

"How many people do you see in the projects making money?"

I thought of Mr. Chapman's winter wonderland and the guys in our neighborhood with the fancy fedoras and shiny new cars—all those things had to cost money. "All I know is I'm going to make enough money to go anywhere I want," I said.

On a Saturday, we took a trip out to the countryside to spend the day with Grandma and Uncle Dick and Harold. We didn't get to visit them often because when we did, Uncle Dick and Harold had to drive out in two cars to pick us all up and then drive us back the same way, so usually they just stayed at our house for visits.

Situated on a narrow country road with long stretches in between houses, their house was painted white and had windows that swung out on hinges, a screened-in porch that looked out at tall trees, wide wooden stairs, and creaky, planked floors. Best of all, it had Uncle Dick and Harold's workshop in the back, filled with old metal machines that Grandpa—who died when I was four—bought long ago to make elevator parts. When we arrived that day, Grandma greeted us at the door as usual and, with her typical mild-mannered cheer, offered us glasses of water. Even the water at their house tasted different from our city water—metallic and icy cold straight out of the faucet. "That's because it's well water," Grandma told us.

Within minutes, Ern, Marji, and I beelined out the back door to the shop, which was a tall, flat-topped brick building that smelled of machine oil, sawdust, and danger. Everything inside was covered with a layer of dust and metal flecks, and the place was overrun with spiders and feral cats that occasionally let me pet them. Marji liked to follow around a tabby she called Tigress.

"Let's ride the elevator first!" I said. That was the hardest part about those initial moments when we entered the shop and stood looking up and around at the grandness of space and metal machinery—which thing to play with first. Sometimes we went straight for the machines, drilling holes into pieces of wood with an enormous drill press or pulling the chain on the one-ton hoist system to lift random metal parts and pipes we connected to the hook at the end of the chain. Once, I brought the drill bit down right between my fingers and watched with awe as it cut into the wood under my hand. Another time a huge pipe fell off the hook halfway to the ceiling and came crashing to the ground beside us.

The three of us climbed onto the elevator's rusty platform. Because it had been built long ago to load gigantic parts and equipment onto trucks, the elevator was stationed on the outside of the building, and it had no railings around the platform, which was one of my favorite things about it. To make it move, you had to press and hold a button on a metal pillar that rose from an outer corner of the platform, and if you let go, the elevator would stop midair. Because I was the first one on, I got to the button first, with

Ern and Marji jumping on behind me. I sometimes liked to wait a few seconds before pressing the button, to let the anticipation build, but the elevator scared Marji, so she always wanted to get going before she had too much time to think about it. "Let's go!" she said, so I pressed the button, and the elevator shook itself into motion. As we began to rise, I looked down at the empty ground below and imagined the Peals standing there, looking up at me. *Sorry*, I would say, *but dumb kids aren't allowed on the elevator.*

When we reached the top, I stared out at the blue sky, which was stippled with tiny white puffs of clouds, and I felt like a small god among the spiders, cats, and kittens—formidable and just. I thought maybe that's how hawks feel as they look down upon the earthbound rest of us, and while Ern and Marji were guessing how many feet up we were—Ern said forty, while Marji guessed one hundred—I spread my imaginary wings.

When we came back down, the elevator landed with a clang. At the same time, I saw Uncle Harold lumbering over, already laughing his goofy laugh as if life were one big shimmering sea of happiness. "What are you kids up to?" he asked.

Marji ran over to him. "How high does the elevator go, Uncle Harold? Is it a hundred feet?"

Uncle Harold peered up at the top of the building. "Probably a thousand," he said.

"It's a miiiiiiiillion," said Ern, running off to gather rocks. This was always the second part of our elevator escapades—to line rocks along the steel edge of the pad beneath the elevator and then watch them get smashed to smithereens when we brought the elevator platform down on top of them. Marji and I went into the overgrown grass behind the shop and joined Ern, all of us filling our hands with stones. Beyond the overgrown grass was a farm that grew corn and soybeans, and the plows had dumped heaps of rocks between the planted field and the workshop. Uncle Harold raised the elevator a few feet so we could place the stones beneath the platform. Once the stones were on the ground, the three of us joined Uncle Harold on the elevator. This time Ernie made it go, rising in a single sweep and then immediately ushering it back down.

We were going at a good clip when Marji yelled, "Stop!"

Ernie immediately let go of the button, which made the elevator jerk to a halt, and we leaned over the edge to see a gray-and-white striped kitten prancing below the elevator.

"You can just keep going on down," said Uncle Harold.

"But..." I said, confused. "Don't you see the kitten, Uncle Harold?"

He looked down and nodded. "We've got too many of them. Tomcats everywhere. I had to drown five kittens just the other day. They'll starve otherwise. This way it's quicker." He let out a more subdued laugh then, like a reflex he couldn't control.

I looked at the hands of this man I loved—the knobby knuckles, the dirty, jagged nails—and my knees felt wobbly. Meanwhile, the kitten had slinked off, and Ernie resumed our descent as we all peered over to watch the rocks explode.

An eerie feeling stayed with me that day and into the next. That night, after we all put our shoes out at the bottom of the stairs like we did every Saturday night so Mom could shine all thirteen pairs for church the next day, I lay awake, turning from one side to the other. "Ern?" I finally whispered. I wanted to ask him if he thought maybe Uncle Harold had just been kidding about the kittens, but he responded with a snore.

"In Heaven, you want for nothing, for everything is satisfied," said Father Schmelzer in church the next day. "All is equal and just, and contentment reigns." And I wondered, if that were true, why was earth so different? I knew what the answer would be—that Adam and Eve sinned, and that caused all the suffering on earth—but that didn't assuage the part of me that wanted an answer I could truly understand.

After church, Mom gathered up her booklets of food stamps and the coupons she clipped from the newspaper, and Dad took her to the grocery store, leaving us older kids to look after the younger ones at home. A few hours later, I watched Mom get out of Terry Bryant's car in front of our house. He lived two houses away with a single mom, two sisters, and three brothers, and though his younger brothers often seemed to be getting into trouble—I'd even seen one of them get taken away in handcuffs by the police—Terry was always soft-spoken and friendly. Marji and I ran out to help Mom bring in the groceries, and Marji immediately asked, "Where's Dad?"

Mom shrugged her shoulders. "I waited and waited for him to come back, but he never did. Luckily, Terry here was kind enough to offer me a ride. I don't know how else I would have made it home with all these bags in the heat."

"My pleasure, Mrs. Seeman," he said as he got back into his car. Even his smile was gentle.

About an hour later, Dad came home, reeling on his feet and slurring. "Wheerreshe?"

I was sitting on the floor, drawing my third anteater of the day. By then I'd come to understand Dad's beer-talk, so I answered him. "You mean Mom?"

"Uhhhcourse I mean Mom. Whooooelsewoulduhmean?"

"She's in the kitchen."

Because our house was so small and there were so many of us, there was almost no such thing as a private conversation unless you whispered, and even then, there was no guarantee you wouldn't be heard. "I cameuhgetyou, but you weren't there." Dad's gravelly voice was always the loudest in the house, and it reminded me of the black smoke that billowed out of tractor-trailer trucks.

"I waited and waited, Harry, but it was getting late, and I had to get home to the kids."

"How'd...how'd yougitallathose bags home then?"

"Terry Bryant saw me sitting outside and asked if I needed a lift."

"Yoooou!" He was yelling now. "You rodehome...witthat pimp!"

"Oh, Harry, he's not a pimp. He's a perfectly nice fellow who did a kind thing."

"Bullshit! Heezza pimp, and that makes you a whore!" I didn't know what the words meant, but I knew that they were bad and that they made him small. They made all of us small.

Rich started crying. Ernie came running down the stairs and stormed into the kitchen. "Don't talk to Mom like that!" he cried.

I ran out the front door and tore down Bronson Street, turned right on D Street, and kept running without thinking about where I was going. I only knew that I was going *away*. Eventually, when I got tired and slowed to a walk, I found a stick in front of a house and picked it up, striking my open palm with it as I went. "This is what I'm going to do to you next time you call Mom a bad word," I muttered under my breath. But then my words seemed like Dad's words, and I worried that Mother Mary could hear me, so I let the stick go and instead entertained other kinds of fantasies. I imagined going to the bar and telling the bartender that he couldn't serve my father anymore. I imagined smashing his beers on the concrete like they used to do in our old neighborhood. I imagined all of us pinning Dad down and making him promise to stop. But then I realized that my fantasies were just that. So instead, I made a promise of my own, as I walked farther from home: *For the rest of my life, I will never take a drink of alcohol.*

I walked for hours that day. I walked until the sky turned pink. I walked until the pink gave way to lavender and then to smoky blue. I walked until a sliver of moon appeared just over the tops of houses belonging to people I didn't know. I walked from one thought to the next—black and white, cat and killer, Mom and Dad—and I wondered if I would ever go home again. But soon my stomach was rumbling, so I made my way back.

When I went inside, it was as if nothing had happened. Susie and the twins were playing with paper dolls; the older girls were making paper clothes for the dolls; Ern was lying on the floor looking through the *Book of Saints*; Joe was babbling in the play-pen; Dan was rolling a small plastic car back and forth with Rich. I found Mom in the kitchen, sewing Ern's initials into his socks, which she did for all of our socks and underwear so she could tell them apart. Dad was gone—back to the bar I assumed. "You must be hungry," she said, pushing the needle down through one hole and back up through the other. "Want me to fix you a fried bologna sandwich?"

I was very hungry by then, and that was one of my favorite things to eat, but suddenly I just wanted to sit near her. "Do you think you could teach me to sew?" I asked.

She stopped sewing and let her hands rest in her lap as she looked at me. A woman some might call a natural beauty, Mom never wore makeup—except for the deep burgundy lipstick she wore to church—or fussed with her chin-length hair. She had a warm and ready smile, radiant skin, and a lazy left eye that was imperceptible to most people. "Why sure, Tom. What would you like to sew?"

"I don't know. Maybe a vest for my yellow teddy bear? A red one, with buttons?"

"Okay," she said. "You go get my fabric scraps and button jar, and we'll make your bear a vest."

And with Dad not there to order us to bed, my siblings continued doing what they were doing while I sat with Mom in the kitchen, just the two of us, and planned the design for my bear's vest. I chose three blue buttons with red eyes, and after Mom measured my bear and cut the fabric, I was soon working the needle as Mom showed me. It was rare to have her undivided attention. There was a lightness in the air that night, maybe because we all sensed Dad would be gone a while, and in our quiet space together, I wanted to ask her questions. I wanted to know how it made her feel when Dad called her names and why she didn't tell him to stop. But I was afraid to upset her and ruin the magic of the moment, so we sat together the way Mom and Grandma sometimes did, easing in and out of silence, and with her guidance, I sewed on the last button.

That fall, my fourth-grade teacher, Mrs. Lambert, asked us to write down the greatest thing each of our parents had given us. There were so many things I wanted to say about Mom, but when I thought about Dad, I came up empty. The only thing I could remember him ever giving me was his "drops" from the bottom of his beer bottles, but that didn't seem like something "great." And as my classmates stood up, one by one, and said flowery things about their parents (sometimes to the point of sounding fabricated) I knew that what

I was about to say was going to be different. When my turn came, I stood up and cleared my throat. "The greatest thing my mother has given me is that she's always there to help me. And the greatest thing my father has given me," I said, nervously clearing my throat again, "is an example of what I don't want to be."

Several kids gasped. Mrs. Lambert looked at me wide-eyed, and I wasn't sure if she was stunned or sad. And while what I'd said may not have been what anyone expected to hear, it was the truth, and it marked the beginning of a new kind of life for me.

EIGHT

Mr. Noble, our neighbor across the street, who lives with his wife and three daughters in a project house identical to ours, is taking us fishing. *For no reason, for no reason,* I play in my mind as Ern and I sit in the back seat of Mr. Noble's car. One of the younger Peal kids from next door, Roy, sits up front. There are things I know about Mr. Noble, though I've never heard anyone say them: he's a hard worker; he's strong but gentle; he's steady and kind. And there are things I suspect: his three daughters don't care for fishing; he wishes they did.

When we arrive at the lake, I'm convinced Mr. Noble has taken a wrong turn and that we're actually at the ocean. Waves of corrugated blue rush over the shore, bringing sand, taking sand. But no, I saw the sign when we drove in—Crane Creek State Park—and I know that's on Lake Erie because it's where Uncle Harold likes to go to be alone and "soak up the sun." His eyes always go dreamy when he mentions it, and now I see why. Next to the sky, I have never seen anything so big.

Mr. Noble has brought a fishing rod for each of us. He explains that the sinker sinks to the bottom and the bait floats a few inches above. For bait, he's brought an old bean tin filled with wet earth and worms—nightcrawlers he calls them, a term my siblings and I use for every large worm we find, though we don't find them at night, and they don't crawl—and when he shows us how to slide the worm over the hook longways, I shake my head because I don't want to skewer a living thing. Mr. Noble makes it look easy, sliding the worm onto the hook as if the purpose of its life has always been to become a hook-shaped sheath on a sharp piece of metal. I don't know how to reconcile the dead worm with the TV cartoons I've seen in which worms on hooks are smiling as they wriggle at the end of the line, happily teasing a fish. "They don't feel anything," Mr. Noble assures me, but when I pierce one and it writhes, I have my doubts.

Ern and Roy don't seem to have any problems with the task, threading their worms onto their hooks as if their fingers were built for exactly this purpose. I've been learning that a boy can't be a "sissy" if he wants to live without black eyes and a perpetual torrent of projectiles aimed at his head. So I fish.

"It's nature," says Mr. Noble from underneath a straw hat I've never seen him wear on Bronson Street. "One thing eats another. The fish will eat the worm; we'll eat the fish. That's the cycle of life."

A man and woman walk by, holding hands and staring at us. I suspect what they're seeing is a Black man with three white kids and nothing more. *We're fishermen*, I want to say.

In the silence, in the waiting, while the waves lap at our ankles, I wonder what it would be like to have a father like Mr. Noble, who says wise things, who helps you unsnag your hook from a piece of driftwood that you excitedly think is a fish, who guides you when you finally do catch a fish, telling you how most catches are lost close to shore, so it's important to be steady and calm but also quick and "no-nonsense about the whole matter." It's my first fish, and my voice turns falsetto with the glee of holding its weight in my hands. Something hardwired in me turns on—a rush that comes in with the waves and makes me forget to feel bad for yanking the fish from its life.

"You got a perch," Mr. Noble says as he takes the rod from my hands. Pulling the hook out of the fish's mouth is tricky, so he does that for all of us. Mr. Noble catches a walleye with a downturned mouth and sharp spikey teeth that make it look sad and fearsome at once. "You don't normally catch walleye so close to shore," he says.

The knife Mr. Noble uses to chop the walleye's head off has teeth like the walleye. It seems brutal, but Mr. Noble says that if everyone ate this way, we wouldn't waste so much. He runs the serrated side over the fish, raining scales onto the sand. Then he slices open the fish's belly, scoops out its innards with his hand, and tosses them into water. "For crabs and other fish," he tells us.

There are things I'm learning about life, though I've never heard anyone say them. I'm learning that when you take, you can also give back. I'm learning that sometimes a man you hardly know takes you fishing for no reason, and when you bring the fish home and your mother fries them in a skillet, you can taste a different kind of life.

NINE

When the Elvis movie *Loving You* re-aired on television, the Jarvis family, who lived on the other side of the Peals' house, let some of my older sisters and me pile into their living room to watch it on their new color television. As soon as Elvis appeared on the screen, my sisters swooned. His guitar was like a magic wand, and as he played, I found myself slipping my hands into the air, fingers working invisible chords as if I were strumming along.

I decided it was time that I, too, started playing the guitar. I could already envision myself swaggering past my classmates during recess at St. Vincent's, guitar strapped across my chest, girls in my class looking on as I begin to serenade them and make playground history right before their eyes. The only problem was that I didn't have a guitar. And I didn't know anyone who had a guitar. And I didn't have any means of getting a guitar.

No problem. I would make my own. I figured that if the Peal kids could build a miniature house that stood level within the branches of a tree, I could certainly construct a string instrument. I began by asking Uncle Dick and Harold to bring some scrap wood from their workshop, from which I chose a short piece of a two-by-four. Then I visited the Random Screw and Nail container we kept on the shelf above the washing machine and proceeded to pound five random nails into each end of the two-by-four, over which I stretched five rubber bands. I took a moment to admire my handiwork before giving it a strum. And when I did, it didn't sound much like a guitar—it sounded more like five rubber bands.

"What the hell are you doing over there?" Dad poked his large beak over his book and peered at me as I knelt in the corner of the living room and made pinging sounds with my new instrument.

"I'm assembling a guitar." I had recently taken to reading the dictionary and liked to impress myself with my polysyllabic vocabulary.

"That doesn't look anything like a guitar. Doesn't sound like one either."

"It's my first try," I explained.

For my second prototype, I tried to make my instrument look more guitar-like by sawing a square piece of plywood and nailing it to the bottom of the two-by-four, but the rubber bands still refused to make music. I played my guitar for Mom, and she explained that real guitars have a hollow box on one end to make the sound reso-nate. So I un-nailed the plywood and taped an empty tissue box to the end of the two-by-four. But once I got the strings over the box, the guitar still wouldn't make music. I ditched the rubber bands and tried attaching scraps of twine instead, tying them as tightly as I could, but they made even less sound than the rubber bands. And that cemented the end of my would-be music career.

In the meantime, I started selling tabletop Virgin Mary statues door-to-door to raise money for our school. Carved into a piece of translucent glass secured to a plastic stand, Mary gazed up from behind her veil as if she were looking through a shaft of golden light at God himself. The contemporary design of the statue looked odd to me—her eyes too big for her face, her neck too skinny for her head—but she had a peaceful look about her, and she came nestled in a special, white paper box with a cross on it.

Naturally, my immediate goal was to sell more Marys than anyone else in my school. Then I would raise the most money for our school, and I'd be the leader of my class, and everyone would be proud of me. Maybe even Dad would be proud.

I decided I would start at the end of Bronson Street and work my way back toward home, and I arrived at my first house with a pep to my door-knocking, a box of Virgin Marys in my arms, and the confidence of a would-be president/heavyweight champion. A woman with curlers in her hair and a cigarette in her mouth cracked the door open a few inches and peered at me warily from the small opening. "Hi," I said with a smile. "I'm selling these statues of Mary for St. Vincent because we need to raise money for our school."

"I don't want that," she said, closing the door.

I stood in a puff of smoke in the morning sun, half expecting her to change her mind. But after several cars passed by and the door stayed closed, I continued making my way along Bronson Street, where occasionally a potential customer would ask to see the Mary "doll," as one woman called her. "She's pretty," said the woman, handing Mary back to me, "but I don't have the money."

"It's only a dollar," I said in my best television commercial voice, but soon I was looking at another closed door. By the time I'd gotten back to our section of Bronson Street, I'd sold a total of zero peaceful Marys. My once-zealous knock had dwindled to a lackluster tap as I stood outside the Nobles' house, wondering why my box seemed even heavier than when I began. When Mrs. Noble's friendly face appeared, I thought I might cry. "Hello, Tom. What can I do for you?"

I shifted my box of statues from my right side to my left. "I'm selling these Virgin Mary statues to raise money for my school, and I thought maybe you might like to buy one."

"May I take a look?"

"Oh yes, sure," I said, reaching into my box, opening one, and handing it to her.

"Is that real glass?"

I felt a small surge of hope rush up. "Yes," I nodded. "Real, genuine glass."

"How much?"

"Only a dollar. It's for charity," I added, lest she forget.

Mrs. Noble flashed a kind smile. "I'll take her," she said.

That year, I became an altar boy at church, and while I'd always been competitive, there was something about mentally separating myself from my father—claiming in front of my class that he was an example of what I didn't want to be—that amped up my innate drive to be the best at everything I did. Whether it was ringing the bells in church when the priest raised the host and chalice— three quick turns of the wrist, left-right-left, before placing the bell back on its cushion without letting it make another sound—or perfecting the precise swing of the thurible to bless the priest with incense during special holidays, I was quick to volunteer for any job he had, determined to prove I could do it better than anyone else. And that spring, on Palm Sunday, Father Schmelzer gave me an unexpected job.

During communion that day, I was distracted with questions— that was the other thing afoot inside my almost-ten-year-old mind: a seemingly endless litany of questions about everything—and on that day, I was puzzling over how, exactly, transubstantiation works.

When I asked Father Schmelzer, he told me the bread becomes the real body of Christ, not just a symbol. But *how*, I wondered, did these little white circular pieces of bread that came in from a factory by the hundreds turn into the *actual* body of Christ? And if all the pieces of bread consecrated during mass (and stored inside the tabernacle for safekeeping) become the body of Christ, then what makes the single host in the monstrance more special than all the other hosts? And why would we want to eat our Lord and Savior in the first place? I was so absorbed in my questions that I didn't hear the retching sounds or notice the kid throwing up his breakfast, along with the host he had just eaten, onto the church's beige carpet.

"We can't throw it away," explained Father Schmelzer after the service, as he led me to the brownish pile. He was carrying a plastic tub of water with a small towel inside. "Now that the host is part of it, we must take special measures."

"Special measures?" I asked, alert and ready to be the best at special measures.

When Father Schmelzer read the Gospel, he had a habit of placing his hands on the lectern and rocking his body back and forth, and he was doing a version of that now. "Yes," he explained, extending his arm toward the vomit as if it were a gleaming tower of gold. "This is now Jesus Christ. Do you see?"

I looked, and sure enough, amid the unidentifiable chunks, the pieces of host shone like a pearl inside an oyster. "Yes," I said. "I see."

"What we'll need to do is get every bit of this up and into this tub. Then we'll need to add more water until the host completely dissolves. Once the host has dissolved, we'll empty the tub out back in the bushes. It's very important that we don't pour it into the sink or toilet—we can never send Jesus into the sewer pipes. Do you understand?"

"Yes, Father Schmelzer," I said, giving him a single authoritative nod to let him know he'd made the best choice in selecting me for the job.

I quickly learned that what he'd meant by "we" was "you," and after he disappeared into the rectory and I told my family not to bother waiting for me because I'd walk home later, I got to work sopping up the vomit from the carpet. I even went to get a second tub of water so that I could wet my towel and ring it into the first container, making sure to do as Father Schmelzer said and get all of it. The smell was putrid, but it didn't bother me, maybe because I was used to the constant changing of babies' diapers. If anything, I felt a sense of pride in my work, watching as, bit by bit, I made the carpet clean again.

That afternoon, I found Mom in the kitchen when I got home. She was baking peanut butter cookies while the washing machine spun and pots bubbled on the stove. "Mom?" I asked.

"Yes, Tom?" she asked, glancing at me over her shoulder.

"How come the host has to be dissolved before you pour it into the bushes?"

"I don't know what you mean."

"Father Schmelzer said I couldn't pour the throw-up into the bushes until the host was dissolved."

Mom pressed a fork onto the cookies to make little cross-hatches. "Why were you pouring it into the bushes?"

"Because you can't put Jesus in the sewer pipes."

"I see," she said, starting on a new pan of cookies.

"So how come it has to be dissolved?"

"I don't know."

"Do you know why there's a special host in the monstrance? What makes that host different from the other hosts?"

"That's just how it is," she said.

"Mom?" I asked again.

"Yes, Tom."

"What does monstrance mean? Is it like monster? Because we should fear God?"

"I don't think it means monster. I know sometimes in church they say we should fear God, but I think God is there to take care of us."

"But if it doesn't mean monster, then what *does* it mean?"

"Why don't you ask Father Schmelzer? He'll be able to give you a better answer than I can."

"Okay," I finally said, swiping my finger inside the bowl for a taste of cookie dough before going out the back door.

Outside, it was one of those spring days when the sudden brightness of the sun belied the chill that still spoke of winter, so I went back inside and grabbed a thin cotton blanket, spread it out on the ground in the backyard, lay at one end of it and then rolled myself into it so that even my head was covered. Lying on my back, I could still see little slivers of sunlight through the cotton threads, and I stayed like that, alone with my thoughts, until I got too warm and poked my head out of my cocoon. The wind came in shifts—huge gusts that seemed to rise up from nowhere before falling again into stillness. New bits of green were starting to appear amid the winter-brown fallowness of the field, and in the distance, I saw Fred and Jim popping their heads in and out of their tree house. I turned to face the other direction and waited for the next gust. As it blew in, I turned my face toward it and closed my eyes. I loved the feeling of it washing over me, the feeling of movement while sitting still, the sound ruffling my blanket and hair. *I'm being touched by the invisible*, I thought. And that made me wonder how many other invisible things there were—like energy, like the Holy Ghost, like thoughts.

That April, right before my tenth birthday, my brothers and I came home from school to find a man in the house with Mom. He was even sitting right where Dad would have been if he hadn't been at work, and he had several books spread out on the floor. He was a thin man dressed in a plaid suit that was several sizes too large for his body, and beside him sat a brown, pebbled briefcase.

"Mr. Parker here is selling encyclopedias," Mom explained, handing the man a glass of water.

"Please, Mrs. Seeman, call me Phil." He regarded Ern, Dan, and me, while Rich squealed in his playpen and the twins worked on their only puzzle—a picture of Goldilocks and the Three Bears—for what must have been the hundredth time. "Looks like you boys came home just in time. A large family like this is perfect for a beautiful set of encyclopedias." He opened one of the books on his lap, and a map of India appeared on its glossy pages. "You've got the whole world in these books. You want to travel to India and—*poof!*—you're in India!"

Now he had my attention. "Can I look at it?" I asked.

"Now boys, as I told Mr. Par—*Phil*—we just can't afford something like this."

"It doesn't cost anything to look, does it?" said Phil, handing me the *I* volume. The first thing I noticed was the inky smell of the pages as I gazed at the colorful map and the people of India. I pored over photo after photo, page after page, captivated by how different their world was from the world I knew. There, men shaved their faces in the streets, cows meandered through cities, and the Taj Mahal loomed like a magical palace. As I sat on our living room floor, I read about the Hindu caste system and how you can never leave the caste you're born into, and about the many languages spoken in India—one hundred and eighty of them—which meant a person could travel to another town and not be able to understand what people were saying. I studied the brightly colored clothes people wore; I peered into Gandhi's eyes; I beheld a sacred river where everyone bathed together. With my finger, I traced the lines of the map, wondering what life was like in this little city or that little city, astonished by the vastness, not only of India but of the world, and curious about every speck of it. Though most of my siblings were in the room, some paging through the other volumes, I felt as though I were in a world by myself. Maybe the ability to block everything out is a trick that most kids born into crowded families come to master—this journey into the imagination that can make almost anything, at least for a brief time, seem to disappear.

"Each volume is organized alphabetically," Phil explained, "and you're looking at *I*. That's the great thing about purchasing a set like this. You only have to pay for one book a month, so you get the whole collection over time, in a way that's completely affordable."

"Do you have *P*?" I asked. I knew that I was half Polish on my father's side, but I didn't know anything about Poland.

"You're in luck!" said Phil, handing me *P*.

I flipped to Poland and saw more pictures of people who looked different from us but also very different from the many different people in India. "Their houses are usually one- or two-room cottages," the book pointed out. "Everyday clothing often is drab." As I read, I delighted in the slippery feel of the pages and the fluttery sound they made when I turned them. These were the most amazing books I'd ever held in my hands. "Look, Mom!" I said, holding the volume up over my head so she could see. "They have a map of New Mexico to show how big Poland is!"

"That's not very big at all," remarked Mom, looking at the clock on the wall.

Worried that she would soon tell Phil to leave, I started turning pages quickly but stopped when I came upon the section titled "Paintings." Aside from Mom's three paintings, I'd never seen much art, and now I was looking at works by Van Gogh, Rembrandt, Wyeth, and more—artists from all over the world who lived at different times, now all in one place. One of the first things I noticed was how different the painting by Mondrian was from all the others, and then I became intrigued by the old storefront in Edward Hopper's "Early Sunday Morning" and by the top hat and odd clothes the man was wearing in van Eyck's "The Marriage of Giovanni Arnolfini and Giovanna Cenami," which were again so different from anything I'd ever seen. I wanted to ask Phil if he had the *T* volume with him so that I could look up time machines, because I wanted to know if I could go back and see how people lived all through time, but I also couldn't take my eyes off Homer's "The Gulf Stream" because I was worried for the man in the capsizing boat surrounded by all those sharks, and I couldn't stop wondering if the red in the water was blood and if it had come from others who had once been in that same boat. But then my eyes fell upon a stormy image by El Greco. "Mom!" I called out again. "Look! It says here, 'View of Toledo!' He painted our city!"

Mom knelt down by where I sat on the floor and looked over my shoulder at El Greco's painting. "I think that's Toledo, Spain," she said. "Though it sure would be nice if we had a castle like that here, huh?"

"Wow, they have a Toledo in Spain too?" I turned and looked at Mom, and she looked at me with an expression I hadn't seen before—a combination of sadness, hope, and what may have been a wisp of mischief. Then she turned toward Phil. "What happens if I can't save enough?" she asked him.

Phil saw his opening and wasted no time. "There's no rush, no commitment—you can pay for the next volume whenever you're ready! Nothing better than the gift of knowledge, that's what I always say!"

I'm still not sure why Mom even let the encyclopedia salesman in the door that day, let alone why she allowed him to arrange his wares on our floor, while sitting in Dad's spot on the sofa. Maybe it was because I, too, had recently become a salesman, selling my Mary statues door-to-door. Or maybe it was because Mom had finally become exasperated by all the questions I asked, particularly those for which she had no answer, and these magical books would give her a reprieve. Or maybe she didn't need the salesman to tell her about the gift of knowledge. Maybe she already knew something about the freedom knowledge can bring, which was why she'd found a way to get us into a school we couldn't afford. Maybe she remembered her own school days, when she painted the three pieces of art that hung on our walls, or her job in a photography studio where she colorized giant photographs by hand—in those days before she met my father, before she gave all of her days to her children, before she stood inside a kitchen inside a house in the projects of Toledo, Ohio, where each day, a tidal wave of other people's needs washed over her, pushing her farther and farther from the shore of her old life, from a once-dreamed future that would now never be hers. I will never know exactly what Mom's thoughts were that day as she looked at me, her cheeks smudged with flour, but I do know that when she said yes, there was a sparkling moment when she smiled and I saw in her face what I saw in my Mother Mary statues: peace.

That evening, after we kids went to bed, I heard Dad start yelling and knew that Mom must have told him about the encyclopedias. "Aww balls, Ginny! You know we can't afford some fancy set of books. You always do this! You always put the kids first. You give them the best clothes. You even give them the best food, and you save the worst for me. And now this!"

"Oh Harry, that's not true at all. There is no best food, and you always get to choose which part of the chicken you want first. And they get donated clothes just like you do. We buy them so little, and I thought it was worth buying books for their education. It's only one book a month, and we can skip months if—"

"Isn't their Catholic school enough?"

"But we're not paying for that. You know that."

"Yeah, that's another thing," he said, his voice getting louder. "Why don't you tell me again—remind me, Ginny, what you did to get all these kids into that school for free."

"I asked."

"You asked? She *asked*!" His voice jumped into a falsetto then, and I felt my heart begin to thump against my ribs. I hated when he yelled because there was nothing I could think about—not even the most exotic animals in the most distant lands—that could stop his voice from finding me. "Just like that, and *poof*—is that what you're telling me? Or is there something you're not telling me?"

"I asked Father Schmelzer," she said, her voice as steady as if she were reading a cupcake recipe, "and when I told him where we lived, he said they would work something out—that the kids could work to cover some of it."

"And did you *work* for the rest of it?"

Suddenly Ernie, who I thought was sleeping, startled me as he leapt from our bed in a single movement. "What are you doing?" I whisper-yelled.

"I'm standing up for Mom," he said.

I jumped out of bed, too. "Me too!" I said.

The two of us ran down the hall, adding our voices to the mix. "Don't talk to her like that!" I yelled.

"Yeah," said Ernie, "we're sick and tired of you being mean to Mom!"

A bedroom door opened upstairs, and Marji called down, "Can everyone stop yelling?"

Dad squared his shoulders and faced Ernie and me. "You get the hell out of here, you little shits, before I give you a couple of knuckle sandwiches! All of you, back in your rooms!"

Marji closed the bedroom door, and Ernie and I retreated to our own bedroom. But our warning had worked: Dad stopped yelling at Mom.

A few nights later, Dad came home in a surprisingly affable mood. "I've got a special treat for everyone," he announced as he staggered toward the kitchen carrying a paper bag. "Ginny, heat this up on the stove," he said, and Mom got right to it.

"What is it, Dad?" asked Mary Jo as she followed him into the kitchen. Several more of us crowded in behind them to get a look at the special treat Dad had brought home for us—something he hadn't done since the crayfish fiasco.

"It's a delicacy," Dad said with a hint of pride.

"What's a delicacy?" asked Susie.

"You damned kids ask too many questions," said Dad. "Just grab a bowl and sit down at the table."

We all did as we were told and gathered around our two mismatched tables, waiting for Dad's delicacy.

Mom brought the heated pot over and set it down on a potholder, making sure to serve Dad first. "Looks like dark tomato soup," observed Dan.

"Nope," said Dad, unable to keep his secret any longer. "It's duck blood soup."

"Ewwww!" said several of my sisters in unison.

"You mean real blood?" asked Marji. "From a duck?"

"That's what I mean," said Dad, giving his soup a stir with his spoon. He seemed pleased that it shocked us.

"No thanks," said Ernie.

Dad looked at me. "I'm not really hungry," I said, pushing my chair back.

"More for me then," he said, slurping a spoonful with his outstretched rubbery lips, while we all left the table.

Later that night he called to me from his spot on the sofa. "Hey Tom," he said, holding a beer bottle up, "want my drops?"

I looked at him for a moment, unable to answer. I had always accepted those last dregs of his beer when he'd offered them to me, and yet I had made a promise to myself that I would never drink alcohol. But there he was, my father, frozen in this second of time, a nasty drunk with nothing to give his children but duck blood soup and a trickle of beer mixed with his saliva, a man who had once been a boy like me, a man who sat with a sheen of hope in his eyes as he held out a nearly empty bottle to his son. "No," I said, turning my back to him and walking to my room.

Right before bedtime, Dad called to me. "Hey, Tom. Get in here. It's time for your haircut."

Because we didn't have the money to get haircuts in a barber shop, Dad always cut our hair with electric clippers. Ours had an attachment that enabled him to cut all the hair on our heads to the same length simply by running the clippers in strips along our scalps. As I came into the room, I saw that he'd already set up by pulling out a kitchen chair and placing it on the newspapers Mom had put down on the floor. I wondered why he wasn't cutting anyone else's hair, since my siblings and I usually all lined up for haircuts. But I knew better than to ask questions, so I simply sat down in the chair. "Your hair's getting long. You don't want to look like a girl, do you," he said. It was not a question.

"Now sit still," he ordered, turning the clippers on. He made his first pass from the base of my neck to the crown of my head but then stopped. "Oh," he said, turning the clippers off. I looked down at the floor and saw what seemed like too much hair. "I forgot to put the attachment on," he said, clicking it into place. I touched my hand to the back of my head and felt what I already knew to be true. He had shaved that strip of my head bald. I started to cry.

"Cut it out and stop crying," he said. "It's no big deal. It'll grow back. Now sit still, goddammit, and let me blend it in."

For days I wore a stocking hat to school to cover my bald strip. But by the end of the day, my head would be so hot and itchy that I'd have to take it off. On our walks home, Jeffrey and Eddie took advantage of that by walking behind me and trying to outdo each other teasing me about it. "You could land a plane on that strip," said Eddie.

"His head's so white I bet it glows in the dark," observed Jeffrey.

"His head's so white you can see it from outer space."

"His head's so white it makes Casper look black."

And so on. I tried to laugh—it was kind of funny after all—but it would have been even funnier if the bald strip had been on one of their heads instead.

Life has a way of righting things sometimes, though. Not long after my haircut, I came home to two surprises. The first surprise was the first volume of the *World Book* encyclopedias. I couldn't wait to look at it, but first I had to take out the trash, which is where the second surprise appeared: a small, matted Collie rooting around the base of our trash cans. "Hi," I said softly, remembering my last encounter with My Dog. "Are you hungry?" She must have found something on the ground because she was making loud chewing sounds. "What did you find down there?" I asked. "Taffy?" As if to answer, she wagged her tail energetically and came to me, then nuzzled her face against the side of my leg. I knelt and ran my hands along her ratty fur, and she licked my face. "You're a good girl," I told her. She wagged her tail and buried her face between my knees. "I bet you don't care about my bald spot, do you?" I wanted to go inside and find something good for her to eat, but I was afraid she'd be gone when I got back.

"Why is there a dog in our kitchen?" Mom asked when we came inside.

"I found her by the trash cans."

"And what do you think we're going to do with her?" she asked as she bent over to pet her.

"Keep her? Just for a little while? She's hungry. And her name is Taffy," I said. As if on cue, Taffy nuzzled up to Mom and shimmied her body back and forth—a gesture I would come to learn was her favorite way of showing affection.

"You know we're not allowed to have dogs here, Tom," she said, kneeling to pet Taffy some more.

"But we could keep it a secret! No one would know. Lots of people have dogs here," I said, using my most persuasive voice, though I could tell by the smitten look in Mom's eyes that she'd already been hooked by Taffy's charm.

By then Susie and the twins had come in, and soon the older sisters joined, and it wasn't long before we were all in the kitchen, united in a sudden celebration with Taffy. And once again, Mom— who managed to feed so many of us with so little and who couldn't turn away the scruffy little dog who desperately needed a meal and a bath—said yes.

TEN

There is a popular stunt where people turn themselves into human flags by grabbing onto flagpoles with both hands and lifting off the ground so that their bodies extend sideways. In our neighborhood, I've seen only one person do it.

Even a father like mine can be a hero. Frozen in the scrapbook of my memory, here he is, suspended in the air, defying gravity like a magician: he has gripped the cold steel of a narrow light post, hoisted his body up, and is now horizontal—a solid flag made of flesh and bone. He holds himself there in a perfect calisthenic harmony of muscle, technique, and determination for an indeterminate amount of time—probably only seconds, though it feels like the span of an afternoon. Time is not what matters. What matters is that something has driven him off the earth in this most unexpected way. What matters is that we didn't know he could be so strong.

ELEVEN

Because our new dog wasn't a bag of M&M's, my siblings and I couldn't call "first" on whose room Taffy would sleep in. After we gave her a bath and ran our fingers through her newly fluffed fur, we all wanted to snuggle up to her and claim her as our own. "But I'm the one who found her," I argued, giving her a scratch under her chin, while Beth, who was patting the top of Taffy's head, reminded me that the last animal I'd been responsible for had gotten loose and scared the living daylights out of Mom. Susie, now six, ran her fingers along Taffy's downy tail and reasoned that Taffy should sleep in the little kids' room because she was "very good at brushing hair," while Mary Jo argued that Taffy should sleep in the big girls' room because she was the oldest and had seniority. But it was Marji who made the most passionate plea for the big girls' room: "I've always wanted a dog since the day I was born, and I've wanted one more than any of you!" she said. Meanwhile, Taffy lifted her head and closed her eyes as she received the vying strokes from our tangle of hands while we huddled around her, not wanting to let go.

"She can't sleep in anyone's room," Mom interjected in her most gentle voice. "She's going to have to sleep outside. And I have no idea how your dad is going to take this."

"But how can we keep her outside if we don't have a fence?" asked Marji.

"I suppose you'll have to tie her up," said Mom, picking up our baby brother Joe and handing him to Beth for a diaper change.

We wasted no time visiting Mom's bag of scrap clothing, cutting off part of an old belt and using a knife to puncture rough holes in it for Taffy's new collar. Then we took a rope and tied her to the T-bar Mom used to hang laundry. At first, I had misgivings about keeping her tied up, especially considering how sad My Dog had been, but then I thought about the burned cat and decided that at least Taffy would be safe with us.

And for a time, she was. We brought her our breakfast scraps and our dinner scraps, and I wrapped her up with me inside my blanket in the backyard when the chilly spring winds came. I told her what I was discovering in our new encyclopedias, and I tried out the latest words I'd plucked from the dictionary: "Taffy, I'd like to convey to you that I relish the information I've ascertained about the life of Caesar. Did you know that he was told to resign as a general because he was gaining too much power, but instead, he used his army to take over all of Rome? And when he was on his way to attack, he had to cross a river called the Rubicon, and once he crossed it, he couldn't go back. Then later, his own people stabbed him to death! It must have been really dangerous to live back then." Taffy, my loyal audience, wagged her tail and peered into my eyes as if she understood.

I started checking the *Adventures of Tintin* out of the library and daydreamed about the adventures Taffy and I might have some day. Like Tintin and his dog Snowy, we would travel abroad, ready to solve mysteries and unearth treasures and possibly even change the course of history. Maybe we would find a gleaming meteorite in the field behind our house or an alien hiding in the Peals' tree house or an entirely new species of animal no one knew about.

Taffy followed me on my treks into the weeds and stood by to see what I might uncover. One day, I lifted up an old refrigerator door, and a milk snake coiled back in self-defense. Taffy let out a bark and pounced at the snake, which lunged toward her. "C'mon, Taffy," I warned, "let's leave that guy alone." Bringing our family dog into a dangerous world alone suddenly felt overwhelming, but as I turned to walk back toward the house, Taffy followed in lockstep right behind me. "Good dog!"

"Hey, Seeman!" one of the Peal brothers called from the window of their "KEEP OUT" tree house. They had recently affixed another sign that read "DETECTIVE SERVICES." I looked toward them without giving them the satisfaction of an answer. "Whose dog is that?" Jim poked his head out the window.

"Ours," I called.

"Can we pet him?"

"It's a her," I said. I wanted to add that there was no reason I should let them pet my dog after they wouldn't let me into their tree house, but instead I walked Taffy over, and they climbed down to run their hands through her thick fur. "She's a collie, I think."

"She's so soft," said Fred. "I think she's called a *toy* collie because she's so small," he added. I admired how the Peal brothers always seemed to know things about animals.

"It looks like she's smiling," said Jim. "I think she likes me!"

"She only smiles at people she likes," I said, realizing that I was no longer mad at my neighbors.

Maybe everyone needs something that's just theirs, I thought, as I walked home with Taffy by my side. And after I reattached Taffy to her rope and rubbed her chest, I turned to make sure no one was around before I pressed my mouth to her furry ear and whispered something I'd never said before. "I love you." And those words, which had also never been spoken to me, warmed me like light.

That summer, we did something unusual for our family: we went for a cookout at Uncle Ben's house. He came to fetch the older half of our clan, and Mom and Dad drove over a while later with the little kids. A farrier and father to four, including a son who suffered brain damage from contracting meningitis shortly after birth, Uncle Ben was another of Mom's older brothers and was one of the friendliest people I knew. "Harry!" he exclaimed, putting his arm around my sour-faced father and snuggling him in close. "I've already got a burger on the grill for you, my friend. Come and have a seat by the pool!" Dad, who looked as if someone had just clanged a huge bell over his head, mumbled something unintelligible as we all made our way to the backyard.

The pool Uncle Ben spoke of was an above-ground circle of blue heaven, a beckoning aqua oasis, a shimmering godsend, which is to say that, though I had previously jumped with glee into the cold spray of a hose, I had never been in a swimming pool.

On the other side of the yard, an enormous weeping willow swept the grass with graceful fronds, and the scent of sizzling hot-dogs and burgers wafted through the air. Aunt Lois greeted us all with hugs and high-pitched exclamations: "Tom! It's so great to see you!" And their kids—Ellen, Mike, Chrissy, and Jerry (who hollered with excitement from his wheelchair)—all welcomed us as if they were genuinely happy to see us, which, given the logistics and cost involved in having thirteen people descending upon a single home, was a big deal. In fact, they were the only people who had ever invited us over for a meal.

As I watched the sun cut thousands of diamonds onto the surface of the pool, after we marveled at the novelty of paper plates and grill-cooking and filled our bellies with as much as we wanted, after Uncle Ben taught me how to hold my breath underwater, after I hid under the canopy of the majestic weeping willow and imagined digging up hidden treasures with Taffy in a yard like this, I decided to pray. Everyone was always saying that if we really wanted our prayers to be answered, we had to "pray hard," though I didn't really understand what that meant. How does one pray hard? Was prayer length a factor in this equation? Ferventness? Originality? No one ever told me. Nevertheless, I wanted to be the best at it. I wanted my prayers to win so they would be answered—a goal that the elderly women in the front pews of our church made seem almost impossible as they slipped their rosary beads through their fingers with quick precision and fiery expressions of determination. How could I compete with *them*, I wondered? They were doing so many prayers per minute—I couldn't possibly keep up. Sometimes I prayed to my Guardian Angel or to Mother Mary, and sometimes I went to a particular saint or straight to Jesus for something really important, but this time I readied a cache of my new vocabulary words and prepared to address all three in the hopes of earning triple prayer-credit, and in the hubbub of cookout bliss, in this magical place Mom called "The Suburbs," I issued a silent prayer: *Dear Jesus, Mary, and my Guardian Angel, I beseech you: please bestow upon me a domicile just like this someday, with a swimming pool and a weeping willow and paper plates we don't have to wash and a grill and charcoal of my very own. In the name of the Father....*

Father Schmelzer was so impressed by how well I cleaned up the holy vomit in church that he asked me if I'd like to take on a summer job with "a lot of responsibility": cleaning St. Vincent's school. Mom had told us we'd have to work in exchange for free tuition, so I wasn't surprised, and in that moment, I didn't think about giving up huge swaths of my summer playtime or about whether I would get paid anything at all (I wouldn't) or about how much work it would be (a lot). What I thought was how lucky I was to be asked to do such an important job. I took pride in knowing that Father Schmelzer saw something special in me, something my own father couldn't see.

After my first few days on the job, I walked beside Mom in the grocery store, my hands next to hers on the cart's cool rail. She was pregnant again. "You wouldn't believe it!" I told her. "I poured buckets of soapy water all over the floors and sloshed it all around with a mop, and then the head janitor, Mr. Murphy, showed me how to use this big scrubber machine to strip off all the old wax and then suck up all the water with a hose and nozzle!"

"That's nice," said Mom, inspecting a carton of eggs.

"The machine was really big, but since I'm probably going to be the heavyweight champion of the world, I was strong enough to handle it."

"Mmhmm."

"We had to move all the desks out into the hallways, and I got to put down the new wax with a special mop. And next he's going to show me how to use the buffing machine!" I held my arm out to the side and flexed my bicep. "Do you think my muscles have gotten any bigger?"

Mom was sorting through the stacks of coupons she'd clipped from the newspaper. Some days, she composed her grocery list before she shopped, but other days she didn't have time. "I'm trying to figure out which peas I have coupons for."

"Well, I think they're definitely getting bigger," I confirmed, giving my arm one last flex.

By the time we got to the checkout line, I'd managed to recount every bit of minutiae about my new job that I could think of, while Mom, who spent the lion's share of her life cleaning, listened patiently as I enumerated the joys of janitorial work. The store was bustling that day, with whining toddlers and crying babies, price checks being called out over the intercom, and long tails of lines wagging out into the store. As we approached the front of the line, Mom accidentally dropped her coupons, which cascaded in several directions all over the floor. I immediately got down and began to gather them, scuttling past grocery cart wheels and people's legs, while farther back in the line a woman with the kind of hair-sprayed hair that a gale-force wind couldn't disrupt complained in an arthritic voice, "Hurry it up already, I don't have all day." And when I stood back up, everyone was looking at us.

Mom handed the cashier her coupons, and when it came time to pay, Mom took from her wallet neither cash nor a check like other people but instead booklets of colorful food stamps. She tore along the perforations from each booklet until she'd paid enough, and as the check-out woman gave my mom her change—also in food stamps—my cheeks got hot, my throat got dry, and suddenly I had the urge to hide. I felt as if everyone could see, through the window of the food stamps, into our lives—the rats jumping out of our trash cans, my father slurping duck blood soup and slurring profanities, my mother silently swallowing his every word.

That summer, I scoured the grime off the surfaces of St. Vincent's School. I washed the cinderblock walls, working my sponge into every crevice. I cleaned the bathrooms, including the girls' bathrooms—that forbidden place of pink walls, heart-shaped pen-marks, and strange metal machines bolted to the wall—which I found both thrilling and unnerving. I moved hundreds of desks in and out of classrooms. But my most challenging task was learning to use a buffing machine to shine the floors. For one, the machine was exceptionally heavy, and if you revved the motor too hard, it could get away from you in a flash and easily crash into a wall, which, supposedly, had once happened. But more than that, the buffing machine required a level of finesse and attention that, according to Mr. Murphy, even some adults struggled to master, which automatically made me want to learn to do it as soon as possible. There was an art to leaning the buffer forward to make the machine go right and tipping it back to make it swing left, and to navigating the seamless transitions between the two directions so that I could make a beautiful back-and-forth design on the floor while allowing the machine's own power to slowly pull it forward or backward. Once I'd mastered it, the hours sped by, and as the buffer pad spun new life into those old floors, I saw my future play out on the screen of my mind. I could see the golden gleam of a medal hanging in mid-air as the announcer's deep voice resonated through the crowded stadium: *Ah wait, Seeman seems to be executing a double buff-back. This has never been attempted before in competition! No one's floors are so shiny! No one can transition as smoothly! And the gold medal for the Buffer Olympics goes to...Tom Seeman!* The crowd roared, fireworks mushroomed through the sky, and miles of linoleum tile shone like wet glass.

I'd always heard Dad complaining about work. "Fucking work" this and "fucking work" that. But I liked working. I liked being trusted with responsibilities. I even liked reaching behind the toilets to clean the places no one could see, even if no one else knew it but me.

I took a second job that summer, working in my fourth-grade teacher's garden. Mrs. Lambert had been my first teacher who wasn't a nun, and she had silky blond hair and a pretty smile. When she asked me if I had any interest in doing some work for her once school let out, I said something along the lines of, "Yes, absolutely, yes, for sure, yes." I liked telling myself that she chose me because she saw what a dedicated student I was, always acing my tests, always raising my hand to answer questions, always paying attention, but I suspected it was more likely that she'd gotten wind of my family's financial situation and figured I could use the work.

After I cleaned the school during the week and helped Mrs. Lambert on Saturdays, I came home and told Taffy about my days—how I had to take my shoes off when I waxed the floors so I wouldn't scuff them and how I had to put newspaper between the desks when I stacked them so that they wouldn't get scratched. "You have to protect things," I explained, and Taffy peered into my eyes as though she understood the deeper wisdom of my words. I told her how the girls' bathroom had a machine that sold something called a sanitary napkin and that I didn't understand why girls needed to buy special napkins. I told her how I used a shovel to dig up the grass in Mrs. Lambert's backyard and how we planted a vegetable garden, pushing some seeds into the soil a whole inch deep and others barely below the surface. "We planted a funny vegetable called kohlrabi. I'd never even heard of it before!" Taffy shimmied her body and licked my face. "On the seed package, it looks like a green ball floating just above the ground. A green ball vegetable—isn't that funny?" Taffy started panting, which made her appear to be smiling. "And then Mr. Lambert brought me lemonade. Have you ever tasted lemonade? I hadn't. It's so good! What an amazing day!"

A week later, something else amazing happened: Mrs. Lambert paid me in cash. She gave me five dollars, but it might as well have been five thousand, such was the intoxication of holding actual paper money in my hands. As soon as I got home, I ran to our room—which I was relieved to find empty—and studied the five bills, each with its own unique number, each featuring the same picture of George Washington. Though I had already learned the basics about our country's first president in school, I looked forward to reading about him in our encyclopedias when the *W* volume finally came. What did it take, I wondered, to be important enough to get your face on paper money, or even a coin?

"I'm planting a vegetable garden in the backyard," I told Mom after I hid my five George Washingtons in my sock-and-underwear drawer and came down into the kitchen, "so you won't need to use so many food stamps."

"That's very sweet, Tom," she said. Grandma was over, and they were rolling meatballs. "But unless you can raise chickens for all the eggs we go through and a cow for all the milk you drink, I think we'll still need that help for a bit."

"There's nothing wrong with needing a little help," Grandma said. "Everyone needs help at some point in their lives."

I wanted to ask why Dad didn't do more to help or why Mom had more babies than anyone else we knew, but instead I said, "I'm planting watermelons. Mrs. Lambert gave me seeds. Also lettuce, cucumbers, and kohlrabi. It's a green ball vegetable."

"Seems like you really know your stuff," said Grandma.

Mary Jo and Marji came into the kitchen and joined me in nibbling on apple peels. "I like your campanulate bottoms," I told Marji. She stopped mid-chew and looked at me askance. "Excuse me?"

"Your pants," I said, as though it were the most obvious thing.

"Can you please repeat in English?"

"That *is* English. Campanulate is another word for bell-shaped. I learned that in the dictionary."

Mary Jo started laughing. "He means he likes your *bellbottoms!* That's so cute!" And soon all the women in the kitchen were laughing at how cute (or possibly how annoying) I was, so I left them and went outside, where Taffy jumped into the air as if her paws were springs. "You're the best dog ever," I told her. "You understand everything I say." I pulled the half-used packages of seeds from my back pocket and gave them a shake. "We're planting a garden," I told her. She spun in three energetic circles, letting me know she was ready.

I used rocks to mark the four corners of my four-by-eight-foot plot in our backyard near the edge of the field, and I broke ground with a rusty shovel. Taffy contributed by sniffing the dirt with gusto. As the smell of turned dirt told a story of fresh starts, I thought about how lucky I was to have so many seeds in my pocket and a yard to plant them in. Dad often complained that our house was too small or that we didn't have enough, but I didn't see it that way. I never had. Maybe kids just have a way of finding what shines, no matter the darkness around them. And as I planted my garden, spacing the seeds the way Mrs. Lambert showed me, the sun reddening my arms, Taffy pressed her nose on the places where I pushed the seeds into the soft earth, giving the seeds one last pat into the soil.

Mom came out with the metal filter from her percolator, full of thrice-steeped coffee grounds. Grandma said they would help fertilize the soil, so I scattered the dark flecks from end to end. I collected sticks I found at a trash-strewn marsh not far from our house (where I also spotted a snapping turtle, which I immediately added to my Wild Animals I Have Seen list), and I constructed an interlocking stick border around the garden. "Very intricate," Grandma said, folding her arms with a decisive nod.

One day, Donald and David Quinton, known in the neighborhood as the Quinton Twins, came walking across the field. They were a year older than I was and lived three blocks away from us on the same side of Bronson Street. The rumor was that they, along with their other two brothers, had both been in "juvie," which is how the kids in our neighborhood referred to the juvenile detention center. Whenever I saw them, I always got out of their way, as did most people in our neighborhood. "What are you doing?" one of them asked as they passed by our yard.

"Just watering my kohlrabies," I said, offering a small nonchalant shrug.

"Kohl-who?" asked Donald.

"Rabi," I said. "It's a green ball vegetable." I looked down at the tiny green seedlings, at once so tender and tenacious, and felt suddenly protective of them. "Or they will be, one day. Right now, they're just sprouts."

The twins started laughing. "Just so long as they aren't blue balls," said David, and I laughed, too, as if I understood the joke.

By the end of summer, my garden was in full bloom. We indulged in the crunch of fresh cucumbers and thinly sliced kohlrabi, which tasted like a mild, peppery broccoli. I tossed dark green "leaf lettuces" into a salad, but we all preferred the texture of the iceberg lettuce we were accustomed to. Only one small watermelon grew, and on a day when Dad took Mom to the grocery store, I pulled it from the vine. When no one was looking, I took a kitchen knife and went upstairs with my melon. My siblings and I always shared everything, but I wanted this for myself, so I hid in the bathroom, sat on the toilet, and split the melon open with the knife, savoring every second, even the resonant sound of it coming apart.

When I was finished with my watermelon, I took my newfound stealth one door over and entered my parents' room. Because it was a place I almost never entered, it felt like an exotic land. At first I prowled around, just looking. Every few steps I became very still and listened for any sounds of my parents coming home, certain that I would make a better detective than either of the Peals. My heart pounded as I opened a drawer in Mom's dresser, which was perfumy and filled with boring white undergarments. Soon, I established a rhythm: open a drawer, rummage, stop, listen, proceed to the next. Just as I searched the field behind our house for hidden treasures, I hunted through my parents' belongings for the unknown. I opened boxes on the floor of their tiny closet. I skimmed through a collection of photographs from Mom's childhood, including one of her on a horse smiling in a way I'd never seen her smile, as if her happiness had another gear I didn't know was there. Dad's drawers were no more interesting than Mom's, except that instead of harboring the scent of perfume, they emitted Dad's unmistakable musty odor, which the laundry soap Mom used could never quite eliminate.

I was beginning to feel pretty lackluster about the whole investigation until I got to the small, square drawer at the bottom right of Dad's dresser. Unlike the other drawers, this one didn't hold any clothes. At first, the contents seemed as uninteresting as everything else in the dresser—a stack of papers, an old wallet that had split in half, a set of keys—but beneath all that I discovered the steely gleam of something new: a handgun. I took the wood-grain handle into my hand and ran my fingers along the smooth black barrel, noting how cold it was to the touch. There was a little button on the left side that, when I pushed it, unhinged the chamber with a slick click. I emptied all six bullets into my hand as though I'd done it a hundred times before. Then I reloaded them, pushed the barrel closed, and repeated the process over and over, imagining how I, like Tintin, could use the weapon to exact good over evil. *Stop right there,* I said in my fantasy, in which I'd time-traveled back to Halloween 1967, *and give us back our candy!* As I held the weight of the pistol out in front of me, I could imagine the candied heft of our pillowcases being returned to our hands. *We're sorry,* the thieves would say. *We won't do it again.* I could imagine also the later darkness of the night and a faceless boy holding a gas can and matches. I'd come running at him, my gun drawn, and he would drop the gas can and matches on the street and run away. I could imagine a black cat, lithe and lustrous, skimming the edge of the field, free.

The tree in the field went up like paper that September in 1969. Everything burned—every leaf, every beam, every sign that pointed to the imagination of two boys who'd nailed every piece of wood themselves. The flames swallowed the tree as if it were the smallest thing and licked up at the sky in spectacular leaps, filling the air with thick black smoke. Fred and Jim had managed to shimmy down their ladder rungs in time and run away, only to stand, as we all did, helpless against the destruction, awestruck by its strange beauty.

By the time the firetruck arrived, the tree was gone. I never asked them how they'd accidentally set it on fire, and they never told me. Eventually, the thick, charred stump became something we stopped noticing.

For a time, my days were marked by goodbyes to Taffy in the morning, as we cut across the field on our way to school, and exuberant hellos when we returned home. "Rrr-rhrrr-rhrrr-rhrrrrr!" I'd call to her, starting from the moment I came around the corner from Central Avenue onto D Street, when I could first see her small, fluffy shape from way across the field. As soon as she heard me, she'd start springing into the air—all four paws off the ground—and spinning in circles until I reached her. I had never before known that a bond could exist between two beings who made each other so happy.

Then things changed, on the most ordinary of days. On one of those ordinary days, as I came around the corner onto D Street, I didn't see Taffy's small, fluffy shape from across the field. I made my usual call to let her know I was coming, but I saw no wagging tail. I immediately took off running toward the house, thinking maybe she was hiding, but when I got there, her rope lay empty on the ground. "Where's Taffy?" I asked Mom, arriving out of breath into the kitchen. And, in her usual calm manner, she said the words I wanted to run back across the field away from: "The Housing Authority came and told us we couldn't keep her anymore. Taffy's gone."

TWELVE

I don't remember Dad ever petting Taffy, let alone acknowledging her in any observable way. But after the Housing Authority told Mom we had to get rid of Taffy or else they would take her to the dog pound, it was Dad who found Taffy a new home. He'd put out the call for a free collie while he was dispatching at the cab company, and one of the drivers volunteered to take her. "A real nice fellow, with a family," he told us. And though I knew I should be grateful that he'd spared Taffy the potential horrors of the pound, the thought of other kids getting to pet Taffy and play with her and tell her their secrets was an injustice I couldn't accept. "How could you just give Taffy away like that?" I demanded as soon as Dad walked through the door that day. He reeled back on his heels a little, as if someone had just hit him. Then he slammed the door. "This is the thanks I get for finding that mutt you weren't even supposed to have in the first place a new home, you little shit?"

My voice came out part squeal. "You didn't even let me say goodbye!" I tried to swallow back the tears, but they poured down my cheeks anyway. Several of my siblings were in the room, as usual, and Mary Jo spoke in a soothing voice, "It'll be okay, Tom. You'll see." But suddenly I didn't want any of them to see me crying, and I didn't want to be told something would be okay when it didn't feel okay at all. I knew they missed Taffy, too, but I didn't respond or even look at anyone as I got up and ran out the back door. I ran past Taffy's empty rope and onto The Path. At the end of The Path, I picked up a palm-sized rock and a stick that was almost the length of my leg and carried them with me.

So this is how it is, I said to God as I walked. *When I finally get something I love, I lose it. Is this some sort of test, like Job? You want me to get tougher, is that it? Well, fine.*

I moved briskly through the streets without any sense of where I was going—maybe because I was never going anywhere. I had no destination. But that wasn't the point. The point was solitude and the scenery that flashed by, marking my distance as I went. Though it was a sunny day, I preferred to walk in the rain, when the wash of nature was like a reset button and I had the streets to myself. Sometimes I'd return home completely soaked through, but Mom never said a word. No one ever asked where I had been or why I would walk out in the rain in the first place.

Sometimes when I walked, I had this sense that we lived behind a hidden wall and that, if I walked fast enough or far enough, I would find it and break through. On the other side would be all the places I'd read about in our encyclopedias—places other people lived with all their possibilities, cities that towered to the sky, rippling mountains, turquoise seas, pink dolphins in the Amazon River—the world alive with all the wild animals of my dreams. Sometimes I would walk for hours, thinking about that wall and how I could get to the other side. If I were president, I would just command that the wall be taken down; if I were the heavyweight champion of the world, I would knock it down myself; if I were the richest man in the world, I would buy an airplane and fly over it.

I figured things out when I walked. And on that day, as I palmed my rock and swung my stick and traced through the neighborhoods that rippled out from Bronson Street until I was in what seemed like a faraway land, I figured out how I might be able to get

Taffy back: I would write a letter to the Housing Authority, asking them to change their no-pet policy. For a moment, hope flooded me, and I forgot to be sad.

I composed the letter in my head until it got dark, and when I got back home, Mom was in the kitchen putting pans of cookies into our old tin bread box. She asked if I was hungry and then heated some spaghetti and meatballs on the stove while smoke from Dad's cigar plumed in. Between bites, I told Mom about the letter I was planning to write. "Maybe the Housing Authority doesn't realize that it's good for kids in the projects to have dogs," I said, "and also good for the dogs because the dogs we get are strays, and they would go hungry if we didn't feed them our scraps, and then our scraps would just go to waste. So it's good for everyone." While Mom zoomed around the kitchen, she nodded and occasionally peeked over her shoulder at me to let me know she was listening. "Plus, when you have a dog, you have someone to hug," I added, "and that's important."

This time Mom turned all the way around and looked at me for several seconds. "Yes," she finally said, though it came out sounding more like a question.

My letter didn't bring Taffy back, nor did it persuade the Powers That Be at the Housing Authority to change their policy, but it might have had something to do with why Mom came into our room a few days later. Ernie was out, and I was lying on my stomach on our bed, reading one of our trusty encyclopedias, when I heard her voice. "Hi, Tom," she said, which for some reason seemed like a strange thing for her to say. She sat down on the bed beside me and then did something she'd never done before: she patted my back—an awkward combination of a pat and a slap delivered in rapid succession between my shoulder blades. I didn't know what to do in this uncharted territory of touch, so I kept my eyes on the ruffed lemur while Mom changed her approach and started scratching my back with her fingernails, which felt kind of good and kind of odd. We stayed like this for several silent minutes, save for the sound of her rapid scratching, before she gave me one last pat-slap and left the room.

Maybe Mom's silence in the language of affection was passed down through her Germanic heritage, because Grandma didn't give hugs or offer professions of love either. Or maybe, like Grandma, Mom's language of affection was spoken through her hard work in keeping the family ship afloat. Maybe it was spoken in the artistry of using saved fabric scraps to make my sisters' color-block Easter dresses or my teddy bear's vest, or in her perpetual hunt for new recipes to cook for us, like the one she called *soutzoukakia*. Maybe love lived in the magic she wove into the tapestry of the ordinary so that we could grow up in the projects rarely noticing that we were poor, and seldom feeling sad.

THIRTEEN

Ern and I started playing football, as most of the St. Vincent's boys in the fifth and sixth grade did. Our new football coach, Gary, was irrepressibly enthusiastic, often patting our backs or smacking our butts as he exclaimed some version of, "Go get 'em, boys!" during practice at Wilson Park—a small city park about eight blocks from our house. "Nice one, Tommy!" He was the first person who had ever called me Tommy.

Perpetually clad in polyester coach shorts, Spot-Bilt shoes, and a silver whistle strung around his neck, Coach Gary cared about our team in that inexplicable way that drives some coaches to devote their free time and even their own money to the cause. And because Jeffrey and I, and one other kid named Mark, were big for our age, our coach's cause was to help us lose weight so we could make the weigh-in to play in the league. With his own money he bought us plastic track suits. Similar to normal two-piece sweat suits, these were designed with one major difference: to make you sweat. And as if the non-breathable plastic weren't enough, the suits were also equipped with tight elastic bands around the waist, wrists, and ankles to ensure no amount of air could ever reach the person sealed inside.

On the weekend before we were due to step on the scales, Coach Gary picked us up and took us and our new plastic, navy-colored suits to Pearson Park. I hadn't been there since Uncle Dick and Harold had last taken us there to feed the ducks, and as we drove in on the wooded road, I felt that same excitement I'd felt before as I peered into the piney distances for glimpses of the wild. "We might see a groundhog," I informed Jeffrey, "or a fox."

"Or a goofball in a plastic suit," Jeffrey said, to which I used the old "you must be looking in the mirror" line. And then we started to run.

As we sped along on the soft gravel-and-pine-needle path around the perimeter of the park, each of us trying to be in the lead, my animal quest soon waned as life inside my plastic suit got hot. Sweat stung my eyes and my lungs fought for air as I secured my position in the lead, while Coach Gary charged behind us, looking as unruffled as a man I'd once seen on TV sipping an umbrella drink in a lounge chair. "How many miles have we gone already?" Jeffrey gasped.

"You fellas are doing great! You're almost at the half-mile mark!" Coach Gary cheered. "Just keep going!" And though the reality of how far we'd actually run was demoralizing, his encouragement made me run a little faster.

His encouragement also, I believe, helped us hit our target weights. Before the first football game of our lives, Ernie and I suited up in our uniforms and carried our helmets proudly to Wilson Park, where the coaches and some of the parents (mostly from the White House) all met to drive in a convoy to our game. Maybe because we were such good sports about the plastic suits, Coach Gary let Jeffrey and me ride with him, while Ernie rode with one of his sixth-grade friends. During the drive, Coach Gary quizzed us on plays, and Jeffrey and I shouted out the answers, envisioning our imminent victory. We arrived at the fields—a huge open area next to St. Francis de Sales High School lined with about five or six football fields—where people and teams were milling everywhere and games were already being played.

"This is where we're going to play all of our games this year," said Coach Gary. "On Saturdays, they've often got five games going on at once."

As we stepped onto our designated field about thirty minutes later, I looked out at the sidelines, which seemed so far away, and at the white chalk line-markings that made the field look official compared to the unmarked grass at Wilson Park, and I realized we were on our own. The coaches and parents couldn't do much to help us anymore. And when our opponent, St. Pius, walked onto the field, I had the unfamiliar feeling of being small.

Maybe because of the many times Dad had referred to St. Vincent's as "that fancy fucking school," I was under the impression that our school *was* fancy. I'd never thought to question why we had recess in a parking lot, why we didn't have any grass to play on, or why we wore used uniforms that didn't fit quite right. I just assumed that was how it was for everyone. But as I stood next to Ern and Jeffrey and beheld the matching black-and-white striped socks that climbed all the way up to our opponents' kneepads and the matching helmets they wore—sleek and shiny and bolstered with intricate cages that covered their entire faces—and the pristine white uniforms that seemed tailormade for their bodies, and then took stock of our plain white crew socks and naked shins, our mismatched helmets with only two bars across the face, and our dingy pants, I saw us for the ragtag bunch we were. And suddenly, any bravado I'd reveled in with Jeffrey Huxley in the backseat of Coach Gary's car fizzled as I faced the calm assuredness of St. Pius. It was as if their very uniforms were stitched with victory.

Right before the first snap of the ball was about to herald my first seconds as an offensive tackle, I shot a glance at Ernie next to me on the line, and he gave me a little nod as he sunk down into his stance. Then I peered into the eyes of the guy across from me. He stared back and opened his mouth, and for a second I thought he was about to say something. Instead, he let out a resonant burp that spoke of the bacon he must have eaten for breakfast. I wanted to turn my head away, but any movement at all on the offensive line could be called as an offsides penalty, so I kept my head still in the invisible bacon cloud.

My mouth went dry as I realized how completely opposed he and I were. His goal was to travel as far into our backfield as he could or to occupy the gap he was assigned to fill, and my sole job was to stop him from doing his assigned job. I hadn't given this enough thought, I realized. I wasn't ready for this pure and direct opposition to my goals, and from a kid who was so very different from me, no less. Sure, our team had practiced dozens of times, but how could I compete against someone like this, I wondered— someone who had all the trappings, things I didn't even know about? What else did he know that I didn't?

When our quarterback called the count, I stopped thinking. My opponent lunged into the gap on my left, which was right where the ball runner was going. I used his momentum to push him past the hole, which wasn't how we'd been coached to do it, but it worked nonetheless, and on our next play I was no longer intimidated by his socks.

"Close game, close game!" Coach Gary cheered later, after the final score sent the other team high-fiving off the field. "You guys have 'champion' written all over you! Those other guys might have ritzy uniforms, but you guys have something they don't—you've got grit. You didn't let up, and that's what'll make all the difference in close games!"

Though I questioned just about everything, I didn't question how our coach could see us as champions when we'd just lost the game. Instead, I believed him.

That evening in bed, in the dark, I asked Ernie, "Do you think Coach Gary was right?"

"About what?"

"That we have 'champion' written all over us?"

Ernie didn't answer right away. I'd always sensed a cautiousness in him that, combined with a certain slightness in his build, I attributed to the year he'd had rheumatic fever. He'd had to stay home his entire second-grade school year, and mom helped him with his homework. We still lived in Ravine Park then, and though my memories of that time are hazy, I remember that his joints were so painful that he had to go up and down the stairs on his butt. The cross the priest used when he came to give Ernie his First Holy Communion was made of wood with a ceramic Jesus attached to it, and the top came off to reveal a hidden compartment inside that housed holy water and two white candles. Dad's mom, Mary Magdalene—whom we called Grandma Joker because she had a little dog named Joker—had given Mom the crucifix kit, and when the priest lit the candle, I couldn't take my eyes off it. I'd only ever seen candles in church, and as I watched the flame dance and flicker as if it were alive, I didn't notice the brusqueness with which the priest gave Ernie his sacrament or how he barely regarded Mom at all (though Mom would tell me about his rudeness many years later). But it was obvious that Mom was upset after he left. She, who rarely complained about anything, said, "Just because we live in this neighborhood doesn't mean we're different on the inside," as she hung the cross back on the wall.

Sometimes when I looked at Ernie, my only older brother, I wondered what was inside *him*—if maybe he had his own hidden compartment with a burning candle I would never see.

"Yes and no," he finally said.

"Yes *and* no?"

"Well, obviously we're not champions now, so if it's written on us, it's not in a way that anyone can see. Like, maybe it's written in invisible ink, and Coach Gary is the only one who can see it. But one day, everyone will be able to see it."

"Even Dad?"

Ernie paused again. I could almost hear the gears of his mind turning. "Maybe not everyone," he finally said.

That fall, as the daylight waned and the jack-o'-lanterns burned and our pillowcases filled with candy that we ushered safely home, as the inhabitants of the field behind our house died off or disappeared into deeper shelter, as I crossed the line between age ten and eleven and felt the power of my body strengthen on the football field, I started noticing things I hadn't noticed before, like the way Claire Kowalski, who sat next to me in class, twirled her hair and sometimes inexplicably sniffed the inside of her textbooks. But it wasn't just girls; it was a new world of subtleties that were coming into my awareness, such as the way Mom sometimes stared off as though she were looking out the window of a train—a departure that always seemed to end almost as quickly as it had begun. It was as if everything had somehow taken on an extra dimension that I hadn't perceived before, like the gratifying crack of a hardboiled egg or the way the autumn light cast long shadows on the streets

as we walked home from school. And though I'd always been one
to ruminate, my ruminations also seemed to be gaining a dimension. I could walk with my rock and stick for hours, puzzling
over existential questions—*Why am I here?* Or, *How can I get* there?
There was still a nebulous place, or rather, an amalgam of things
on the other side of my imaginary wall, including the far-off wilds
I longed to explore, a house with a pool like Uncle Ben's, and the
state of bliss I'd once seen when Uncle Dick played his saxophone.
There was a feeling as much as a place—a sparkle in the mysterious
darkness—and I began to orient myself to it like a star.

Because the priests seemed to have the answers to all of life's
questions, I started paying more attention in church, not only to
how intensely the front-row pew ladies prayed but also to what the
priests were actually saying in their sermons. They talked about the
Ten Commandments, and it struck me that if following the rules of
God could get you into Heaven for all eternity, maybe it could also
help me get to the other side of the wall. But how could I follow
ten rules I didn't fully understand? I brought my conundrum to
Coach Gary. "What does it mean to have other gods?" I asked him
one crisp day after practice at Wilson Park.

We were jogging back to his car in the early dusk, and his
whistle thumped against his chest with each step. "Sorry Tommy,
but I have no idea what you're talking about."

"The Ten Commandments," I explained. "The first command-
ment says, 'Thou shalt not have other gods before me.' But how can
you have another god if God is the only god?"

"Oh, I see!" he said. "Sure, sure. That just means you shouldn't
worship fake gods, like maybe a statue or something."

"Or ghosts?" I'd been working on a report for school based on
the life of Sitting Bull, and I'd just read about the Ghost Dance, a

Native American religious movement that invoked the ghosts of their beloved dead to come back and fight wars on their behalf.

"You don't believe in ghosts, do you?"

I squinted my eyes and stared into the rosy distance to see if I could spot any ghosts. "I believe in Guardian Angels. There's one right behind me now," I said. "Aren't they a kind of ghost?"

Coach Gary stopped jogging, though we hadn't reached his car yet. He turned and looked at me in that strange way Mom sometimes did when I asked too many questions. Then he looked behind me, as if to acknowledge my Guardian Angel. "You know, I'd never thought about that. But I suppose you're right!" He was still smiling as he picked the jog back up and I jogged alongside him, looking for phantasms in the Toledo sky.

It was a busy fall, made even busier when I got my third job. I'd learned from a kid in school that his friend was selling his paper route for the *Toledo Blade*, and I jumped on the opportunity to deliver papers seven days a week. The kid who sold me the route allowed me to pay him over time with my earnings, which Uncle Dick said was a great way to start a business. *I'm a businessman*, I'd think, pulling a paper from the white canvas sack I'd purchased from the *Blade* and tossing it so that it landed just so on the customer's front step.

In the beginning, I walked my route of sixty houses, for which I paid sixty dollars. After I paid off my route, I bought my first bike—a second-hand, banana-seated, high-handle-barred, one-speed that I spray-painted gold—and began perfecting the art of timing my throw without slowing down my bike, a challenge that made my job endlessly exciting, especially when the paper landed in such a way as to make it appear that I'd carefully walked over and placed it there. Sometimes I gave imaginary television interviews as I rode between houses. "Tell me," the interviewer would say, "how do you achieve such precise results? Is there a secret to your throwing motion?" "Well," I'd say, answering myself as I pedaled, "it takes a lot of preparation, meaning you have to fold the papers very tightly. But most of the expertise is in the rotation of the paper through the air. Eventually, you create a reliable paper delivery system that," I often paused for effect, "makes people happy." I liked to sound official during my interviews.

But I didn't only talk to myself while I delivered papers. When Saturday came and it was time for me to collect payments door-to-door, I talked to my customers too. At first, several of them cast a skeptical eye at me, wanting to know where their usual paperboy was. But after I started getting up at 5:30 a.m. on the weekends so people could have their papers in time for breakfast (the most important thing, I quickly realized), and opened a jar of peanut butter for a grandmother with weak hands, and helped a man carry a heavy concrete bird bath into his garden, my customers warmed to me, and I stood in their doorways, breathing in the particular scents of their homes—blueberry muffins, garlic, cigarettes, mildew, perfume—and learned about their lives. When I told the man with the bird bath that I'd built a backyard garden that summer, he warned me to be on the lookout for aphids, which had destroyed many of his plants last year, and he gave me several packets of seeds to save for the spring. Another customer asked if I'd be interested in shoveling her walkway that winter, and that led to more shoveling jobs later. And a pretty woman answered her door wearing only a T-shirt and underwear, which, perhaps by design, distracted me from the fact that she didn't have the money to pay me that week. I was learning a lot about how other people lived and about how to run a business—for instance, how long was reasonable to continue delivering to a customer when they didn't pay (I had to pay *The Blade* for every paper each week, regardless of who paid me) and how many special requests I should accommodate, such as placing a paper behind their screen door. I had to accommodate some, since people gave tips at Christmas, but if I accommodated too many, I'd be late for football. One constant was that if a paper came damaged or got rained on, that was the one I'd keep for our family, much to Dad's chagrin.

Just when it seemed I couldn't add one more thing to my days, my fifth-grade teacher, Mrs. Willis, nominated me to take free art classes every Saturday morning at the Toledo Museum of Art, a gift for which I had my report on Sitting Bull to thank. For the cover of my report, I'd drawn Sitting Bull's face, then cut all the pages out in the shape of his head, punched holes in the pages, and tied them together with wire twist-ties mom had saved from bread bags—details Mrs. Willis said were "inspired" and "above and beyond." And while it was true that I compulsively sought my teachers' approval, it made me genuinely happy when I, like Mom, went "above and beyond" to make things special.

When Dad dropped me off for my first Saturday morning class at the museum, leaving me at the curb in front of the enormous neoclassical building that boasted the grandest steps I'd ever seen, I gazed up at the sixteen marble columns that spread like teeth across the front of the building and felt a similar feeling to the one I felt the first time we stood on the football fields next to St. Francis: the sensation of being small. My excitement, however, loomed large, as did a red stegosaurus-like sculpture that towered like a mascot on the landing between staircases as if to say, "Mystery awaits you inside."

And the stegosaurus was right. Though I had peered at every painting featured in our encyclopedias, seeing paintings in real life—large, textured, illuminated, bold—invoked in me an indescribable sense of mystery, as if each painting were a secret world you could magically enter. I especially liked the paintings showing people living in different times and places, because I liked thinking about different kinds of lives. I tried to notice everything—the clothing, the furniture, the buildings, the tools. I wondered, what was the woman in the painting thinking at that moment of her life? What did she do with the rest of her day?

Our class of ten was held in the museum's whitewashed basement, in a cavernous room messy with canvases and huge tables strewn with paints and clays and charcoal pencils and brushes and enormous drawing pads. We were led by a young woman named Lauren who wore rings on all her fingers and peered deeply into our eyes. Before we got started making our own art, Lauren gave us a tour through a few of the museum's galleries, asking us what we thought of various works of art, pointing out uses of shadowing, perspective, color. In one painting, when I leaned in close as Lauren instructed, I noticed that the artist had created the lace with a precisely stippled arrangement of tiny dots. I often thought about that later—how something so intricate could also be so simple.

That Saturday morning, Dad knew he wouldn't be able to leave his job dispatching taxis to pick me up, so he sent a taxi from his company instead. As the driver took the turns that would bring me home, Dad's gravelly voice sounded from the taxi's radio like a familiar song you can't quite place. Only it was different too; taxi dispatching had its own special shorthand language, so I couldn't understand everything he was saying, and each time he stopped speaking, the radio made a staticky sound that abruptly cut off his last syllable. I had never heard my father in command, with people responding to him as though his words were important. He told drivers which roads to avoid, which shortcuts to take, what time traffic would start in different parts of town. I felt proud of him, this man who carried an intricate map of Toledo in his mind and who made it seem so simple, this man who almost seemed to care about the drivers he was directing. *That's my dad*, I thought.

But nothing is static. Tree houses turn to ashes in minutes; dogs appear and then are gone; a garden is fecund and then fallow. And not long after Dad reigned heroic on my short taxi ride home, he was stopped by police for "drunken driving." And just like that, Dad was gone to "the state hospital to dry out," Mom said.

While Dad was away, I'd taken my paper route customer's advice and looked up aphids in my encyclopedia so I could be prepared if they appeared in my garden in the spring. I learned that aphids' mouths are shaped into sucking tubes, that the males have wings but many of the females are wingless, and that they produce a sweet fluid called honeydew, which ants lap up. Some aphids give birth to unhatched young from unfertilized eggs within their bodies, thus bearing generations of fatherless aphids—an occurrence known as parthenogenesis. *Parthenogenesis.* I repeated this word several times, as if the word alone could make Dad stay away forever and I, too, could become fatherless.

FOURTEEN

He was a stranger when he came home—pale and thin, his hands shaking, his voice a husk of its former timbre. "Welcome home, Dad!" several of the girls called as he made his way in the front door with Mom, who looked solid and strong next to his hunched and tenuous carriage. The rest of us watched, frozen in place. Susie and the twins had been playing jacks on the linoleum at the edge of the living room rug, and the jacks lay scattered and shiny; I'd been arguing with Dan and Marji over a game of just-toppled pickup sticks; and others peered over their open books and partially assembled puzzles as Dad trudged over to his corner of the couch and slowly lowered himself down. He looked around the room at all of us as if we, too, were strangers, and he pulled a cigarette from a pack in his shirt pocket—an odd sight, since we'd only ever seen him smoke cigars. He clenched the cigarette between his teeth while he fumbled for his metal flip-top lighter, and when he sparked it, his hands shook so violently that he lost the flame twice before he was finally able to light his cigarette. Mom said he hadn't been allowed to smoke cigars in the hospital, so he'd taken up cigarettes instead. And it seemed fitting—his cigars slimming to cigarettes, reflecting how he, too, had shrunk.

But I felt, as I looked at my father in his newly timid and diminished state, a sense of hope. I thought that maybe with the alcohol stripped away, he might be a better man. I remember repeating those words in my mind—*a better man*—as if they were a boat that would ferry us into a new future. And as we all sat silent with our thoughts, Dad began to cry—a soft whimpering that erupted into violent sobs. His body quivered as tears shook loose from his eyes and his face contorted in monstrous ways, reminding me of the red-faced babies I sometimes saw bawling in church or in the grocery store, all while the cigarette burned down between his fingers and the ashes fell to the floor without him even noticing. "It's okay, Harry," Mom said in a wisp of a voice, but that only made him cry harder. Wide-eyed and unsure, my siblings and I looked at each other, while Mom sat down beside Dad and smoothed the tops of her trousers in long strokes toward her knees, as if that were the most comfort she could offer.

In the weeks Dad was away, Mom had started learning to drive. "Because I don't want to be left waiting for Dad to get me anymore," she'd said, visibly weary from all the times he'd left her stranded so that he could go to a bar. Her cousin's husband, Walter, had been taking her out to practice, while Grandma came to look after us. She and Uncle Dick and Harold had also been taking Mom to the store, taking me to and from art class, taking us to church. They stayed for dinner; they laughed; they asked us questions about our days; they were the living antidote to the years of Dad's grumbling and barking, of his distance and anger. They, like Uncle Ben, were windows into another kind of life, an oasis in the desert that had been our father. But now, as he sat in his usual spot, a changed man in a cloud of smoke and torment, I felt guilty for having wished him away. "We're glad you're home, Dad," I said, secretly wondering whether lying for a good cause was still a sin.

Dad smashed his cigarette out in the ashtray with so much force that the side table shook. "Get the hell out of here, all of you!" he cried. "Scram!"

Old Dad is back, I thought, and like a handful of dropped coins, my siblings and I dispersed, marking the end of Dad's homecoming celebration. I went out into the field, where I soon realized my T-shirt wouldn't be warm enough for the brisk fall weather. But I didn't want to go back home to get my jacket, so I turned on Central instead and entered the Ontario Store, a discount department store set back off the street. Fred and Jim's mother worked inside, and she spotted me immediately. "Oh hi, Tom!" she said, reaching out to pat my shoulder with her long fuchsia nails.

"Hi, Mrs. Peal," I said, trying for the nonchalance of a boy whose father wasn't a hysterical alcoholic fresh out of a state hospital.

"What are you looking for today?"

I didn't know what to say—I'd been saving my paper route money in my sock drawer along with the money I'd earned at Mrs. Lambert's house, but I didn't have even a penny in my pocket—so I shrugged and moseyed away.

Mom sometimes shopped at the Ontario Store for underwear or other things we needed, like my husky-sized pants, but now I was free to roam the toy section at my leisure, bouncing basketballs when no one was looking, squeezing stuffed bears and dogs, pretend-firing toy guns. Each one I picked up surprised me with its lightness compared to the gun in Dad's drawer, which I'd revisited more than once while he was gone. Now when I snuck into my parents' room, I went straight for the pistol, loading and unloading this most secret of toys.

The fake guns quickly lost their appeal, so I headed to the part of the store Mom discouraged us from entering: the candy aisle. "No sense in looking at what you can't have," she'd say. But now I looked with abandon at the gleaming offerings—the pastels of candy necklaces, the packs of Camel-brand candy cigarettes, the palm-pleasing rolls of Life Savers and the waxy wrappers of Necco Wafers, the rattling boxes of Good & Plenty and the bins filled with Hershey's bars and Milky Ways and 3 Musketeers and Charleston Chews and M&M's—a hypnotic symphony of shapes and colors promising the sweetest delights. But it was a bag of Tootsie Rolls that invited me to pick it up and press it to my nose. I could smell the chocolate through the paper, and I imagined what it would be like to have the whole bag to myself—no piles, no counting, no siblings to share it with. I contemplated breaking the bag open and eating one right there, but instead I returned it to the bin and left the candy aisle.

Then I came back. And I shoved the bag of Tootsie Rolls down the front of my pants.

My heart drummed inside my ears as I made my way to the exit doors and scuttled out into the autumn air. Outside the store, everything was going on as usual—car doors opening and closing, people coming and going, traffic susurrating in the distance—all impervious to my crime. But I felt different. I'd never stolen anything before, and as I turned toward home, I felt like a version of Dad—a stranger to myself.

"Hold it! Hold it right there!" a voice shot at me from behind.

I froze. Two men rushed up behind me and grabbed my arms with enough force to make me yelp. "Do you have something you want to give us?" one of them asked, pulling my arm back behind me.

Terrified, all I could do was squeak, "No."

The other one firmed his grip on my arm. "Come with us," he said. He was taller than the other one and had a deeper voice, but I couldn't look either of them in the eyes.

As they led me back into the store and I kept my eyes on the ground, I could feel people staring at me. I could even feel their thoughts: *Just look at that evil boy. He's headed straight for Hell!* I bit my lip to keep from crying.

The men took me to a back room with a desk and a couple of metal chairs and told me to sit down. "Are you sure you don't have anything you want to show us?" the taller one asked in a way that sounded more like an order than a question.

"I'm sorry," I said, extracting the candy from inside my pants. Now the sobs came unbridled, and as I hid my face in my hands and heard myself, I heard my father too. I heard the sound of shame.

Mrs. Peal came into the room, and I wiped at my eyes and tried to appear stoic, worried that she would tell Fred and Jim about my crime's craven end.

"I'm very disappointed in you, Tom," she said.

"I understand," I said between sniffles. "I've never done this before."

"Do you want us to call the police?" the shorter man asked.

Images of cold prison bars and dank cells besieged my mind with a terror so sobering that I was no longer even able to cry. Now I would become just one more boy from my neighborhood gone to juvie.

Mrs. Peal clicked her bright pink nails on the desk, one after another, and appeared to be considering it. "Nah," she said. "I know this boy. He's not a criminal."

I was glad she was there to save me, but then she glared at me. "I'm going to have to call your mom. You know that, right?"

"I guess," I said, starting to cry again.

"I want you to go straight home now, okay?"

I nodded. "Okay."

As I walked back home on E Street, I was too busy hatching escape plans to notice the cold: I would run away and live in the forest with Bigfoot; I would find a new dog and finally embark on my own Tintin-inspired adventures; I would sneak into the church, where I would sleep in empty pews and dine on hosts; I would go to Coach Gary's house and convince him to be my new dad. But when I looked across the field at the back of our house—Mom's laundry lines, the frame of sticks I'd built around my garden, an old ball my siblings and I had kicked countless times—I yearned for that little house in a way that made me feel as if I'd been gone for a very long time. I just wanted it to be the house from yesterday, before I had committed my crime, when the cares I had didn't seem as imposing.

I braced myself as I entered the back door, prepared to hear Dad threatening all manner of knuckle sandwiches upon the sight of me. Mom would probably be crying, maybe even fainting over my betrayal, while my sisters and brothers would be sharing a collective head-shake of disappointment. But the scene I walked into looked a lot more like ordinary life—Mom bustling around the kitchen, Dad settled in behind another paperback, the kids milling about as if nothing had happened. It was obvious that Mrs. Peal hadn't called yet, a relief I knew was only temporary. "Wanna play Concentration?" asked Susie, holding a deck of cards. But all I could think about was the imminent ring of the phone and the tsunami I felt roiling in my stomach, so I told Susie I'd play with her later, grabbed my jacket, and slipped out the front door.

Some days our street was as quiet as a ghost town, but on other days, especially on weekends, one might step out into an almost parade-like atmosphere, as I did that Saturday. The sun had broken out and warmed our autumn-gold patch of Toledo, where the cool cats in their white patent leather loafers and thick-n-thin socks strutted up and down the sidewalks, and the neighborhood's car-obsessed characters cruised slowly along in their tricked-out Cadillac Devilles, Delta 88s, Grand Prixes, and "Deuce and a Quarters"—each car gleaming under the sun with freshly buffed wax and flashy hood ornaments and polished chrome hubcaps ringed by whitewall tires—as they scoped for opportunities to stop in the middle of the street and talk, often greeting their friends with special high-fives and handshake sequences that made it seem like their hands were dancing and that I secretly tried to memorize by practicing in the air when no one was looking. They often conducted their greetings at shouting volume, regardless of how close or far apart they were, as if every encounter were one grand celebration worthy of exclamation.

That day, the sun seemed amplified too. Sunlight fell on Viola, an older girl whose arm was looped around her mother's as she walked her up and down the street. Sunlight touched her mother, who was debilitated by an unknown muscle disease, as Viola led her carefully over the part of the sidewalk that had buckled from tree roots growing beneath. Sunlight struck the sidewalk and illuminated the tree's last yellow leaves. It shone upon Keelie, a friendly girl about my age who often wore multicolored butterfly barrettes in her many braids and who was up the street smiling and waving at the boys in the cars while Sly and the Family Stone pumped out of bass-heavy speakers, directing the world to "dance to the music." Sunlight landed on the backs of the Bryant twins, who lived two houses away from us and who both habitually leaned forward like pecking chickens when they walked and who now rushed into the street to ogle one car's green paintjob. Flurries of wind dipped down, loosening leaves, wafting the smoky scent of meat through the crisp air, straight from the grill of Mr. Hobo—which is what everyone in the neighborhood called the kind, older man who lived on our block with his wife June and who, with summer now in the rearview, was still having cookouts in his backyard. Sometimes, if we ventured over, he'd offer us a taste of his barbecued ribs, but on that Saturday I stayed on our front stoop and watched the action.

Soon Beth came out with Jane and Judy and drew a hopscotch grid on the sidewalk with a piece of chalk. The twins were four years old by then and looked like miniature versions of Mom, with their straight bangs and chin-length hair. Though Mom had to leave their hospital bracelets on for weeks when they first came home from the hospital because no one could tell them apart, we could now easily distinguish between Judy's thinner face and Jane's slightly rounder one. Despite their perceivable differences, however, I think most of us saw them as a single entity, living half in our world and half in that exclusive world of intertwined thoughts and private jokes only twins know.

As if to complete the Bronson Street rollcall of twins, the Quinton twins made a brief appearance with a basketball as they headed down D Street to the new park the city had just finished building. Situated next to the field on the other side of D Street, it was often bustling with boisterous basketball games. Several times I'd started to venture over, but each time I'd lost my nerve. The few white kids in our neighborhood just didn't play basketball on that court—that appeared to be the unspoken rule.

Jane and Judy got busy hopping, and Beth sat down beside me on the front step. "Who are they?" she asked, looking at a group of four boys I didn't recognize. They were heading west on Bronson on our side of the street. "Maybe they came from across the highway?" I wondered. They were dressed in dark clothes and smoking cigarettes, walking with their chests puffed out and that menacing look in their eyes. I'd seen that look enough times now that I could spot it from afar.

As they neared our house, they slowed their pace and sized us up, holding their gazes on Beth for too long. "Wonderbread," one of them said. Then he flicked his cigarette onto our walk. It landed about a foot away from the twins' hopscotch grid, though they were too engrossed in the game to notice. "Hey," I said, standing up. "Don't throw your cigarette butts on our sidewalk."

It was the unusual harshness of my voice that stopped Jane and Judy mid-hop.

"You could have burned one of them," I added, pointing at my little sisters, who looked at me as if I'd just ruined their game.

The cigarette-flicker flicked me off and kept walking.

"C'mon," whispered Beth. "Let's go inside."

Instead, I ignored Beth and walked toward the boys from the porch. The cigarette-flicker turned back toward me and stepped onto our walk. "Tom, c'mon," urged Beth. But I didn't want to back away. I balled my fists and walked as menacingly as I could toward my opponent.

In my mind, this was just another game of football.

In reality, he'd pinned me to the ground before I'd even gotten to the end of our walk.

With both hands, he latched onto my hair and knocked the back of my head against the sidewalk again and again. I tried to fight back, but my arms flailed like a couple of earthworms. I could hear Beth and the twins screaming, though their voices sounded far away. On either side of the boy's head, bits of blue sky started to go fuzzy and turn black.

Then there was another voice. "What the hell is wrong with you? You get the hell off him right now!" Someone was pulling the cigarette-flicker off of me. I wanted to yell "Stop!" because the flicker's fingers were still latched onto my hair, which had grown long since the incident with Dad's trimmer, but I couldn't find a single word; there was only the intimate ripping sound of my hair, loud in my ears.

As the guys scattered, my hero emerged: the neighbor from across the street who'd once taken us fishing, Mr. Noble. He leaned forward and offered me his hand. "Let's get you up off the ground," he said. Mom must have heard the commotion, because she came out in time to thank Mr. Noble before he made his way back across the street. "Why don't you go in the house," she said. It was only then that my earlier trouble at the Ontario Store came rushing back into my awareness. I scanned Mom's face for any sign that Mrs. Peal had already called, but my head ached, and everything sounded loud and muffled at once, so I couldn't get a read. "I'll be in in a bit, and you can tell me what happened. Your Dad's very jumpy today, so..." she trailed off.

We came inside, where Dad's position was unchanged and my sisters and brothers were busy carrying on as if nothing had happened, and I sulked my way to our bedroom. As I lay on the bed I still shared with Ernie, I wondered what Mom had meant when she said I could tell her what happened. Did she mean at the Ontario Store or on the front walk? The more I thought about it, the more my head hurt. Mom had never been prone to coddling, and yet I had never wanted it more. But I had no idea how to ask for it, let alone how to explain to her the terrible ripping sounds of my hair being pulled out or how much it hurt, maybe because

I could already hear her telling me what she always did—that it would be okay.

Then the answer occurred to me in the form of Mom's sewing scissors, which were on top of the sewing machine she kept in our room. It was such a dazzling stroke of genius that I felt a moment of pure glee. But I needed to act quickly before she came in.

When she finally entered the room, it seemed as though an entire day had passed while I lay there on my pillow with a careful arrangement of my own freshly cut hair placed in tufts around my head. I figured that showing her what had happened would have greater impact than telling her. As she approached, I put my hand on my head and moaned a little for good measure.

"Is that hair on your pillow?" she asked, sitting down beside me.

I nodded. "That mean kid pulled it. I think it's still falling out," I said.

"That's not good."

"He almost hit the twins with a cigarette. I was sticking up for them."

"I see," she said.

"It hurts," I said.

She reached out and touched my head so softly that I almost didn't feel it. It was the second time she'd ever touched me affectionately, and it unleashed a torrent of tears I wasn't expecting. She patted my hand and waited for me to finish before she spoke again. "You know, you're not the only one who's hurt," she said.

And then I knew she knew. I swallowed hard, afraid to say something that would make her take her hand away.

"Do you have anything you want to tell me?" she asked.

"I tried to steal candy," I blurted out, "and I'm sorry." And though I truly was sorry, I thought I'd remind her of a little bible scripture for good measure. "Jesus said let those who are without sin cast the first stone."

Mom was silent for a moment as she kept her hand on my hand. "Yes, that's true, Tom. But I don't want you to commit that particular sin again, okay?"

In my ten-and-a-half years of life, I'd set one life-rule for myself—to never drink alcohol—but on that day, I set another. "I promise, Mom."

"Good," she said, giving my head one last pat and collecting the hair from my pillow. She got up and started toward the door, but then stopped and turned to face me again. "What was it, anyway?"

"What was what?"

"The candy. What kind was it?"

"Tootsie Rolls," I said, feeling a new sheet of shame slide over me.

"Okay," she said. And then she left me alone.

But the consequences of my crime were not over. "Forgive me, Father, for I have sinned," I said, fidgeting in the confession box a few days later. "It's been six weeks since my last confession."

"Go ahead, son," said Father Schmelzer.

Sometimes during confession, I combed through the weeks' minutiae for things I suspected might not even be confession-worthy—vague things like "I didn't finish my bean sandwich" or "I played with my brother's toy car without asking"—because I felt like I couldn't go in empty-handed. Just as I sometimes compared the quality of my praying to the more zealous praying of the old ladies working their rosaries in the front pew, I also fretted over the quality of my confessions, never knowing exactly what an A-grade confession might be. But now that I had an indisputable sin to confess, I missed the lightness of my usual concerns. I was wearing my scapular as a special show of deference, and the itchy tag scraped against my chest under my shirt. I looked at the translucent screen that separated the priest and me and let him have it. "I yelled at my siblings three times. Istolecandy. I had two bad thoughts." There. If I couched it between two more ordinary things and said it really fast, maybe he wouldn't notice.

"Did you say you stole candy?"

Darn. "Yes, Father."

"And why did you do that?"

Once again, I worried over what the best answer might be. "I don't have a good answer," I finally said.

"The truth is the best answer," Father Schmelzer said in his deep sermon voice.

I took a deep breath. "Because they smelled good and I was hungry and I didn't have any money with me."

"That sounds like the truth to me," he said. "Say two Rosaries, five Our Fathers, and five Hail Marys." Then he said a prayer of absolution and sent me on my way.

That night, I kneeled at the side of our bed and offered God my penance, praying silently, as Ernie and I always did. "Were you praying for Christmas presents?" Ern asked when I finally finished and climbed into bed beside him. "Cause you sure were down there a long time."

"Yes," I lied, not wanting to tell him the truth. And once he was asleep, I got back down on my knees and offered one last Hail Mary for lying to him.

That November, our football team had its fourth win. We'd been working on pop passes and screen passes, a departure from our usual approach of running the football, and we'd smoked the other team. "We're on our way, men! Just keep at it, just keep at it!"

Coach Gary sang, patting our butts as we walked victoriously off the field.

When Ern and I arrived home that afternoon, I couldn't help but beam to Dad. "We won!" I announced, giving my cleats an extra swing. "Against St. Joseph's!"

Dad put his book down on his lap and eyed our uniforms. He was drinking a Fresca instead of a beer, something I still wasn't used to seeing, but he'd returned to his King Edward cigars. "So now you think you're some kind of bigshot?" he accused, molding his lips around his cigar. He reminded me of the proboscis monkey I had seen in the encyclopedia.

"We're just happy," Ern said. "Not that you would care anything about that."

We headed to our room while Dad yelled at our backs, continuing even after we closed the door. "You better watch your mouth, or one of these days," he called, "you'll get the knuckle sandwich of a lifetime!"

And though our football victory that day was still sweet, it was dampened—not as much by Dad's expected string of insults and threats as by the realization that it wasn't only the alcohol that had made him mean. That's who our father was, even sober.

Sometimes I wonder if I'm forgetting something important about him, some moment when he was tender or supportive, anything that would have indicated that, despite his anger and indifference, my father loved me. I wonder if maybe I've inadvertently cast him as a two-dimensional, two-bit player on the stage of my memory, if in letting go of all that was hurtful about him, I somehow let go of some gems too. Memory is a faulty thing after all, and Marji, if asked now, would tell you that she was deeply loved by our father and that he often told her as much. She even quotes him as using her nickname: "You know I love you, Mudja." She remembers him tickling her. She remembers him playing games with her. But to my knowledge, the rest of my siblings have no such memories. Mom tells me that, even decades later, as she took care of him in his final days, he didn't thank her or tell her he loved her: "Nothing, never, not even at the end." As for me, what I remember most is the architecture—those lines I drew around my life by making rules that were, in many ways, inspired by him, by all I wanted to reject in him. Those rules gave my life a structure, within which I felt safe.

Early that December, Mr. Chapman's animated front yard marked the beginning of the Christmas season, as did one of the four holidays a year when my siblings and I got candy: St. Nicholas Day. Passed down from Mom's German heritage, this was the holiday on which, if you cleaned and polished your shoes and placed them outside your bedroom door on December 5th, St. Nicholas would come in the night and fill them with candy. Though I was nearing eleven years old and had heard kids at school say it was all done by our parents, I still believed in St. Nicholas, just as I believed in Santa Claus and the Easter Bunny. Mom once told me that if you stop believing, they stop coming, so I tapped into a wellspring of faith that still endured.

On that one night a year, we kids would open Mom's shoeshine tin and clean and buff our shoes. Everyone thought my brown-and-white wingtips were ugly, but I liked them because I'd never seen another pair like them. I was being careful not to let the brown polish get on the white parts. Mom was bringing in the laundry from outside. Because we didn't have a clothes dryer, our wet clothes often froze solid on the line, so Mom would have to bring them in, all rock-stiff, and arrange them across the kitchen chairs to let them defrost before rehanging them back outside on the line again, in multiple cycles. As she brought in another load, I heard Dad say, "Your hands are bleeding again."

"It's just from the cold," she said. "It'll be okay. I just have to keep the blood off the clothes." Several of her fingers were cracked and bleeding, but that didn't stop her from heading right back outside. And as she went, I promised myself that when I grew up, I would buy her a dryer.

The next morning erupted in a cacophony of happy squeals after we leapt from our beds to find our shoes, all of us shouting out at once about our different treats—"I got Good & Plenty!" "I got Life Savers!" "I got a 3 Musketeers!" As for what was in my own shoes, St. Nicholas was good to me that year: tucked into each fastidiously polished wingtip were a few Tootsie Rolls.

"Let me get this straight," said Jeffrey Huxley. "Some magical person—"

"St. Nicholas," I interrupted. It was snowing, and we were attempting to build a snowman in our front yard, but the powdery snow kept collapsing.

"Some magical person named St. Nicholas comes to your house when it's not even Christmas and puts candy in your *shoes*? Those ugly things you put your nasty old feet in? Those white-and-brown things on your feet right now?"

I tried packing another mitten full of snow onto our mound. "You are correct." The snow scattered like glitter.

"How come he comes to your house, but not to mine? How come I've never even heard of him before? I think you're full of shit, Seeman."

"I think it's because I'm half German," I explained.

Jeffrey studied my face for a moment to see whether I was telling the truth, and then he kicked our feeble mound, sending a puff of snow skyward. "What if I say I'm German too?" I appreciated that Jeffrey still believed, just like me.

"But that would be a lie," I said. "And St. Nicholas would probably know, like Santa knows stuff."

Jeffrey thought for a moment while snowflakes collected on his hat. "What if you adopt me as your brother? Then I could say I'm German."

That seemed logical enough to me, so under a snow-filled sky, in the snow-cushioned quiet of the day, I adopted Jeffrey Huxley. "You are hereby my brother, and you are hereby German," I proclaimed. We shook mittens to seal it, and then we tackled each other to the ground and shoved each other's faces in the snow.

FIFTEEN

With the lowering of a glittering ball in Times Square, we lifted off into a new decade. It was 1970, the year that would bring us Apollo 13, the Boeing 747, the inception of Earth Day, and the disbanding of the Beatles. That January would also bring us Barbara, the newest addition to our family. While other kids in my class beamed with excitement over their new baby brothers and sisters, the baby-having business had become commonplace for us. Mom had been pregnant for half of my life (having given birth to all twelve children in fifteen years), so when she brought Barb home, we took her into the fold—changing her diapers, holding her bottles, wiping the spit-up from her chin and our shoulders—with little fanfare.

But that wasn't all 1970 brought us. By spring, Dad had returned to his true love, Pabst Blue Ribbon, and soon after, he came home from work at the cab company as happy as I'd ever seen him. "Well, everyone," he boomed from the front door. "What are you waiting for? Come outside!"

Mom gave Dad a quizzical look, and then we all scurried outside to see what the fuss was about. Dad strolled halfway down the sidewalk and then stopped and held his arm out like an arrow. At the end of that arrow was a twenty-two-foot-long 1962 Checker Aerobus. "I present to you our new car!" he announced. The chalky-white, eight-door station wagon stood on the street in front of our house as though it were lost. "It's an airport taxi. A limo really. Now everyone can have their own window!"

Mom blinked quickly at the vehicle, as if at any moment it might evaporate the way things do in dreams, but the Seeman-Mobile, as it would come to be known, stayed put. "I got it for a steal from work. They were selling all the old ones for almost nothing, and they said I can pay a little each week from my paycheck," Dad said. "Get in. Everyone, get in!"

It was a lot to process—both the car and Dad's unprecedented excitement about it—but my siblings were quick to join in with enthusiasm. "Wow," said Dan, "it's humongous!"

"It's a funny-looking bus!" said Susie.

"What's a limo?" asked the twins in tandem.

Dad's eyes curved downward into thin crescent moons as he smiled. "It's a big car for fancy people. Most ordinary families don't have a car like this. You won't see another like it anywhere around here, that's for sure! But I was able to get one. Why? Because I have connections!" He puffed his chest out and patted the limo proudly, as if he'd built it himself, while Mom ran back inside to gather up the rest of the kids.

Then we all dutifully piled into the car. With its rigid seats and peeling vinyl, it didn't feel particularly fancy to me, but I still tried to share in the festiveness. "Now Mom can drive too!" I said, raising my voice so that they could hear me from my fourth-row seat. I could hardly see out the front windshield from way back there.

"Nah," said Dad. "Too complicated for her. Too big to turn."

If Mom, who was holding Barb and looking blankly out the window at the road ahead, had an opinion about what Dad said, she didn't show it. Instead, it was little Susie who spoke up. "Mom can do anything!"

Dad responded by clearing his throat with a series of forceful hacks, and with that, we took off on our maiden journey. Like the neighborhood guys with the flashy cars, Dad inched slowly down Bronson Street, looking out the window and nodding at no one while we all peered out of our respective windows. It seemed like it would take forever just to reach the corner, but eventually Dad turned on D Street, where there were actual people for him to nod at, including the Quinton twins, who were on the basketball court with several other guys from our neighborhood. Dad struck a pose, resting his arm on the open window while offering the world a self-satisfied smirk, which spurred the kids on the court to laugh unabashedly and point at us. Marji, Beth, Mary Jo, and Ern all ducked down and tried to hide, while Dad continued to tour our neighborhood. And, after our mile-long laughingstock adventure was complete, Dad eased the Seeman-Mobile back to its new resting spot in front of our house, where he slumped out of the car—head down, smile gone—without saying another word.

I turned eleven that April, and Uncle Dick and Harold came over with Grandma for Sunday dinner. "How's the newspaper business going?" asked Uncle Dick as he handed me a card with a bunny on it and two dollars inside. It was their custom for each of us on our birthdays, just as it was Mom's custom to bake us any kind of dessert we wanted. My favorite was chocolate and vanilla marble cake with chocolate frosting, and as I eyed my cake, which sat tall on the counter, calling to me in all its chocolatey triple-layer glory, I found myself torn between wanting to tell Uncle Dick all about my paper route and wanting to rush through dinner so that my cake and I could finally be united. But dinner in our house was never a fast affair when Uncle Dick and Harold were there. The sixteen of us wedged in around our two tables as we did most Sundays, scooting our chairs forward in a flurry of chitchat and hunger. Joe, now two, squealed from his high chair while Barb cooed and kicked her feet in the wooden playpen that had housed us all through the years. Uncle Dick asked Dad about work, football, the weather, while Dad offered monosyllabic answers. Uncle Harold sat between Rich and me and tickled us both, each time laughing harder than we were. Susie always wanted to play the name game, so Mary Jo kicked it off: "I'm thinking of a name that begins with an A."

Susie shouted out, "Amy!"

"Abigail," I said.

"Nope," said Mary Jo, and I often wondered whether she changed the name she was thinking of if we guessed right.

Grandma, who still wore her long braids wound into tight coils on each side of her head, removed her apron while Mom served everyone, buttering one piece of bread after another and then tossing them with a spin from her place at the head of the table onto our plates. She rarely missed—not even the little kids' plates that were farthest away against the wall—and she always landed the bread butter-side up. I thought they should make bread-tossing an Olympic category, but Mom never seemed impressed by her aim the way I was when I landed my newspapers just so on people's doorsteps. She just kept on serving.

Dad liked his slabs of butter almost as thick as his bread, and now that the years had brought him dentures, his teeth clacked with each bite. He breathed heavily when he ate, as if he were in his own Olympic race to shovel in the contents of his plate faster than anyone, but on that night, dinner seemed to stretch on forever as Uncle Dick and Harold enjoyed second and then third helpings and my siblings started another game and Mom and Grandma talked about recipes, all while my cake beckoned from its lonely place on the counter.

But, like all things in life, dinner did end. And the funny thing is, after all that impatience, all that yearning and distraction, I don't remember eating the cake. I remember the little things—that Uncle Dick smelled like his vanilla pipe tobacco, that Uncle Harold was careful not to tickle us too hard, that Grandma smiled softly at everyone—and how I'd wanted to rush through all of it. If I had known then that Grandma would die the following year—if I had understood then that one day those Bronson Street dinners would be a dim star shining through the great distance of my past—I believe I would have savored the moments more. I would have asked more questions. I would have appreciated my family, and those times, more. I would have said thank you.

We didn't say thank you very much growing up. I don't remember hearing any of the adults in my family saying it, or anyone in our neighborhood—not even the Nobles, who were the best across-the-street neighbors anyone could ask for. Maybe for those who are poor, the words "thank you" point, in an indirect way, to all that is lacking—a deficit that pulls on the threads of shame that people in need try to keep hidden. Or maybe it has something to do with pride and self-reliance—a need to resist having any need at all. Whatever the reason, those two words were not part of my daily vocabulary growing up. But if I could go back now, I would thank so many people, including Mrs. Willis, who nominated me for the Toledo Museum of Art classes; Lauren, my first art class teacher who doled out approval from what felt like an endless well; and Mrs. Lambert, who gave me my first paying job because she knew I needed it.

When I showed Lauren my most recent creation—a city I built inside one of Dad's empty King Edward cigar boxes—she pressed her silver-adorned hands to her heart and exclaimed, "Oh my gosh, Tom! I love what you did here! And I see you've used the little nuts and washers to make a variety of buildings. And is that a *car*? It's *terrific!*" I explained my idea of night falling on the city when you closed the lid and the sun rising when you opened it, and she said I was brilliant.

I suspected her praise was over the top, but she celebrated my ideas and abilities in a way that no one in my family did, and, like Coach Gary's encouragement, her support gave me confidence and inspired me. I woke on Saturday mornings in a rush of excitement about what we would do in art class that day. Would we use pastels? Watercolors? Clay? Something entirely new? Would we tour a new gallery in the museum, peering closely at the paintings' mysteries and revelations? Would we learn another new concept like chiaroscuro or impasto, realism or surrealism?

The first time Dad picked me up from art class in the Seeman-Mobile, I hung my head when he pulled up in front of the museum, hoping no one would notice our embarrassing car. But when the following Saturday's class was over and I stood outside the museum with all the other kids, watching them get picked up one by one, I scanned near and far for the Seeman-Mobile, but each car that came and went wasn't it. I was used to Dad being late to pick up Mom from the grocery store and the welfare office, so at first I wasn't worried. I busied myself with my city, which I'd just put some finishing touches on that morning. I lifted the lid and closed it again, whispering, "day, night, day, night...," while the area in front of the museum, where just minutes before dozens of kids had been milling around, slowly thinned out. *There are still six other kids left*, I thought. As long as there were other kids also waiting, I had nothing to worry about. *There are still three other kids. There's still one other kid.* But then I was alone.

I looked in the windows of the cars whizzing by on Collingwood Avenue and was envious of every kid I saw tucked inside a back seat. I don't know how long I stood there holding my cigar box city, but at some point, I began to cry. A police officer who was directing traffic spotted me and walked over. "What's the matter, son?" he asked. He had a short afro and a depth to his eyes that made me feel less embarrassed about crying.

"My dad was supposed to pick me up," I admitted, "but I think he forgot."

The officer pressed his lips together and nodded. "Ah, I see. That happens sometimes. Where do you live?"

"I live at 1209 Bronson Street, Toledo, Ohio, 43608."

"Ah, the zip code even," he said, smiling. "Is that near Woodward High School?"

"Yes, my older sister goes to Woodward."

"That's not exactly close, is it? Do you have any money on you?"

I shook my head no. "Just this city," I said, opening the box so he could see the daytime inside.

But he didn't offer the enthusiasm for my creation that Lauren did. "Have you ever taken the bus?" he asked.

"No," I said, closing the lid. "And I don't have any money."

"Then here's what we're going to do. The Collingwood bus will be coming here any minute now. It's going to take you downtown. When you get to the end of the line, the driver will tell everyone they have to get off. Then you'll have to transfer to the Stickney bus. Ask someone where to get it. Tell the Stickney bus driver to drop you off on the corner of Stickney and Bronson Street. I'll give you the money, and you can repay me by helping someone else out sometime when they need it, okay?"

"Okay," I said. "I will." I tried to look like a future me that would help someone in need, but the truth was, I was scared. There was a lot to remember, and what if I got off in the wrong place? I rehearsed it with him one more time. But what if I couldn't find the Stickney bus? What if the drivers were mean?

Fortunately, both bus drivers were nice. They saw that I was borderline crying, and they listened intently when I told them about the police officer who'd given me my instructions. And though Dad's failure to pick me up would be a regular occurrence, just as it was with Mom, and still hurt every time, at least now I knew how to take the bus. Now I carried change in my pocket just in case. Now I didn't need him in the same way I once had.

So maybe, in a strange way, I had Dad to thank for my budding pluckiness, which I finally took onto the basketball court in the new, small park near our house. After having nonchalantly walked past the park day after day as if I couldn't have cared less whether I ever played basketball or not, I finally strutted onto the court in my cut-off jean shorts. As I made my way over to the guys, I tried adding an extra bounce to each step the way others in our neighborhood walked, a gait I'd always admired because it looked like they were dancing.

"Look," said one of the guys in between plays, "that white boy's trying to walk like a brotha."

All the players stopped and looked at me then, some laughing, some shaking their heads, some just mocking me with their eyes. *Turn around*, screamed a voice in my head as my dance-bounce flattened into a regular walk. *Go home right now!* But I didn't listen.

"That honky must be lost," said a boy with a red bandana tied around his head.

"I'm not lost," I said, pointing toward the field at the back of our house. "I live right there."

"I don't care if you live at the Empire State Building," he said, dribbling the ball back to the half court line.

I cleared my throat—making a mental note to look up the Empire State Building in our encyclopedias when I got home—and shrugged my shoulders. "I was hoping I could play with you guys."

At this, a bunch of the guys broke into a fit of unabashed jeers and laughter. "You hoped wrong," one of them said.

The Quinton twins walked over, stopping at the edge of the court to take swigs from what appeared to be a communal bottle of raspberry wine. Their shirts were off, and their dark, magazine-ready muscles glistened with sweat, while my pasty legs stood out like two thick pillars of snow. "Hey, aren't you the ones with that ugly long white car?" said Donald.

"We have a big family," I tried to explain. "My dad got it from work."

The two of them looked at me then, and I wasn't sure what would happen next. "Let him play," Donald finally said.

And though I had no good moves on the court yet, I was at least strong and tall under the boards, and in time, I would learn how to do a double-pump shot and a sky hook like Lew Alcindor that no one could block. Sometimes it's the small yesses in life that you never forget—those unexpected doors that suddenly open. And though I never thanked Donald for going against the crowd and letting me play, I hope he had a sense of how much it meant to me—that simple freedom of getting to be one of the guys on a piece of blacktop so close to home.

Later that year, St. Vincent's was given the opportunity to send two kids to Camp Storer, an overnight camp near Jackson, Michigan, and they chose Ernie and me. Going to camp was a mysterious concept to me. I'd heard kids in art class at the museum talking about summer camp, but none of them lived in the projects, and I'd never considered the possibility that one day Ernie and I—two kids who had never spent a night away from home—would be heading north for two weeks to a lake nestled among the pines, where we would sleep in cabins with total strangers. It was through the donation of a stranger that Ern and I were about to set out on this "adventure in nature," according to the brochure, which sent me dreaming about what kinds of wild animals I might add to my growing list.

To make sure we came prepared, the camp sent us a list of all the things we would need, such as a large waterproof bag, two pairs of swim trunks, athletic shorts, flashlights, soap dishes, sunblock, and boat shoes, which I imagined were shoes with little boats printed on them. But they neglected to send instructions on how a mom of twelve living on food stamps might come up with the funds to purchase those items. Nevertheless, Mom took the list over to the Ontario Store and came home with bags filled with things I knew we couldn't afford. "I'm sorry," she said, "but I could only get you boys one pair of swim trunks, and you're going to have to bring the shorts you already have. Also, what in Heaven's name are boat shoes? Nobody at the Ontario store knew, that's for sure."

Boat shoes were only the beginning of a long list of things I wouldn't know, like how to shoot a bow and arrow, how to water ski, how to sail, how to ride a horse, or how to paddle a canoe down a river, but when we arrived and I saw the vast lake sparkling between the trees, somehow it all seemed possible. The air smelled of sunlit conifers and lake water, with occasional traces of woodsmoke wafting by, and as we stood next to each other, breathing in this place that felt so far away from home, I heard Ern whisper, "Wow," under his breath. And for two weeks, that would be the most Ernie would say to me because we were placed in different cabins according to our ages.

For the first week, our separation seemed a terrible fate as I suffered the time-honored tradition of homesickness. At night while the other boys played pranks and told stories that pointed to a history of prior summers spent at camp (which bred a familiarity I knew nothing about), I squeezed my eyes shut and wondered what Mom was making for dinner and whether there was anything new in the field behind our house. I wondered what Ernie—the person I'd shared a bed with all my life—was doing in his cabin and if he was as sad as I was. I wondered how the basketball games in the park were going and what flavor wine the Quinton twins were drinking and whether Mr. Hobo was grilling meat and sharing tastes with my siblings. And though a lot of my childhood fantasies had, until that time, been devoted to the adventures I would one day have—gallivanting across the globe, mastering the open sea, getting close to the most exotic and dangerous animals on the other side of the world—the reality of my camp adventures one state away at first proved a lot less fulfilling than I'd hoped. For one, the social hierarchy was different from what I had known. What made a boy important in my neighborhood was whether he was big and strong enough to physically intimidate others, and, if he wasn't, whether he was cocky enough to bluff. What made a boy important at camp was whether he had been to camp before and whether he could perform well in the sports of camp life—none of which I had ever tried before. I was proficient at only one thing during my first days at camp: crafts. I quickly learned to make the most colorful eight-strand boondoggle, and my counselor liked it so much that he asked me to make one for him. But that was cold comfort in a world for which I was otherwise ill-equipped. Until then, I had never even taken a shower before, because all we had at home was a bathtub.

Whether it was the multiple face-plants that pushed distressing amounts of water up my nose every time the motorboat pulled me forward on my water skis, or my failure to duck before the boom came around and knocked me off the boat I was learning to sail, or the horse whose soft neck I stroked for roughly three seconds before she pinned her ears and nipped my thigh, I was ready to pack up my newly purchased duffel bag, with its rubberized interior and special flap beneath the drawstrings on top, and bid farewell to adventure altogether.

But true to the narrative arc upon which countless overnight camp-goers have traveled and will travel for generations, things began to turn around, and my first disorienting days of humiliation were beginning to pay off. I could now stay upright on my skis as we zipped across the lake; I could steer the camp's Hobie Cat at the correct angle to the wind; and I could groom and ride a horse without falling off or becoming intimate with its teeth. I'd even made some friends—one boy had webbed feet, and another was an impressive ventriloquist—and at night, after we gathered around the fire and told ghost stories while stuffing our mouths with toasted marshmallows, we traced fireflies through the damp darkness, running with abandon, as if there were nothing in the world but freedom.

During my first weekend at Camp Storer, I learned how to paddle a canoe. And those skills were quickly put to the test on a four-day camping and canoeing trip down a meandering Michigan river that alternated between rapids and calmer waters. I was now a man of the wilderness who could pitch a tent, build a fire, and use a can opener. I also very nearly caught a fish—a trout, which I knew would make Mr. Noble proud and which, along with a badger, I added to my list. The world was opening to me in its endless array of sensual delights and discoveries, and every experience I had during those two rugged and revelatory weeks formed a bridge between my first eleven years and all that would come later. I'd seen beyond Bronson Street, beyond the farmhouse where Uncle Dick and Harold lived with Grandma, beyond Pearson Park, beyond the football fields next to St. Francis, beyond my Uncle Ben and Aunt Lois's house with its shimmering pool—and there was no going back.

But what I remember most about Camp Storer was none of that. It was the moments after our canoe capsized in the rapids when I realized the duffel bag Mom purchased for me wasn't waterproof at all. In fact, I had to turn it upside down to pour out all the water it had taken in, a casualty of which was the notebook that, for years, had been housing my list of Wild Animals I Have Seen. As I stood in the river's shallow water near the bank, my heart broke, not because all my clothes and supplies were soaked or because I'd lost something that had been important to me, but because I remembered how Mom had walked home from the Ontario Store carrying our bags of stuff—how she'd beamed her happiness upon us as she emptied them on the table, proudly showing us each thing she'd selected, including the "nifty" liner inside our "waterproof" duffel bags, never saying a word about what she might have sacrificed to purchase those things, but instead smiling that generous smile as she did what she always did for us, even if no one was there to help her, even if no one ever thanked her: her best.

SIXTEEN

Though it rarely happened, Mom occasionally reached a breaking point when it came to disciplining us. When my older sisters failed to clean their room despite Mom's repeated pleas, she dumped out every single one of their drawers so that they would have no choice but to address the (now much larger) mess strewn from one end of the room to the other. And when Susie, Rich, and the twins made the same mistake, she dumped a full toybox over their heads. "You little son of a gun!" she once said to me as she punched my leg—winding her fist in circles like a comic book character before letting it land with a tiny thump on the side of my thigh—after I'd told a lie. But, in keeping with her unshakable stoicism, Mom showed little emotion when she doled out these punishments—there was no fire in her eyes, no fury on her tongue. In fact, if you saw nothing but her face while she disciplined us, you'd see the same expression she had when she was doing any other mundane thing, like rolling out cookie dough or changing a diaper. These things—whether pastries or punishments—simply needed to be done.

So when I came home from school to find Mom sobbing at the kitchen table, I felt like the ground was dropping out from under me. I had never seen Mom cry before, and I found myself wishing I hadn't raced home ahead of the others that day. "Mom?" I asked in a tiny wavering voice.

"She's gone," she said, slumping over the table and burying her face in her arms.

"You mean Taffy?" I asked.

She picked her head back up and looked at me dumbfounded, almost offended. "Nooooo," she cried. "*Grandma*. She passed away." Then she let her head drop back down onto her arms and cried some more.

I started to cry, too, even though I didn't yet fully grasp the reality of what we had lost, or what Mom had lost—her one quiet constant, her cheerful co-peeler of apples and potatoes, her best friend, her mother. I tried to imagine what it would be like if Mom died, and the thought sucked my breath away.

I was grateful when my siblings started making their way in the back door, one by one sinking into the news until we were all huddled together in the suddenness and sadness of it all, all of us unmoored by seeing Mom come undone. But when you live in the projects with twelve kids, grief is but another luxury you can't afford, and by dinnertime that night, Mom had pulled herself together. "She's in Heaven now," she told us matter-of-factly as she poured leftover gravy on a slice of bread for each of us—a sign that we were toward the end of our food for the week. "And that's even better than here."

"Why is Heaven better than here?" Susie asked.

"Because there are angels in Heaven," Mom said, glancing up at the ceiling. "And other things."

"Like what other things?"

Mom stopped mid-serving-spoon and considered the question. "No one ever gets sick, for one thing," she said, dipping back into the roasting pan. "And the streets are paved in gold."

"They have *cars* in Heaven?" Jane asked, astonished. She squinted her eyes as if she were trying to see it. "I bet there are a lot of limos like ours!"

And with that, Mom put the pan down and started to laugh. It was a hesitant trickle of a giggle at first, but it slowly began to bubble until tears came rushing down her cheeks for the second time that day, now in a torrent of laughter. And for the second time that day, we joined her, laughing and laughing—laughing because Mom was laughing, laughing at the thought of a Heaven filled with Checker Aerobusses, laughing because laughing is also the underside of crying, laughing as if at Death itself—all except for Dad, who sat by, bemused, an anchor in the wake.

As for our "limo," it didn't survive a year. That fall, not long after I started sixth grade, Dad came home with a rusted green station wagon that Mom could drive too. "Out with the old, in with the new," she said as she set off on her maiden voyage to the grocery store in our new car. And, as if that old adage she uttered were an incantation, I, too, began bidding farewell to the old while looking shine-eyed at the new. After my list of Wild Animals I Have Seen met its end in a Michigan river, I started a new list: Animals I Want to See One Day. Now there were no limits to the creatures I could add—Komodo dragons, killer whales, lemurs—or to the things I could dream. Part list, part sketchbook, my blue spiral notebook was a compendium of the mysterious creatures that lit up my imagination, a guide map to my future.

And that wasn't all that was new for me. As I rounded the halfway point between ages eleven and twelve and sprouted up out of all my clothes, I also began to acquire a new wardrobe for school. I purchased a snazzy outfit from the Ontario Store with my own money—a brown suede fringe vest; a red button-up shirt with a wide black collar, black cuffs with three black buttons each, and puffy sleeves; and brown corduroy pants that were too short but that I purchased anyway because they were on sale. Mom brought her scrap pile of fabrics to the rescue. First, to widen the bellbottoms, she opened the outside seam from the bottom of the leg to just below the knee and inserted a large V-shape of white fabric with a large black houndstooth print. Then she lengthened the pants by adding three inches of the same fabric to the bottoms. When she finished, it looked as though I were wearing two big hoop skirts around my shins that swooshed when I walked.

Around that same time, Mom brought home a new donation bag from the church, and, as was the custom, she dumped it on the floor and let us rifle through the goods. Because I seldom found clothes big enough for me in those bags, I searched hard and fast. As soon as I saw it, I knew, and I quickly claimed an oversized red sweatshirt with a hood and a large kangaroo pocket, which I proceeded to wear almost every day for the next two years. I wore it as I walked the neighborhoods alone, thinking, planning, staying out later than I ever had before—past the time when the sky turns dusty pink and porch lights come on and birds fly home, past the time when pink sinks into indigo and the air quiets and the first stars poke through, gleaming like every wish you ever had. I'd pull my hood far over my head so my face was mostly hidden and walk down the middle of the street with a rock in one hand, hidden inside the kangaroo pocket, and a stick in the other hand. *You don't know what's under here,* I'd think to anyone who passed by. *I'm the heavyweight champion of the world. I'm a ghetto kid. I'm going somewhere.*

Sometimes I walked the streets with my new friends, Tyrone, Frankie, and Trey, who lived on the other side of the highway that separated our neighborhoods and boasted a Quinton-twins-level of clout in their neighborhood—a kind of untouchable power—that appealed to me. I went to school with Frankie, a good-natured and eager kid who sometimes spoke with the hint of a lisp when the guys were teasing him and he was attempting a rejoinder. Though Frankie and I had known each other for years, it wasn't until sixth grade that we really noticed each other, and soon I was crossing the highway to his house, where I met Tyrone and Trey. They attended a local public school with a reputation for being rough, and for me, that only added to their appeal. Quick-witted and funny, Tyrone was the natural leader of the group, and what he lacked in fashion sense he made up for in confidence. Sometimes his humor came with a dagger attached, and I was always relieved when he wasn't pointing it at me. "Shiiiiit," he'd say to Frankie on the basketball court, "you need to take that shot to school." Once, out of the blue, Tyrone called me a "turnbuckle-head-lookin-mothafuckah." When I looked up the word "turnbuckle" later, I had to conclude that sometimes Tyrone himself didn't know the meanings of the words he chose—or he genuinely thought my head looked like a long, skinny piece of metal hardware used to attach boxing ropes to the corners of a ring. Though Tyrone had a seemingly bottomless vocabulary, he tended to cloak whatever words he dredged up from his mysterious repository in the same sorts of phrasing, finding on any given day many opportunities to say something to the effect of, "Check out that googly-eyed-vestibule-lookin-mothafuckah," or "She's one fine-ass-bastion-lookin-mothafuckah"—a one-size-fits-all approach to language that always elicited a laugh from the rest of us. But the guys didn't seem to like it as much when I trotted out multisyllabic locutions of my own, commenting, for instance, on "the splendor of the crepuscular sky" or the "magnanimity of our neighbors across the street," so I learned to keep my aspirational lexicon to myself.

"We should call ourselves the Half-and-Halfs," said Frankie on the basketball court one day, seemingly apropos of nothing. He practically shouted it after making a basket, and he was grinning his high-watt, ever-ready grin, which regularly brought levity to our group. "You know, half Black, half white!" he explained. He was blond and fair-skinned like me, and Tyrone and Trey were Black. "Nah, that's stupid," said Trey. "We should just be *The Halfs*." And like that, we'd given ourselves a name and, with it, a bond.

Unlike Jeffrey Huxley and Eddie Gonzalez, who weren't much more highly esteemed by the tough kids in their neighborhood than I was in mine, it was as if Tyrone, Frankie, and Trey owned the streets. They walked *where* they wanted *when* they wanted, fearing no one, and despite my having adopted Jeffrey as my brother with a skyful of snowflakes as our witness, I began to leave him and Eddie behind as I ventured into new territories—in this case, a neighborhood populated by old piles of decaying wood, small defunct hook-on trailers overrun with rodents, abandoned cars with flat tires, and noxious weeds growing up around it all. We always met at Frankie's house, which was right next to I-280, and to get there I had to take a footbridge across the highway. I often took my bike, carrying it up the concrete slope of the bridge and riding across as fast as I could until it almost felt like flying, then riding down the other side. Because the bridge had been built too low over the highway, the cars and trucks that whooshed by created constant wind on the bridge. Though their neighborhood was only about a mile from mine, there was something about crossing that barrier of the highway that made it feel much farther, and like a totally separate world.

In that year of the new, I purchased a second paper route adjacent to my first, which doubled my customers. Now, when Sundays came, the thicker papers were too heavy for me to carry on my bike, so I had to walk the route instead, pulling everyone's Funnies and Horoscopes and Sports Pages in a wagon. To make sure my customers had their weekend papers by breakfast time, I woke at 5:30, when it was still dark and the rest of my family was still in the deep quiet of sleep. One Sunday morning, I headed out into a snowstorm that had arrived in the night and had already spilled several inches. The snow was coming down so fast that, by the time I got to the end of our walk, it had piled up on my jacket sleeves and eyelashes and on the papers in the wagon. I started to drag my wagon down the street, but it kept getting stuck, and because my only pair of shoes had no tread, I kept slipping and falling. When my wagon wasn't stuck, it seemed to have a mind of its own, spinning away from me, threatening to topple. Still, I continued my slapstick dance down D Street—just me and the muffled hush of so much snow—until I took one last tumble and realized, as I pulled myself back up again, that I needed help. I had to return home.

Back inside our house, the warmth and quiet was womblike, and a wave of sleepiness washed over me as I padded up the stairs and, in slow motion, turned the doorknob to Mom and Dad's room. As I inched their door open, Dad's musty smell, which was tinged with the sourness of beer turned stale, reached for me, and I held my breath as if I were underwater. It was a smell I could never get used to, and for a moment I considered closing the door and taking my wagon back out into the snow. But I knew that was impossible, so I steeled myself and tiptoed to Mom's side of the bed. She was curled up like an armadillo, facing away from Dad, and strands of her mousy brown hair fanned across her cheek. "Mom?" I whispered.

"Hmm?" she sighed.

I got the sense that I'd become part of a dream she was having. "I'm sorry to wake you, but I can't do the paper route by myself this morning. There's too much snow."

In the blueish predawn shadows, Mom opened her eyes, and I felt as if someone had turned on a light. She made short work of getting dressed before we were outside in the snow together, loading up the back of the green station wagon with newspapers. Accompanied by the swish-swish of the windshield wipers, Mom and I developed a rhythm that morning as we inched through the snow-globe world: I'd get out of the car, deliver papers to several houses while mom drove the car alongside me, then I'd pull a few more out of the back of the car and deliver those, and so on. The heater in the car didn't work, but I ducked in periodically to get the wind off me. As we made our way through my route, I liked thinking we were the only two people on earth.

After that day, Mom rose with me in the winter darkness on Sunday mornings and drove me on my route. And as spring bloomed, she kept driving me. I didn't ask her to do it—she simply showed up—and I wondered if she enjoyed our special time together as much as I did, especially now that Grandma was gone. There was so much I didn't know about Mom, and I found that once I started asking questions, a door flung open, and her stories poured out. "I hated moving to the country when I was a little girl," she told me one day. "Sure, it seems beautiful, all those long roads and farmland, but I had friends, you know? And suddenly, all my friends were gone. I missed them. I was lonely out there in the country. I rode my bike around all the time, to nowhere."

I thought of how I often walked without a destination too. But in my mind, I was going *somewhere*. Was that why Mom settled for the likes of Dad, I wondered—had she thought he was *somewhere* when he was just another kind of *nowhere*?

One day I got the nerve to ask her about it. I had just finished the route, and we were on our way home. "Why do you let Dad treat you so bad?" I blurted.

But Mom, in her reliably matter-of-fact way, calmly glanced at me from the corner of her eye and said, "Things aren't always simple, Tom."

"But you're so nice," I argued. "And pretty."

Mom tapped the top of the steering wheel with her index fingers. "Sometimes you don't always know how things will be. When I was young, my job was colorizing very large photos—I felt it was like being an artist—and someone might have looked at me and said, 'she's going to have a career at this,' but they would have been wrong, because I always knew I wanted to get married and have children. What girl doesn't want romance, you know?" she asked.

I shrugged, for this was out of my not-quite-twelve-year-old-boy territory. But I thought about how, on Sundays after church, Mom would sit at the kitchen table with a cup of coffee and a romance novel—something like *The Youngest Bridesmaid* or *Doctor on Horseback*, the cover often featuring a coquettish woman and a dapper man, sometimes donning a stethoscope—and it made sense. For that one hour each week, from her seat at the table, Mom went to a place far from Bronson Street—a place I will never know, a place where maybe she lived a ghost life, haunting the desolate streets of her desires—and it was up to the rest of us to make sure the little kids had what they needed during that hour. Sometimes we took advantage of Mom's brief window of distractedness by asking her for things she would normally say no to. "Mom, can we get chocolate milk at school tomorrow?" we'd ask. "Can we have a pet turtle?" And Mom would absent-mindedly say yes.

"Your Dad was a good dancer, and he looked handsome in his Navy uniform," Mom added, despite my having gone quiet. "Square dancing. I loved square dancing."

I could hardly picture Dad walking a straight line. "Then why don't you dance now?" I asked.

"People change. You know. They have hardships."

"Hardships?"

"I didn't know about alcohol when I met your dad. I just thought everyone drank, and I was too young to recognize that he drank too much. And then his mother and brother died."

I vaguely remembered when Grandma Joker, Mary Magdalene, died. "What happened to his brother?"

"Don't you remember Uncle Danny? You met him a couple of times when you were little. He was younger than Dad—tall, kind of handsome, dark hair, smiled a lot."

I had a fleeting memory of riding on his back once and pretending he was a horse. "Maybe a little, I guess."

"Well, he went to Texas and then to California, and—I can tell you this because you're older now—someone killed him."

Even though I hardly remembered him, I felt gut-punched. "That's awful," I said.

Mom circled around our block to keep the conversation going. "No one really knows what happened. When they found him, his head was severed."

I was used to Mom's no-nonsense manner, but this was a supreme moment of cognitive dissonance for me. How was it possible for her to deliver such horrifying information without so much as the tiniest rise in her voice, a catch in her breath, or even the smallest hint of quickening tempo? "You mean they cut his head off?" I squealed, picturing his severed head lying on the ground, still smiling.

"Yes. It was a big shock for your dad," she continued calmly.

I thought about how devastated I would be if something like that happened to one of my brothers or sisters. And Dad only had one.

When we got home, Dad was stationed in his usual corner with his usual accoutrements, but I saw him a little differently than I had before. Suddenly, he was an orphan, a man who carried hidden wounds that obfuscated what might be a kinder, gentler Dad underneath. "Hi Dad," I said.

He shot me a look from over the top of his book. "What? You too lazy to do your route yourself now?"

"No, I—"

"Papers too heavy for you?"

I stood there blinking at him for a moment in a haze of emotional whiplash. Then I turned without a word and left. I walked through the morning's brisk sunlit air until I no longer recognized where I was. I walked without breakfast and then without lunch. I walked until my legs buzzed. I walked until my new surroundings made me feel new too. And I kept walking until eventually I regained my bearings.

Luckily, I didn't have any altar boy responsibilities that weekend, and that was the first Sunday I hadn't accompanied Mom and my siblings to church—the place that would tell me to honor my father, the place that would say we should treat others the way we want to be treated. I wondered why parents weren't told to honor their children too. And why would someone want streets paved in gold if you could just float in Heaven anyway? It seemed that the more I learned and the older I grew, the less these things made sense to me. Even our encyclopedias were falling short. They could no more tell me the virtues of golden streets than they could explain why an uncle I barely knew got his head chopped off or why my father was like a human snapping turtle.

After walking for hours, my stomach started rumbling with hunger, but I didn't want to go home. Instead, I walked across the footbridge and arrived unannounced at Frankie's house—something I'd never done on a Sunday. His mother, a short pixyish woman, seemed genuinely happy to see me. "Tom, what a nice surprise! Come on in! We're just about to have hotdogs. Would you like to join us?"

"Yes, please, Mrs. Owen," I said as I wondered if maybe I could just move in.

"Hey, Quarter!" Frankie said with a toothy grin. "How's it goin', man?"

"Quarter?" I asked, confused.

"Well, if we're The Halfs, and you're half of one-half, then you're a quarter."

"Come, Tom," said Mrs. Owen, waving me over and handing me a plate. "Don't be shy."

"Yes," echoed his father, a gentle, unassuming man with thinning hair and chubby fingers. "Don't be shy."

So I loaded up my plate with hotdogs and macaroni salad and enjoyed the rare experience of sitting at a dining table with only five other people—including Frankie's little brother Billy, who was a charmer beyond his years, and their little sister—while just out-

164

side the walls of their house, traffic thundered by on the highway, hissing and chattering its persistent language of speed and mass and the varied cries of horns.

Later that day, Frankie and I gathered up Tyrone and Trey and, after a couple of hours on the basketball court, we took to the streets. Out of habit, I pulled a rock from my pocket, and Trey immediately snatched it from my hand. "What's this?" he asked.

"It appears, by my estimation, to be a rock, you rock-head-lookin' mothafuckah," said Tyrone, swiping the rock from Trey's hand. Then he threw it hard. With a spectacular clang, it hit a mailbox about twenty feet away. "C'mon!" said Frankie, "Let's get the hell out of here!" So we took off running through the twilight, and when we were far away and out of breath, we stopped to gather more rocks and then took turns pitching one after another at random mailboxes, keeping score of who hit the most. Tyrone was in the lead when he declared our game over. But I ignored Tyrone and grabbed another rock from my pocket. "If I can hit that bird," I said, pointing to a green mailbox with a carved wooden cardinal perched on top, "then I win." The guys agreed, and I wound my arm back the way I'd seen pitchers do, took a deep breath, and threw my rock with all I could muster. It hit so cleanly that it barely made a sound when the cardinal, for the most fleeting of moments, took flight. The four of us stood dumbstruck, looking at the fallen bird on the street. "You win," said Frankie, but before I could bask in my glory, the front door to the house of the severed mailbox bird slammed open, and a man who reminded me of the Incredible Hulk came running at us full speed. "You little bastards!" he yelled. "I'll fucking kill you!" The four of us scattered, but he stayed behind me. I ran as fast as I could down Manhattan Boulevard, with the Hulk keeping pace. "I'm sorry!" I called out desperately. "I'll never do it again!" My legs burned from the hours of walking followed by the games of basketball we'd played earlier that day, and I wasn't sure how much farther I could run. The man must have known not to waste any breath answering me. The sound of his relentless footfalls was my answer: if he caught me, he would make good on his promise.

Mom's face flashed before my eyes, then Taffy, then the lake at Camp Storer—just the water, gleaming as it had on those days I'd learned to water ski and to sail, as if the sun-dappled surface had been my future, slick and sparkling. But now, as the last of the daylight retreated into the smoky darkness of nightfall, I could feel it all ending.

I cut a quick turn down the train tracks that divided the marsh and instantly regretted my decision when a piece of rebar came flying past my head. The man was so strong that he was able to pick up huge pieces of rebar from the side of the railroad and heave them like spears, one of which grazed the back of my leg. But the hulk's process of arming himself cost him: he was beginning to lag a little behind.

Please God, I prayed as I ran down into the marsh, *let me live. I'll never do it again if you let me live!*

And then, as if by a miracle, the man stopped running. It was almost completely dark now, with only the shadowy outlines of things still visible—the bumpy tops of trees, the jagged weeds erupting from the fetid water, and the man's muscular outline growing dimmer as it moved away.

I was free. I was going back to Bronson Street.

There was no fanfare for my homecoming when I walked through the front door drenched in sweat. In fact, as usual, it was as if no one had even noticed I'd been gone, though Mom noncha-lantly pointed at my pants. "What happened to you?"

I craned my neck around to see what Mom was pointing at. My jeans were torn, and the back of my thigh was bleeding where the rebar had caught me. "I was running around with the guys," I said, trying to push the fabric together.

"I'll put a patch on it," she said.

"Can you use red stitching?" I asked.

"I think we can arrange that," she said with a smile. "Are you hungry? Do you want me to make you a fried bologna sandwich?"

I nodded. I wasn't hungry, but I could never turn down my favorite comfort food. "That sounds good," I said.

Mom never said anything to me about missing church that Sunday, maybe because she'd heard what Dad had said to me and under-stood why I left. The following Sunday, she and I returned to our sunrise ritual of delivering papers as if nothing had happened.

But something *had* happened. When we got home and I went to put the paper route money I'd collected in my sock drawer, all the money I'd been saving was gone. I double-checked, triple-checked, pulled out every sock, every drawer, but there was no trace of my money. Who would steal the money I worked so hard for? Who would do something so unfair, so cruel? And then I knew.

I burst into the living room in tears of fury. "Give it back!" I demanded, standing in front of Dad.

"I'm trying to watch TV," he said, poking his head off to one side so that he could see around me.

"You took it! You stole my money! You drank it all up!"

"I didn't take anything," he said, standing up. He was still taller than I was, but not by much. "But if you don't get out of my way, I'll *give* you something," he threatened, balling his fist.

"Give it back!" I shouted, my cheeks burning.

"If you're missing money, maybe you should ask one of your sisters or brothers. I'm not the only one who lives here, in case you haven't noticed."

I knew then that it was futile. He had taken all my money, over eighty dollars, and I would never get it back. Grief soddened me for days, but I was grieving far more than the loss of the small fortune I'd worked so hard for. I was grieving a pivotal loss of hope: that my father could ever be someone trustworthy or fair—that he could ever be a true father—and I began to hate him for it.

But soon I let that go too. As I walked the streets thinking about it all, I realized that my hatred for my father served absolutely no purpose other than to eat away at my happiness. I thought about something Gandhi had said: that forgiveness is an attribute of those who are strong. And I wanted to be strong—not human-flag-pole strong, but strong of heart and mind—and free.

That evening, Frankie, Trey, Tyrone, and I took to the streets on our bikes instead of walking. As we pedaled single file up Manhattan Boulevard, I wondered what would happen if we just kept going. It was one of those slow kinds of evenings. The sunset spread across the sky in a spectacular show of molten pink and wispy lavender, while silver-lined clouds cast down sunbeams that conjured the hands of God—all of it unraveling across the expanse in such small increments that it seemed we could ride forever under that changing sky, with starlings fluttering their last flights before roosting, peepers turning on their incessant metallic chirping, and the air dipping down cooler, fragrant with honeysuckle.

Even the traffic whispering past seemed to be moving at a languorous pace, tires gripping the road with sibilant certainty, everything poised on the verge of something I could feel but couldn't name.

Without warning, Frankie power-slid his bike to a stop and kicked up a ghostly dust cloud. "I'm gonna be the Marlboro Man one day!" he exclaimed, looking up at the billboard we'd passed so many times that I'd stopped noticing it.

But now we all gazed up through the haze at the cowboy and his cigarette. "So am I," said Trey with a decisive nod.

"You know a brotha can't be a *cowboy*," said Tyrone, leaning back on his bike until his front wheel popped up. "It's not natural."

I thought about the covers of the Westerns I'd seen Dad reading over the years, and realized I'd never seen a Black cowboy. "That doesn't seem fair," I said.

"Yeah," said Trey. "That's bullshit."

"Bullshit!" echoed Frankie, jumping off his bike and finding a rock in the weeds on the side of the road. He threw the rock up at the billboard and hit it dead center.

"Bull-mothafucking-shit!" said Tyrone, leaning his bike on the ground and gathering some rocks of his own. Beneath the light that poured down from the eight long fluorescent tubes jutting out over the billboard, we all began rifling through the weeds to arm ourselves once more with stones while, at some point when I wasn't paying attention, night had fallen. Farther back off the road we found even bigger rocks the size of grapefruits, and with both hands we flung them up from between our legs, careful to avoid them as they came back down on us. "Bullshit!" we screamed up at the cowboy, up at the stars, launching our stones toward the heavens. When one of my rocks hit two lights at once, the gas rushed out of the bulbs in a small explosion and we all cheered as the delicate glass fragments glittered down on us, slow as dande-lion seeds. "Bullshit!" we called again and again until the word lost its meaning. We were a band of sound and muscle, lit with sweat and emboldened by the ease of our destruction. We were the vio-lence of spring—fury and hunger pulsing in our fists. "Bullshit!" we rallied. And one by one, the billboard lights ruptured until Tyrone shattered the last one, leaving us, and the Marlboro Man, in darkness.

SEVENTEEN

"The problem is you can't force people to be good. You have to inspire them to *want* to be good," said Mr. Everett, my seventh-grade teacher, as he stood before us in his tight tan suit. He was both the first male and first Black teacher I'd had, and he was the only other teacher, aside from Sister Mary, who wasn't opposed to corporal punishment—though I would soon learn that his method was far more painful. He was a tricky teacher for an approval-driven kid like me because the straight *A*s and ready answers I'd historically used to impress all my other teachers didn't work on him. When my friends had teased me for being the teacher's pet in the past, despite my outward protests, it always secretly pleased me, but no one accused me of possessing this status during the seventh grade. Since Mr. Everett was also the only teacher I'd ever had who spoke to us about current events, including heated race-related topics, I'd even started reading the newspapers I delivered in the hope that one day I'd knock Mr. Everett's socks off with a casual but insightful opinion on a recent headline. "Take bussing, for example," he continued. "You can say segregation is unconstitutional. You can force the Black children into the white neighborhoods. But what do the white people do? They intimidate our children. They move away to new neighborhoods. They stand in our way. So, if you can't force integration, then tell me class— how do you inspire it? Upon whom do you call?"

Traditionally, I'd shot my hand up before a teacher even finished asking a question, but now I sat in my wooden chair and fidgeted in a cloud of uncertainty. I was used to the solid kinds of questions that had unequivocal answers, such as the year an important historical event occurred or the capital of a state or the answer to an equation, but Mr. Everett's questions often seemed impossible to answer.

Apparently, however, not for Frankie, who blurted out an answer. "The Black Panthers!" His eager grin lit up his face and his eyes sparkled.

Mr. Everett folded his arms across his chest and narrowed his brow. "And why do you call on the Black Panthers?" he asked.

"I, um, because they're...*influential?*" Frankie nodded as though he approved of his own answer.

Mr. Everett shook his head and took a long audible breath, a sign that he was about to deliver one of his soliloquies. "Yes, the Black Panthers *are* influential. And they've done great things, like the Free Breakfast for Children program and their much-needed copwatch tactics, for instance. But my question was about how to change people's minds. And if you can't *force* people's minds to change, then you must *inspire* them, and I think you're more likely to inspire them with a more peaceful approach, like Dr. King's..."

Intrigued by Mr. Everett's passion and his willingness to talk to us in a way I'd never heard another adult speak to children, I typically paid attention when he spoke, but he'd just reminded me of a recent addition to my Animals I Want to See One Day list, and because I couldn't resist the opportunity to seem knowledgeable about at least something, I whispered to Frankie, "Did you know that a blank panther can refer to both a jaguar *or* a leopard?"

"Did you know you're a dork?" he whispered back.

"I mean, there's no actual animal species called a panther," I explained, as if somehow he'd failed to register the wow-factor the first time.

"Mr. Seeman, do you have something important you'd like to share with the class?" Suddenly Mr. Everett was towering over my desk.

I could feel my cheeks turn red. "No, sir," I said.

"Clearly what you had to say to your neighbor here was important enough for you to speak while I was speaking, so why don't you let the rest of us in on your sagacity."

I cleared my throat. I tried to swallow. I shot a quick prayer to Mary to make me disappear. And when it didn't work, I confessed in the meekest voice I'd ever heard myself speak. "I was telling him that black panthers can be leopards or jaguars."

The whole class laughed. And as if that weren't punishment enough, Mr. Everett ordered me to the front of the room. I'd seen other kids endure, often tearily, Mr. Everett's standard punishment, but I never thought I would one day be facing it myself. "Knees on your knuckles. Face the class. Five minutes," he ordered.

I put my hands knuckle-side-down against the cold floor, which I had buffed and waxed a few months earlier, and then kneeled inside my open palms. "Not your palms," he said. "Kneel on your knuckles. I'm watching." Within seconds, the pain was only narrowly trumped by the even greater pain of having to inflict it upon myself. As I kneeled through each agonizing second, avoiding my classmates' stares by peering down at a blur of nothing, my throat burning as I choked back tears, I imagined socking Mr. Everett in the face with my aching heavyweight champion of the world fist. But after my punishment ended and the screaming bones in my knuckles quieted, I stopped being angry at Mr. Everett. Instead, I became determined: somehow, I would solve the mysterious puzzle of how to impress my unimpressible teacher; somehow, I would win his approval.

"Damn," said Frankie to Tyrone and Trey. "Tom got nailed today!" I had just shown up at Frankie's house as I did most school days after finishing my paper route and homework.

"Screw you," I said, giving Frankie a playful push. "It was your fault anyway."

"My fault, ha! In your dreams!" We were warming up on the basketball court, and Frankie swished the ball through the net.

"Black Panthers?" I argued, stealing the ball. "What kind of shit was that?"

He ignored me and continued to share my humiliation with the guys. "Mr. Everett made him kneel on his knuckles in front of the whole class."

Tyrone smirked. "What'd you do, Seeman?"

I saw this as my opportunity to impress Tyrone with tales of wrongdoing, but Frankie answered before I could get a word out. "He was talking to me about tigers and shit while Mr. Everett was teaching."

"It wasn't tigers," I corrected. "It was leopards and jaguars."

"You and your crazy-ass animals," said Tyrone. Then he upped his voice to a tremulous falsetto. "Lions and tigers and bears, oh my!"

Frankie and Trey started laughing, so he sang it again and again—each time a little more dramatic—until the veins in his neck were bulging and even I couldn't help but crack up. Then we pounded that court in the cool November air until the neighborhood quieted and kids scampered home and it was too dark to see the ball, and as usual, we started walking the streets.

I slipped the hood of my red sweatshirt halfway over my eyes and listened to the sound of our footfalls on the ground. Sometimes it seemed that the others were listening, too, as our steps synchronized into a singular rhythm. Occasionally a random car slipped past. A bat flapped against the starry backdrop. A pocket of cooler air moved over us like a ghost. And when we came upon a family of discarded jack-o'-lanterns lying haphazardly against a curb, we tucked them under our arms and headed for the footbridge over the highway. For all our chatter, sometimes we also knew how to share silence, and we stood not saying anything for a while as we watched the traffic rumbling below and making the whole bridge vibrate. We'd never made a plan, but when Tyrone said, "Now!" we all tossed our pumpkins onto the flatbed of a semi-truck as it emerged from under the bridge. In the haze of headlights and taillights, the once jagged-toothed Halloween sentries exploded and scattered in bits all over the highway, and then the four of us scrambled across the bridge, a pack of coyotes yipping into the darkness in different directions—the three of them heading back to their neighborhood while I ran alone in the other direction all the way back to Bronson Street.

Billboard lightbulbs, autumn gourds, the eggs we would later smash against the windows of St. Vincent's—we were becoming practiced in the art of making things explode, though it would be years before it would even occur to me how dangerous our escapades had been that evening. What if we'd hit a car? Caused a wreck? Killed someone? But in the self-absorbed territory of adolescence, we were focused on our own makeshift and muscled minute-to-minute. We were tough and silly, savage and tender. We were on the hunt, primed for adventure. We were learning how to push limits. We were learning how to be powerful.

Maybe my father could sense that power in the new sureness I felt in my step, the confidence I carried across my shoulders, because he started making his presence known in ways he hadn't before, like stepping in front of me suddenly so that, if I was walking from the living room into the kitchen for instance, I'd have to contort myself around him. But sometimes, while I was busy doing my best to avoid him, he leaned in and banged into me with his shoulder anyway.

He started harassing Mom more too. "Miss Fucking Perfect," he'd taunt night after night. "You think you're *soooooo* perfect."

And she continued to answer him with her calmest reasoning, as if there were actual merit to his words. "Not at all, Harry. I'm far from perfect. I just try really hard to do a good job."

At this point, he often mimicked her in a mocking falsetto: "I just try really hard to do a good *jooooob,*" he'd say, straining his vocal chords. And the more he picked on Mom, the more Ernie and I, and even young Susie, began to confront him. "Leave Mom alone!" we admonished. "Stop being mean!" And the more we did that, the more he blocked me from moving around the house.

One night, I'd gone into the kitchen to get a glass of milk, and he followed me in. "Do you realize how much milk costs?" he asked.

I ignored him and took a sip.

"You listen to me when I talk to you," he said.

"I did listen."

"Well then, what's your answer?"

"I'm a growing boy," I said, gulping down the rest and putting my glass in the sink. I started to leave the kitchen, but he stood in front of me.

"Wash it," he said.

I returned to the sink and washed the glass. That had always been one of the few chores we kids had—to wash and dry the dishes, which we did in alternating shifts: one shift washed the breakfast and lunch dishes, and the other washed dinner. The dish-washing ranks were established by age: the younger kids started out as dryers and eventually graduated to washers, but the dryers (there were always two dryers for each washer) had one special power—they could return any dish they deemed dirty and make the washer do it over. "Dirty, dirty, dirty!" the dryers would happily sing, passing the dish back. By necessity, we were a family of routine, but there were some gray areas, such as after-dinner dishes, which often stayed in the sink until morning to join the breakfast dishes. On that night, however, Dad was changing the rules. *Too bad you've never done a dish in your life*, I thought, as I wiped my glass dry.

I tried to leave the kitchen again, and again he blocked me. Thanks to my continued growth spurt, we were almost eye-to-eye now. "Can I get by?" I said, trying to duck away from his cigar-tinged beer breath. But whichever way I moved, he followed, so we entered into a strange football dance beneath our kitchen's most notable item—a frying pan-shaped clock with fried eggs and strips of bacon for numbers. I fixed my eyes on the plastic bacon to avoid looking at my father's face, but as we darted side to side and I felt increasingly trapped, I began to feel a little panicked. "Let me go!" I finally pleaded.

"Make me," he said, thumping my chest with the flats of his palms and thrusting me backwards. I stumbled but caught myself, and then, out of reflex, I pushed him back—a shock to us both. Perhaps it was the strength I'd gained from years of football and basketball that made him seem like one of Jane and Judy's baby dolls—flimsy and will-less against my hands. He fell back against the table, and I watched in awe as the man I'd grown up afraid of stumbled like a cartoon version of himself, knocking down one chair after another in the most protracted fall I'd ever seen, until finally he hit the floor.

Mom and some of the kids came running in to see what the ruckus was about. "What happened?" she insisted, helping Dad up. He looked at me with a narrow glare of warning. "I tripped," he said. "There's no room to even breathe in this house—that's the problem. You've got us all piled up on top of each other like mice in a cage."

"Oh Harry," said Mom, picking up the fallen chairs. "We have more space here than we used to have at Ravine Park, and I for one...."

I began singing to myself as I went into our bedroom and closed the door, so that I didn't have to hear her try to reason yet again with another of his tirades. "Joy to the world, all the boys and girls. Joy to the fishes in the deep blue sea, joy to you and me...."

I had once told Taffy about what our encyclopedias had been teaching me about Caesar. "He had to cross a river called the Rubicon," I'd explained, "and once he crossed it, he couldn't go back." After that, I'd thought a lot about the concept of a point of no return. What if I crossed such a place in one of my walks through the neighborhoods, I wondered, and could never go home? What if the astronauts who landed on the moon could never come back to earth? Knowing this, would I still walk the streets of Toledo? Would the astronauts still rocket up toward the heavens? I never could decide on an answer. But that night, after attempting to dodge my father in the doorway of our kitchen, I knew as I stepped across that threshold, that I had crossed a Rubicon of my own: I had outranked my father. I was no longer afraid of him.

But it didn't take long before a new fear surfaced, one that would send roots down into the depths of my psyche and anchor itself in place for years. It happened unexpectedly one night when the four of us were having a sleepover at Frankie's much older sister Kathy's apartment—a messy little place in an old creaky house. Kathy was an upbeat soul who was always willing to laugh, and she had this way of looking into you when she asked a question. "So, Tom," she asked that night, "how's football?" Like Frankie, she had a smooth, milky complexion, but her face was rounder, almost cherubic.

Naturally, I fumbled over myself. "Good. I mean, good. We went to the Toy Bowl this year. That's the championship. We lost. Coach Gary is our coach. He's great."

She tilted her head to one side and gazed at me like a curious puppy. "Toy Bowl, huh? You must be pretty good."

"I am. Yes, we are."

Unlike the many adults who made me feel like I was wasting their time when I talked to them, she seemed genuinely interested in us. She enjoyed giving us access to the very things most adults forbade, like the bottles of beer Frankie, Tyrone, and Trey were sipping. Having made my vow of abstinence years earlier, I didn't partake, but as I watched my friends grimace and shudder whilst trying to feign nonchalance about the bitterness on their tastebuds, I wasn't tempted at all.

I was, however, almost thirteen, and when Frankie produced a stack of porn magazines, tossing them down in front of us and opening one to some of his favorite pages, holding them out for us to see as if we were in second-grade show-and-tell, I suddenly found myself awash in a maelstrom of sensations. Because Frankie had repeated two grades, he was two years older than the rest of us, and never before had our age difference been more apparent than it was now. While Frankie was comfortable ogling naked women, and more—he claimed to be having sex with his girlfriend—I had never seen a naked woman in my life. Once, at a roller rink, I slow-skated with a dark-haired girl named Pam, and I still regularly relived the thrill of holding her hand, of going around and around to "Killing Me Softly" with a sweaty palm that made me feel linked to someone else in a way I'd never been in my life. But as the glossy pages in Frankie's hands shone in the light and I rode the wave between attraction and repulsion, hunger and embarrassment, I had the opposite feeling: the world was shrinking. My face flushed hot while my hands turned cold. I wanted to look closer, and I wanted to look away. My heart raced, and my mouth went dry, while parts of my body stirred without my permission.

I didn't appreciate it. Whether planting a garden, building a city inside a cigar box, making lists of animals, setting rules and goals for myself, or strapping a coin dispenser to my belt so I could quickly make change for my newspaper customers, I liked things to be orderly in my life, and this was anything but orderly. This was a tsunami. And it scared me.

That night I unwittingly crossed another Rubicon. And suddenly I knew it: I could never go back; I could never unsee what I'd seen. I could never un-feel what I'd felt. I thought of my parents, poor and struggling, popping out baby after baby, and I thought of the girls in the neighborhood who walked around with their pregnant bellies and who were the ages of my older sisters. I thought of the Hell our church promised those who had sex out of wedlock. And that night, as my friends snored in their beer-drunk slumbers and I stared into the darkness, I made a new rule for myself: I would not have sex until I was married—or at least until I was much, much older.

The next day, the guys and I went back to Frankie's house and walked up the train tracks along the marsh. It felt good to be back to ordinary pleasures, like plucking snails from the concrete drain that allowed the marsh waters to flow under the tracks, poking through the pickerel weed and cattails in search of lily-pad-dwelling frogs, picking up snapping turtles by the sides of their shells and giggling while they tried to claw and bite us. This was the real stuff—the dirt and slime of childhood.

When we heard the sustained horn from an incoming freight train pierce the afternoon, I reached into my pocket to see if I had any pennies. We occasionally put pennies on the tracks right before a train barreled through, then marveled at the pennies' supreme flatness. But as the train came ambling toward us this time, Frankie had a different idea. "Let's jump on!"

Everything inside me screamed *NO!* We'd all heard the rumors about a boy who'd slipped and lost both his legs under the wheels, and I wasn't a fan of leaving my own legs on the tracks—but Frankie was beaming his most convincing grin, and soon the train was upon us, a shock of rattling metal. He started running next to the slow-moving train and grabbed onto the steel ladder welded to the end of the box car. He kept running while holding onto the ladder, and then he jumped up onto the rungs and was carried down the tracks. Tyrone leapt onto the next car, followed by Trey. "C'mon Tom!" they called as they moved away from me. "Don't be a chicken!"

That was all my competitive side needed to hear. I ran forward to catch up with the car next to Trey's, grabbed hold, and leapt onto the bottom rung. And then we were moving, sailing past the scrub and the fetid water, past the backs of tiny houses, into the wind. I climbed higher on the ladder, and the others did the same. *Let it always be like this*, I thought, closing my eyes into the luscious rush of air—as I'd once done on the back of Uncle Dick and Harold's truck on the day we moved to Bronson Street, and later on a boat in a lake at Camp Storer—feeling myself come alive, pure as anything being born.

In the sacristy at church a few weeks later, as another altar boy named Sam and I poured water and wine from bottles into the cruets and filled the chalice with hosts, I thought I'd get Sam's take on one of the many questions that had been nagging at me lately. "Do you think your Guardian Angel is watching over you all the time?"

He shrugged and shoved a handful of hosts into his mouth.

"I mean, like every *second*?" I said as he chewed. I'd been concerned about the notion that I might never have a moment of privacy, that my Guardian Angel, or worse—Grandma—could look down on me anytime they wanted and see what I was doing. I had just turned thirteen, and Sam was a year older, so I thought he might have some insight.

He took a swig from the bottle of altar wine and laughed. "What, are you beating the meat, Seeman?" he asked, glancing down at my trousers.

"No! No way!" I protested.

"Then why's your face all red?"

I was grateful that Father Schmelzer entered the sacristy at that exact moment, ready to be dressed in his vestments. And after Sam left to take the cruets and chalice to their place at the back of the church, I took the opportunity to ask a different question—one I'd asked Father Schmelzer years before. "Does the host *really* become the body of Christ?" I hadn't been satisfied with his answer the last time I asked, and now that I was an official teenager, I thought maybe he would level with me. "I mean, his actual *flesh*?"

Father Schmelzer shot me a quizzical look. "Haven't we been through this already, Tom? Of course it is. That's the miracle called *transubstantiation*. Haven't you been paying attention all these years?"

All I ever do is pay attention, I thought, handing him his cincture, which he tied around his underrobe. "Yes, Father. It's just—it doesn't make sense to me. How do those hosts that get delivered here"—I nodded toward the large plastic bag of wafers on the table—"turn into, you know, actual bones and skin and organs and stuff? Scientifically speaking. And why do they just taste ordinary?" I carefully draped Father Schmelzer's stole, an ornately gilded silk, around his neck.

"Miracles aren't scientific," he answered, adjusting the stole. "They're gifts from God."

I finished dressing him by slipping his green and gold chasuble over his graying head. "Well, since the Lord can perform miracles," I asked, "then why can't he stop murders?" I thought of my beheaded uncle, a ghost who was always skimming the edges of my mind. "Or stop people from burning and drowning innocent cats?"

Father Schmelzer looked at the door. "What's taking Sam so long?" He stood up then and, for the first time in our conversation, really looked at me. "God has given us free will, Tom. And that, too, is a gift. You have to choose whether to believe or not."

I wanted to ask about so many things—free will, Hell, rules, whether we can ever escape the eyes of heavenly beings—but Sam returned, and we entered the church, where the music had begun, where my family stretched along the length of a pew and the women in the front row had their rosaries at the ready, and where I led our priest down the aisle and held tightly to the wooden cross I was carrying.

As spring warmed toward summer and seventh grade was nearing its end, it seemed I would never find my way into Mr. Everett's good graces. But then something amazing happened: I signed up for an interscholastic speech contest, for which we had to recite a famous piece of writing from memory. And perhaps because I was one of only a few kids in our school who signed up for the event, Mr. Everett took a special interest in the selection of my speech. When I mentioned that I was thinking of reciting the Gettysburg Address, he told me everyone would be doing that and I should try something different, like a poem. But when I later suggested Frost's "The Road Not Taken," he put his fingers to his temples as if I'd just given him a headache. "I mean something *really* different, Tom. Something meaningful that'll make the judges take notice."

Of course, I was eager to win the contest and to please the teacher who, for the better part of a year, had been impervious to the swiftness of my in-class hand-raises and the correctness of my answers, who had neglected to comment on the extra algebra equations I regularly included with my homework or the drawing of a printing press I included with my paper on the Reformation, so I would have probably recited Mom's grocery list while standing on my head if he had told me to.

But instead, he suggested a different poem. "Can you stay for a few minutes after school today?" he asked, dropping a copy of it on my desk. "To practice?"

"I have my paper route," I told him, and after a moment's thought I added, "but it can wait." And that day, after our classroom emptied out and the clock on the wall ticked louder than I'd remembered it ticking before, I nervously recited the poem for Mr. Everett.

"Do you have to fidget so much?" he asked.

I scratched my head. "No."

"I call it 'the dance,' when someone shifts back and forth on his feet like that. A good rule is to always avoid doing the dance. Now try it again."

So I tried again, but this time he interrupted me partway through. "You think Dunbar would say it like that? C'mon, where's your soul, Tom? You have to put some zest into it. Let's do it again."

I don't know how many more times I read Dunbar's poem that afternoon before Mr. Everett finally slapped his hands together. I thought I'd done something wrong again, but then my stoic teacher offered a hint of a smile. "Now *that* is how you recite this poem," he said.

There it was: my gold star, my hard-won victory, my moment of deep relief. In an empty school, in the waning afternoon, in my sweat-soaked school clothes, I had finally won Mr. Everett's approval.

I recited that poem all the way home, holding the paper out in front of me as I walked, until I had it memorized, and in the weeks that followed I recited it constantly in my head—during dinner, on my walks through the neighborhoods, on the basketball court, in my dreams. And when the Saturday of the competition finally came, I brushed my teeth for an extra-long time and got dressed before waving goodbye to Mom and getting in the car of Claire Kowalski's parents, who were kind enough to give me a ride to the contest.

"Are your parents sick?" her mother asked after a few minutes on the road. I sat shyly beside Claire, whose right knee (I was trying not to notice) bore a tiny red dot from where a boy had stuck her with a pencil in fifth grade. "Is that why they can't come?"

My parents almost never came to any school event, so I hadn't even thought about it. "No, they're just busy," I said. "My dad has a job, and my mom has lots of kids."

"Oh," she said. "I see." And that was the last question she asked me.

When we arrived at Lourdes College, there were so many kids milling about in every direction that I stopped noticing how sweet Claire smelled and started feeling for the rhythm of my poem again, which had now become a part of me. But once we'd all been sorted into various classrooms and the recitations had begun, I said a quick prayer to Mother Mary and then went silent inside, looking down. I noticed their janitor didn't do as good a job buffing the floors as I would have done.

A girl named Sarah was called to perform first by the panel of five judges. "Four score and seven years ago..." began Sarah, with her two springy pigtails.

Mr. Everett was right! I thought.

"Two roads diverged in a yellow wood..." began a boy wearing a crisp white shirt under his navy suit and red tie.

"We hold these truths to be self-evident..." said another boy in another freshly pressed suit.

And then, somewhere between the third and fourth "Shall I compare thee to a summer's day" of the morning, it was my turn. I'd dressed in my spiffiest outfit for the occasion—a light blue shirt with puffy sleeves, a pair of red polyester pants on which Mom had sewn denim knee patches and denim bellbottoms, and my brown suede fringe vest—and as I walked to the front of the room, I could feel the fringe of my vest swaying with each step.

"This is a poem by Paul Laurence Dunbar," I said, making eye contact with each of the five judges who sat straight-faced in a row, "called 'Sympathy.' It's by a Black poet from Ohio, and it's about slavery." I cleared my throat, once, twice, three times. I focused on not doing the dance. And then I began, with all the "soul" and "zest" I could muster.

> I know what the caged bird feels, alas!
> When the sun is bright on the upland slopes;
> When the wind stirs soft through the springing grass,
> And the river flows like a stream of glass;
> When the first bird sings and the first bud opes,
> And the faint perfume from its chalice steals—
> I know what the caged bird feels!
> I know why the caged bird beats his wing
> Till its blood is red on the cruel bars;
> For he must fly back to his perch and cling
> When he fain would be on the bough a-swing;
> And a pain still throbs in the old, old scars
> And they pulse again with a keener sting—
> I know why he beats his wing!

The judges' eyes narrowed, but I kept on as if the ghost of Paul Laurence Dunbar—a poet who, Mr. Everett taught me, was born in Dayton, Ohio, to former Kentucky slaves; a poet who started writing verse at the age of six and later gave readings in Toledo; a poet who died very young—were in the room with us.

> I know why the caged bird sings, ah me,
> When his wing is bruised and his bosom sore,—
> When he beats his bars and he would be free;
> It is not a carol of joy or glee,

But a prayer that he sends from his heart's deep core,
But a plea, that upward to Heaven he flings—
I know why the caged bird sings!

The room was silent. I worried for a moment about what Mr. Everett had said—that no one else would be reciting a poem like this. Some of the judges smiled. Then one began to clap, and the others followed. *Yeah. Like that,* I thought, fringe swinging as I walked back to my seat.

EIGHTEEN

Maybe summer sings the same songs to all children, regardless of where they live. In the projects, in the summer of '72, surely the wood thrush was no less vocal than it was in any other neighborhood. Surely the hawks that circled over Bronson Street were no less majestic than the hawks that circled over mansions, nor were the monarch caterpillars that munched on the wild milkweed any less vividly striped than the monarch caterpillars of other zip codes. The sun lit our shoulders as we kicked cans and balls, same as any other shoulders in any other part of town. And the moon spared no glow for us. But despite my happy ghetto childhood, despite the gospel music that still swelled like surf from the church across the street every Sunday, despite Mr. Hobo's grill on overdrive that summer, casting smokey ribbons through the air like invitations to a party that seemed as though it would never end, I knew that I didn't want to live in the projects forever.

So when it came time to take the Catholic high school placement test that fall, I'd already devoted many nights of solitary walking time to thinking about where I wanted my test results sent. Because my older siblings all attended public high schools, I didn't have anyone to ask, but I figured that the better a school was, the better a student's chance at a successful career—even if, in the shadow of my dwindling heavyweight champion and presidential aspirations, I didn't know what that career would be. By my calculations, there was only one private school I could afford: Central Catholic. But as I prepared to take the test, I saw the little boxes you could check to select the high schools who would receive your results. I checked Central Catholic, and when I noticed the box for St. Francis, I checked that too. I knew their tuition was $700, compared to Central Catholic's $425, and I knew they were known as a college prep school and that the students wore coats and ties. Because of that, in my neighborhood, St. Francis was known as the "sissy school." I also knew there was no way I could afford to attend St. Francis, but maybe because our football team had played so many games on the sprawling fields next to St. Francis, seeing their name on the list of schools was like seeing an old friend.

"I figured out a way I can go to Central," I told Coach Gary as I slipped the new plastic sweatsuit he'd bought me over my regular sweatpants and T-shirt. That year, I was the only kid who needed to lose weight for the team weigh-in, so it was just the two of us at the park. I was already starting to sweat.

"How's that?" he asked, readying his stopwatch.

"Between my paper route and my odd jobs, like mowing people's lawns and shoveling their driveways and washing their cars, I can make $450 a year, which is $25 more than the tuition. And maybe the school will give me a job as a janitor like at St. Vincent's, and maybe they'll even pay me, and then maybe I'll have extra for candy and clothes."

"At least you have your priorities in order," he laughed. "Candy first!" But then he looked at me in a more serious way, letting the hand holding the stopwatch fall in slow motion to his side. "What do your parents think? About your calculations, I mean?"

I shrugged. "I haven't told anyone but you."

"So you just figured this all out on your own? How to pay for high school by yourself?"

"It wasn't hard," I said, puffing my chest a little. "How else am I going to see a Bengal tiger one day?"

Coach Gary smiled. "Yup," he said. "I always knew you were special. That's why you're team captain this year. You're going places, Tommy. Tigers and all." He lifted the stopwatch back up and zeroed it out. "Let's make these miles really count, okay?"

I nodded as I smiled back at the man who'd always had something encouraging to say, who'd led our ragtag team to the Toy Bowl because he made us believe we could do anything, who'd spent his own money on not one but two plastic suits to ensure I'd get to play. Then I fired up my legs and took off into September.

❖   ❖   ❖

Half a year goes by like a scene from a dream. One minute you're playing football on a field in autumn; the next, it's Easter Eve, and you're putting your shoes at the bottom of the steps like you do every Saturday before going to bed. Your mother will polish fourteen pairs of shoes before church the next day. She always finds a way to make elaborate Easter baskets for each of her sweet-toothed children, and she'll decorate the baskets as she does every year, making a bed of paper grass and latching fuzzy pipe cleaner chicks onto the handles. With your shoes awaiting your mother's touch, you lie awake in bed—now on the second floor in a hand-me-down bunkbed from an aunt you almost never see—Ern on top and you on the bottom, free in this new and rare private space. You're only days away from turning fourteen. Something is happening inside you, but you don't know how to name it. You don't know about hormones because no one has talked to you about the things that happen to a teenage body. What you know is that you're drifting into a haze of football plays and pretty girls and rejoinders you wish you'd dished out to your friends, until you slip across the hidden bridge to sleep and travel deep into the forest. The darkness drapes you in silent breezes as you lean into the hum of crickets and katydids, trying to find your way. You walk among the dense trees with your arms out, feeling for what you can't see; you sense that the trees are dancing, that this is their secret. Meanwhile, coyotes yip excitedly, hunting something. An owl screeches. Somewhere a cougar is screaming, ripping open the fabric of nighttime....

The screams were coming from our older sisters' room across the hall. There were thumps and thuds and footsteps down the stairs. Someone had closed the door to our bedroom, something Ernie and I never did at night, and we scrambled out of bed and flung the door open, rushing into the hall. I flipped on the lights and grabbed a baseball bat from the closet. Mom was standing at the top of the stairs, and Marji was gripping her arm, pulling her back. "Don't go down!" she pleaded. "Just let him go!"

Dad wasn't home; he was working the night shift.

"Who? Let *who* go?" I shouted, readying the bat with both hands.

By then, the whole house was awake, babies crying, all of us bleary-eyed and blinking into the sudden brightness as we clustered together in the hall.

"I think it was one of the Bryants," said Marji. "He was hovering over Beth. It was hard to see, but it looked like Odell."

Odell was one of the Bryant kids we rarely encountered. Unlike Terry, who'd once given Mom a ride home from the grocery store when Dad failed to pick her up, or the twins, who could often be found sidling up to the slick guys of the neighborhood with the fur vests and gleaming cars, I'd never seen Odell interact with or acknowledge anyone. He had a way of walking that was more like skulking, and I'd once heard some kids on the basketball court refer to him as "Crazy Eyes."

"He was reaching for my face when I woke up," Beth said, starting to cry. "His hands were so close to my face."

"I'm calling the police," said Mom, scurrying to her night table.

Bat raised over my head, I ran down the stairs, turned on the lights, and found the kitchen door wide open, hanging half off its hinges like a dead tree limb. Both the door and the doorframe were marred by deep gouges where it had been pried open with a crowbar. I looked around to see what other damage the intruder had caused and if he'd stolen our television or our fried-egg-and-bacon clock. But everything seemed to be in order, including the two rows of Easter baskets lined up on the living room floor. "He didn't take our baskets!" I called up the stairs.

Soon the night was invaded by the red-and-blue swirl of police lights and the staticky words that spilled out of the chunky black radios strapped to the officers' belts. "This guy was pretty determined," noted one of the officers as he inspected the damage.

Mom cleared her throat and spoke in a low voice. "My daughter saw who it was. He was in the girls' room. It was dark, but she thinks she knows who did it."

The officer looked Mom up and down. "Where's your husband, ma'am?"

"He's at work," she said. "Why?"

"Unfortunately, without a positive identification, there's not much we can do. You said yourself that it was dark." He glanced at the collection of Easter baskets on the floor. "Who knows—maybe it was the Easter Bunny." He laughed at his own joke, and one of the other officers joined him. "I'll file a report, but in the meantime, I'd suggest you have your husband get a stronger door with a better lock," said the officer. And then they were gone.

Dad never did get another door, and the dents and scrapes, like the hole in the ceiling where Mom's leg poked through, would stay. But the next morning, while Dad was asleep and my sisters and brothers and I whispered excitedly over our Easter baskets, our teeth brown with chocolate, Uncle Dick and Harold did their best to smooth out what they could and reattach the hinges. "The Easter Bunny is so nice!" exclaimed Joe, now five, as he nibbled a bunny ear. We all shushed him for fear of waking Dad, so he said it a second time in a whisper, and we laughed. It was almost as if what had happened in the middle of the night had been a dream, a strange hiccup in the regular rhythm of our lives.

Soon though, despite our careful joy, something woke Dad up too early, and he came stomping down the stairs, his face creased with pillow marks, his eyes puffy. He lumbered into the kitchen, where the uncles greeted him merrily, screwdrivers in their hands. He ignored them, opting instead to open and slam the refrigerator door several times in a row before stomping back up the stairs empty-handed.

He stayed mad for days, harassing Mom at every opportunity. "Dick thinks he's some big man, coming here pretending to be some kind of hero or something. Pretty easy when you have a retarded sidekick to do all the heavy lifting for you." He repeated some version of this after dinner for several nights in a row, and each time it hurt me anew.

"Me?" he said. "I'm out working my ass off so that they can come every Sunday and eat all my food, taking extra helpings even, as if it's their fucking house."

At first, Mom tried to reason with Dad as she always did, treating his accusations as though they deserved credibility. "They come here because they love the kids and they want to help, Harry."

"They come here to eat my food! And strut around with their toolbelts."

But after days of the same conversation, Mom went quiet, scooping leftovers into bowls without enthusiasm while we kids reported for dish duty and Dad lorded over the empty table. "It's *my* house, you hear me, Ginny? *My* house!"

"Leave Mom alone!" yelled Susie.

"Shut the fuck up!" yelled Dad.

"You shut the fuck up!" yelled Ernie.

Dad erupted from the table and grabbed Ernie by the collar. "You ever speak to me like that again and I'll kill you. You hear me?"

I rushed over and put myself between them. I was now taller than my father and Ernie, and we both knew I was stronger. "Get off him!" I said, freeing Ernie from his grip.

"Fuck all of you!" said Dad, grabbing the car keys and rushing out the door.

The following Sunday, after Mom settled in at the table with her cup of coffee and the one luxury she allowed herself all week—a romance novel—he stood over her and yelled down at the top of her head. "Admit it!" he demanded. "You wish you'd married him instead of me!"

Mom closed her book and laid it on the table as gently as if it were a sleeping baby. She smoothed the cover with her hands, then let them fall helplessly to her lap. "He's my brother, Harry."

"Tell that to him! Why do you think we never see him with a woman? Why is that, Ginny?"

Mom's eyes turned watery, and her head drooped forward like a flower too heavy for its stem. It was the second time in my life I'd seen her cry.

Barb, three years old, came babbling into the kitchen carrying a blue wooden block from a set Uncle Dick and Harold had cut and painted in different colors for us one Christmas. "Mean Daddy," she said, throwing the block at his feet.

After walking the streets that night, I came home to more yelling, this time between Dad and Ernie. "Please," Mom was trying to interject, while Dad and Ernie stood in the kitchen, face-to-face, eyes locked, Dad's neck veins bulging. "That's enough. You're upsetting the little ones."

"I'm not going to be disrespected in my own house by this little twerp. Now get out of here and don't let me see you for the rest of the night, or else I'll knock the daylights out of you!"

"Go ahead then," said Ernie in an eerily calm voice. "I'm not afraid of you anymore."

Mom left the kitchen to scoop up Barb from the playpen. Rich and Joe were zooming toy trucks around on the living room floor as casually as if the yelling were coming from the television or someone else's house, while the twins huddled together on the sofa looking at the same book and Daniel stood at the window, looking out. To some degree, I think we were all used to Dad's tirades. But something about that night felt different, and I stood in the doorway, unsure what to do. Dad balled both of his fists. "I mean it," he said. "Scram!"

Ernie held his ground. "I'm not going anywhere. I'm tired of you bullying everyone all the time! We all are," he said, and at that point, his voice cracked. He shot me a questioning look, as if to say, *Are you with me or not?*

"It's true," I said, taking a step toward them. "We're tired of it. Of you."

Dad looked at me, and his face paled. His bottom lip quivered, and for a moment, I thought he might cry. Over the years, the skin of his eyelids had become so droopy that he wore a perpetual expression of sadness, even when, on rare occasions, he smiled. But now, he looked desperate, trapped between two sons who were finally calling his bluff. "I'll show you," he warned, as he stormed out of the kitchen and marched up the stairs.

"I'm glad that's over," I said to Ernie as soon as he was out of sight.

But before Ernie could even finish sighing, Dad was back. "You think you're such tough guys now?" His hands were shaking as they gripped an object I knew well: his gun, which he was pointing at us.

Ernie charged at our father and knocked the gun out of his hand. Dad stumbled backwards, and the gun slid across the linoleum floor—a smooth, cold piece of steel upon which suddenly everything, every life in that house, hinged. I grabbed it. Dad and Ernie continued to holler, now with Mom's voice intertwined in the mix, while I did what I had done so many times before: I opened the gun's chamber and emptied out the bullets.

I took a hammer out of a box of tools on the kitchen shelves, hurried out the back door, and on that starless night, under the glow of our back porch light, I laid the gun down on the back stoop and hammered it to pieces.

Dad was gone when I came back inside. He never asked about the gun, which I threw in our chained-down trashcan along with the bullets.

Big things seem to happen in clusters. Not long after the break-in and the gun incident, Sister Ann, our school principal, wanted to see me in her office. Mystified, I combed my mind trying to think of what I might have done wrong. After our trifecta of vandalisms the year before, The Halfs and I had settled into a more mundane existence together that mostly consisted of basketball, marsh dwelling, and train jumping, so nothing recent came to mind. But I walked into the reception area of Sister Ann's small office feeling sheepish anyway. "Someone's here to meet with you," she said.

As I entered her office, a priest stood up and held out his hand. "Hello, Tom. I'm Father McMenamin, from St. Francis de Sales High School."

Now I was even more confused. "Nice to meet you," I said, shaking his hand.

"Have a seat." He was an officious man with glass-smooth red cheeks and a mouth that was somewhat small for his face. "I'm here because I received the results of your high school placement test," he said. "Tell me, why did you send your test results to Central?"

The test! "Well, I did the math, and I have this paper route and I can work extra, so I figured I could afford Central."

"You'll be paying for this by yourself? With no help from anyone?"

"Yes. My parents don't have any money," I admitted.

He adjusted his spectacles, as if to look at me anew. "Then why did you check the box for St. Francis?"

"Because I heard it's a college prep school, and I want to go to college. And we play our football games there on the fields.

But I know I can't afford it, so I shouldn't have checked the box. I'm sorry."

"What if I told you that you could afford it?"

I looked at him, dumbfounded. Sister Ann smiled at me and nodded.

"Sister Ann has told me that you're an A student, and based on your test results, Tom, I can offer you a full scholarship to St. Francis. But you'd have to work a little at the school. Would you be willing to do that?"

"I love to work!" I said, practically springing out of my chair.

"That's good news. I hope you come to St. Francis—we could use a hard worker like you."

"Yes, Father. I will definitely choose St. Francis!" I said.

And with that one short conversation, my life had changed, though I did not yet know how much.

That day, I ran all the way home from school. Mom was in the kitchen when I burst through the back door out of breath, threw my bookbag on the floor, and blurted out the news. "A priest came from St. Francis and told me I can go to St. Francis for high school next year! He said he would pay for the whole thing!"

"Oh, that's wonderful," she said, tapping the tops of a pan full of cookies to see if they were still hot, then pointed toward the counter. "Could you hand me that spatula?"

"It's a college prep school," I said, placing the spatula in her hand. "To prep kids for college."

In quick lifts, she began emptying the pans. "That's really terrific, Tom."

"When kids score high on the placement test. Which I did." All my years of extracting approval from teachers and coaches, friends and their families, couldn't take the place of what I most yearned for: to hear my mother say she was proud of me. Even admitting that now wakes up the shame-angel in me, the one who sits on my shoulder and points accusingly at my face. *Isn't that petty?* the shame-angel says. *Didn't she do enough for you? Wasn't she miraculous enough?* And though the answer must always be yes, as the fifth of twelve children, I couldn't help but long for things that were impossible. I still do.

Soon my sisters and brothers piled into the kitchen, and as we loaded up on snickerdoodles and milk and the house filled with chatter and laughter and the clinks of glasses and the day unfolded like most other days on Bronson Street, I kept my news inside, quiet as a birthday wish.

NINETEEN

"The question is, do we really have free will?" asked Barry, a fellow freshman at St. Francis who wore the same orange-and-purple plaid jacket to school most days and who never missed an opportunity to have a debate, especially about politics or religion—though he'd gladly argue the reasons why "Yesterday" was the best Beatles song, why Lady Jane Grey was the most interesting royal in English history, or why the O'Henry was the most perfect candy bar on earth. He was one of a group of four new friends I'd made at St. Francis, the five of us grouped together by our high school placement tests (our homeroom had scored the highest), and now we sat packed together at our lunch table as if we'd known each other all our lives. "Or is everything we do already prewritten? Like the way I eat this particular fry, for example," he said, inserting a saliva-covered french fry into his mouth. The saliva was his solution to the St. Francis French Fry Walk of Shame, whereby the meeker students were regularly subjected to bullies who shamelessly swiped their fries as they hurried to their lunch tables. Barry had lost many handfuls of his lunch that way, until one day, in a moment of uncharacteristic theatric aplomb, he spat all over the golden lot of them as soon as he paid for them. He continued this ritual until everyone in the school knew about it, and from then on, all Barry's fries were his to keep.

"Yes, I'm sure God wrote in detail about the exact constituents of your lunch tray," said Gene, who had a businesslike appearance that belied his silly nature. "I mean, what else does God have to do all day?"

"If you ask the Calvinists," said Joel, whose comb-over and disheveled shirt and jacket made him look like the medieval history professor he would one day become, "they'd say that everything is already decided because of predestination. If God is omniscient and knows the future, He already knows everything we'll do, so do we really have a choice? You're either destined for Heaven or destined for Hell, and that's that." He adjusted his glasses on his slender nose and cocked his head to one side as if to consider the profundity of his own statement.

"Of course we have free will," said Gary, the least argumentative and most socially buoyant of the bunch. Otherwise, what's the point of following the Commandments or going to confession?"

"Or being baptized," I added, eager to contribute to the discussion.

"Hey, Seeman," Gene interjected, "why do you always hunch over your food like that? You think someone's gonna steal your radishes and lettuce leaves?"

The guys laughed, and I laughed, too, as I sat up straighter. I didn't tell them how hard mom worked to collect coupons and stretch her food stamps for the food she packed for me each day. I didn't tell the guys a lot of things at first. Instead, I sat quietly, repeating the word *Calvinist* in my mind until I was sure I would remember it long enough to look it up in our encyclopedias when I got home. This was often how I spoke with my new friends—inside my own head. Notwithstanding that the majority of my conversations had historically happened that way, usually while I walked the streets alone and pondered the meaning of life, I was now being exposed to new ways of thinking—to words like "Calvinist" and "rhetoric," to kids who tossed words like "constituents" into casual conversation—and I needed time to process it. These kids had parents who discussed politics, who pondered philosophy, who read magazines like the *New Yorker*. They had basements with game rooms, and they didn't have to chain their trashcans down to keep them from being stolen. Most of all, my new friends had a lightness of being that was somewhat foreign to me.

In the early days of our friendship, I spent a lot of my time with the guys, quietly observing. And they watched me too. Though I was the only varsity-caliber athlete in our group, my new friends came to my football games and cheered for me and the team. By then I was six feet, three inches tall and weighed 240 pounds. One of the guys on the team—a somewhat oafish but naturally gifted tackle who'd taped a picture of a bikini-clad blonde to his locker— once asked me why I hung out with those "nerds." He wasn't mean about it—just curious. "Because I think they're going somewhere in life," I told him. And that's what I wanted for myself, even if I still didn't know where "somewhere" was.

There was more, of course, that I didn't say—that my new friends made me laugh; they made me think; they cared about things. And once, when a well-off sophomore pointed at me and announced to everyone within earshot that I was wearing his father's unmistakable twenty-year-old green glen plaid jacket, which I'd bought for two bucks at a St. Francis rummage sale, the guys stood up for me by pointing out that it gave me character and that I had better things to spend my money on anyway.

It didn't matter that I came from a neighborhood where one could purchase drugs or sex on a street corner or that my father was a foul-mouthed alcoholic. It didn't matter that I presided over my food like a vulture or that I was the only one of the five of us who had to work in the school office to cover my tuition. These guys accepted me as I was, with my watchful eye, my second-hand clothes, my radishes.

❖　❖　❖

"It smells like something died in here," whispered Trey, pinching his nostrils closed.

"It smells like a *lot* of things died in here," whispered Tyrone.

We had just broken into an abandoned travel trailer two blocks from Frankie's house because curiosity finally got the better of us, and because Tyrone reasoned that nobody had been showing it any love anyway, and because we were bored. We'd walked past the dilapidated camper dozens of times on our rounds through the neighborhood and had stopped more than once to marvel at it. Standing knee-deep in weeds on the edge of a yard littered with yesterday's joys—a rusty bike, a deflated basketball, a bent and peeling lawn flamingo, and various unidentifiable objects peeking through the greenery—the camper boasted the name *Shasta* in windblown script across the front, and we wondered aloud what was behind its broken windows and mold-speckled aluminum. A kitchen? A bathroom? A family of racoons? We told stories aloud about the Shasta, detailing our future lives in it—one day we'd fix it up and move in. We'd live in secret, sleeping by day and emerging with the owls and cats and coyotes at night. One day, when we were old enough to drive, we'd hitch it onto a car of our own and venture off to vacation destinations we'd heard about—the Grand Canyon, Old Faithful, the Everglades. The "Everglaaaades" we'd say, making it more real with each incantation.

I'd never been to Tyrone's house—meeting up at Frankie's had always been our default, and Tyrone never mentioned his family—so I could only guess at what he meant when, during one of our street-side reveries, he quietly, almost dreamily, said, "It could be a *real* home." He stepped back then, almost as if he'd surprised himself by accidentally speaking his inner thoughts out loud, and quickly added "Mothafuckers!" so that we'd all laugh.

It was dusk when we opened the camper's bent door and climbed inside, sending scores of mice scurrying into the shadows. Even in the faint light, I could see how this had once been an actual miniature home. "Look, guys," I whisper-yelled, "it's got a real stove and everything!" The setting sun struck one last rosy chord that poured into the camper's little windows—casting a fog of warm light over the stained seat cushions, the bumpy layer of animal feces crusted onto every surface, the holes gnawed into the wooden drawers, the broken glass and rodent bones scattered upon the floor—before going out like a candle. As we rifled in the near dark through the camper's drawers and cabinets and announced our finds—a plastic spoon, a deck of cards, an ice cube tray—I couldn't help but wonder what my new friends would say about what we were doing. "You guys," I whispered, "do you think we're in this camper because our lives have already been decided for us? You know, because of *predestination*?"

"Predesti-*who*?" said Frankie, crunching over a pile of broken glass.

"Predestination-lookin' mothafuckah," Tyrone blurted out to no one in particular.

We kept even our laughs to a whisper—Frankie, Trey, and I were as reliable an audience as Tyrone was a jester—but in that same moment, as our camper dreams sank into the grime and disrepair of reality, I knew I would be spending less time with The Halfs and more time with my new friends. I felt a little guilty about feeling myself drift and for not being able to tell them about it, but I couldn't help it—a greater force was pulling me away.

The last time we jumped onto a freight train was also the last time I hung out with The Halfs. We'd done it enough times by then that the fear of slipping under the wheels had waned, but the thrill of the brazen leap was as alive as ever. The November air that day was bright, laced with smoke from a burning brush pile and the promise of winter. High, puffy clouds meandered in slow motion across a vivid blue sky, while the world below was patched in shades of russet, pumpkin, gold—and the occasional vermillion-colored splashes of leaves still holding on as we were holding on. As we sailed along the tracks into the wind, I noticed that the sliding doors on my boxcar were open a few feet. I leaned back on my ladder, extending my arms fully, and looked inside. A man was sitting on the floor right next to the door with his back against the wall. He wore an oversized flannel shirt and a dirty baseball cap, and when he turned his head and our eyes met, I knew he was one of the homeless people I'd heard about—*hobos*, we called them, or *bums*—who took shelter in the box cars when they were empty on the backhaul. As I looked into his eyes, I saw his sadness, and I had the feeling that if I stared too long, he might break.

I quickly looked away, and the train carried us forward.

❖   ❖   ❖

"So you're basically a secretary now?" Dad was stationed at his corner of the sofa, peering up over another paperback. It seemed that every day his eyelids drooped a little more, an unfortunate progression in his laxity of skin that now gave his face the impression of melting. I'd been standing in the kitchen doorway, telling

Mom about my work in the school office—filing, stuffing envelopes, running the addressograph, the mimeograph, the letter-fold-
ing machine, and the envelope-sealing machine—when he'd felt the
need to weigh in. "Proud to be a secretary, are you?" he added.

I turned and looked at the thin brown slits of his eyes. I wanted
to look away, but I didn't let myself. "I'm proud to be able to pay
part of my tuition," I said, flexing my biceps a little, "which is more
than you can do."

Dad receded slowly back down behind his book like an eel
down into a water cave. "Cocksucker," he muttered half-heartedly.

I shuffled upstairs into the bedroom Ern and I shared and
lay on the bottom bunk, thinking that someone should make a
Halloween mask that looks like the back of an open book. Then I
stared up at the bottom of the top bunk and wondered about my
new friends' fathers. I could almost see them, animated against the
mattress above my head, calling their sons by names like "Son"
and "Champ" and "Buddy." They donned baseball mitts, aprons for
cooking burgers on the grill, and warm smiles. They laughed like
Santa Claus.

"I'll kill you, fucking motherfucker!" Someone was yelling outside, an ordinary occurrence but one that nonetheless wiped my
mind clean of fathers. I glanced down toward the door, next to
which four Virgin Marys stood on my side of the dresser, posi-
tioned randomly on a white doily Mom made when she was young.
For each year I'd sold the statues for St. Vincent's, they'd given me
one as a gift, and because we never threw anything out, my side
of the dresser seemed like as good a place as any to display them.
But I'd never really studied them until now—Mary in angelic pro-
file, white ceramic matronly Mary, slightly hippie-ish long-haired
Mary, etched glass serene Mary—as I climbed down from my bed

to get a closer look. With a new appreciation for her many moods, I settled on matronly Mary, the toughest looking of the bunch, and said a little prayer, pressing my palms together under my chin. "Dear Mother Mary, please help my dad be less of an asshole. Amen." I heard another sound from outside—this one a strange grunt—and I ran downstairs to the window. Out in the street, two guys were whaling on each other with two-by-fours.

This sometimes happened in our neighborhood, usually involving carloads of two-by-four-wielding guys from other neighborhoods. Sometimes they also had chains, nunchucks, or baseball bats. Occasionally, the police came and threw somebody in the paddy wagon, but most of the time, the intruders squealed off as they arrived, and whoever got the brunt of the beating just hobbled on home without fanfare. This fight outside my window, however, was different. They fought with a ferocity that seemed primal, even biblical, as they made each other bleed and knocked each other to the ground.

❖   ❖   ❖

Spring came and brought my fifteenth birthday, along with the "1974 Super Outbreak" of tornadoes, Hank Aaron's 715th homerun, the infamous photographs of Patty Hearst robbing a bank, and a paper on the Quran I was writing for my freshman history class. When Mr. Robinson—a teacher who doubled as the school's basketball coach—had given us the assignment to write about a famous book in history, I remembered the Dunbar poem Mr. Everett had coached me to recite and how special I felt knowing that I'd done something nobody else had. So instead of writing about the Bible or *To Kill a Mockingbird* like so many of my classmates, I spent two weekends in the Toledo Public Library learning about Islam, the religion Muhammad Ali believed in.

I don't know what I was expecting when I began my research, but it certainly wasn't discovering a religion that was, in many ways, a lot like Christianity. There were differences, of course, and I found them interesting enough to experiment with in my own life. When Mom asked me if I wanted a fried bologna sandwich when I came home from the downtown library where I'd been learning about Ramadan one Saturday, I told her that I was fasting to "share the hunger of those less fortunate," though I didn't mention I was thinking specifically of a man I'd briefly locked eyes with on a train. And when Ernie asked me why I was turned away from my bed instead of facing it during my bedtime prayers, I explained that I was facing Mecca, as if that were the most obvious answer in the world.

"Who knew the Quran had so many beautiful things in it?" Mr. Robinson said, placing my paper, on which he'd written a large red A+, on my desk. "I learned a lot of new things." And though my exploration of the Quran ended when I tucked my paper into my book bag, the question it left me with persisted: How can our religion be so sure that our book is the only true holy book, that our key is the only key to Heaven, that it was Moses and the disciples and not Mohammad—or even some other prophet—who received the true word of God?

One place I didn't wonder about these things as much was in the Catholic Club, a community center in downtown Toledo where I worked Saturdays that summer as a janitor. During the summer weeks, I worked as a janitor for St. Francis, I still had my paper route, and I still mowed lawns and said yes to any other odd job that was offered to me, but the Catholic Club job was my favorite because I snuck glances at one of the camp counselors there whenever I had the chance. Tall and willowy, Clara had the kind of blonde hair that looked sunlit even on cloudy days, but what I found most appealing about her was her confidence and the way the little kids gazed up at her with so much trust. I'd never spoken to her and had only come to know her name by overhearing it, but she was at the center of my thoughts that summer.

One weekend, I was asked to clean the building's coal chute by climbing into a ten-by-ten-foot wooden bin with a thin paper mask and a shovel, "to prevent explosions from the coal dust," I was told. This struck me as a very important job and one they wouldn't ask just any old janitor to do. *I'm basically a hero*, I thought, thrusting my shovel into the coal dust. *Nobody else I know has a job like this!* Once I'd removed the bulk of the coal dust, I swept out the rest with a broom and dustpan, and because I was the kind of janitor who reached behind toilets to clean the places no one could see, I spent half a day in a black cloud, sweeping up every speck of dust from every surface I could. When I emerged, I had so much coal on me that I could see it in my eyelashes when I blinked. I wore the dust with pride, as proof of my hard work.

By then, I knew that Clara took the kids into the gym on Saturday afternoons, so that was when I always tried to time the emptying of the gym trashcans. And that day, I was in luck. Clara was cheering the kids through a volleyball game when I whisked out a fresh trash bag from the depths of my pocket with the flare of a magician pulling a scarf from his sleeve. Usually she didn't notice me, but now, she and several of the kids turned and looked at me with wide eyes. I raised one still-blackened hand and waved, and for a moment, they seemed frozen in place. *They know I'm going somewhere,* I thought, emptying the trashcan closest to Clara. And then I spoke my first—and last—words to her: "I'm just emptying this trashcan." Clara nodded politely and smiled, and I went on, filling my cart with trash.

TWENTY

And then, on a seemingly ordinary day, I knew where "somewhere" was—or rather, *what* it was: the tallest building in the world. There it stood, some thirty feet tall—the height of the movie screen at the Showcase Cinema where I sat in between Barry and Joel, our hands plunging into popcorn—its sleek glass gleaming like a promise. We were watching *Towering Inferno*, but before it became an inferno, the building sparked something in me. I wondered about the people in the building, making important decisions in their suits and fancy offices, where brothers didn't beat each other with two-by-fours and fathers didn't bellow insults from behind a haze of smoke, where nothing was broken or dirty. I wondered how those people came to work in this neat and gleaming place, how they'd come to achieve success. *Success.* This word— this abstraction, this flagpole that waved in the darkness of my possible future—was a word I'd been thinking a lot about. *Success.* Just the sound of it was like a key opening a lock, and I repeated it in my mind until it became a kind of incantation—another kind of train that would carry me forward. And now I had a destination.

The summer before junior year, the guys and I had seen so many movies that we fancied ourselves expert moviegoers. We learned about the tortured life of Lenny Bruce; we traveled on the Orient Express; we watched Keith Carradine sing his hit song for the first time in *Nashville*. Gene, who was a year older than the rest of us, had gotten a car, which enabled us to spend as much of our free time together as possible. Soon after, Barry got a car, too, and both of them would drive miles to the projects to pick me up and drop me off. Instead of walking the streets as I'd always done before, now we drove, sometimes for hours, debating the finer points of a movie we'd just seen—such as whether "success is nothing without someone you love to share it with," as Billy Dee Williams said to Diana Ross—or belting out Styx's "Lady" with the windows down, generously serenading anyone within earshot.

We sang about girls, and we sang about love, but I don't think we ever considered spending a Saturday night anywhere else but in one another's company, thereby forgoing even the possibility of romantic pursuits—because we were all, in our brotherly way, a little bit in love. And most of us were also a little bit terrified of girls.

"The thing about girls is," Barry started, slathering on the Coppertone as he lay back on his towel, "they don't like guys like us." We were at Centennial Quarry, a defunct granite quarry fed by a natural spring that kept the water at a temperature cold enough to turn your lips blue and shrivel whatever confidence you may have had when you jumped in. We had just unfurled our towels onto the sun-parched patches of grass when we saw a beautiful girl in a lime green bikini plant a kiss on an older guy's neck. "His *neck!*" Barry had exclaimed in a whisper. We both suspected that a kiss that intimate could only mean one thing: they'd crossed the line into territory that was still completely foreign to us. "They don't like guys like us because we're too nice." Barry scratched the fuzz on his chin and looked at me. "But you're a football player, so maybe you stand a very small chance," he said, and we both laughed.

"I just don't understand," I said, eyeing the guy's muscled body and his trifecta of tattoos: an eagle, a dagger, and a leopard. How had I never added an eagle to my list of Animals I Want to See One Day, I wondered as I watched him flex his tanned biceps each time he drew his cigarette to his lips. "Why wouldn't they want someone who's going somewhere?" I looked down at my own biceps: no matter how much I went in the sun, my skin, at best, turned the color of bologna. "He's not going anywhere," I said, gloating a little. "Just look at him. You can tell he'll never be successful."

"Well," Barry shrugged. "I kind of think he already is."

He had a point. And though the tattooed guy's sexual success represented the very thing I'd vowed to avoid, that didn't stop Clara and every other pretty girl I knew from promenading through my mind at all hours of the day and night.

That summer, I often went to the weight room with a guy named Jack, another St. Francis student who also worked as a janitor. A closet-sized space tacked onto the St. Francis gym, it boasted a single piece of equipment—a universal weightlifting machine with several stations, one of which had gained cult-like status in our school: the bench press. There were just a few students who could bench the entire stack of weight, and they often strutted into the tiny room like celebrities. The small group already in the room would invariably whisper the same question: *Do you think he'll bench the stack?* Benching the stack wasn't always a given if the room wasn't full—at capacity, it could accommodate about seven people, maybe eight if we really squeezed in—and sometimes the known stack-benchers chose to tease us by putting the pin lower and lower with each lift but then ducking out before the denouement. Of course, this only made it more special when they did bench the stack, sometimes even twice or three times in a row—a feat we'd watch in awe before patting them on their sweaty backs, as if that momentary touch might confer some weightlifting magic upon the rest of us. That summer before my junior year, I tested the magic by descending upon that benching station after every janitorial shift. I lay on my back and closed my eyes as I gripped the handles and pushed a torrent of hope and ambition and desire up toward the cobwebby ceiling. And with each lift, the mostly abstract notion of *success* that I carried with me like a partially drawn map continued to sprout roads into the land of the specific: one day I would work in an imposing high-rise building filled with successful people doing important things, and one day I would bench the stack.

Though I was still nowhere close to accomplishing either goal, I did get some extra practice lifting weight when I found Jack with my locker open and his hand in the little bag of chocolate chips Mom had packed with my lunch. "Hey, man," he casually said when I caught him, as though we regularly helped ourselves to each other's food. Over the years, I'd had lots of things stolen, but this was different. It was like stealing directly from Mom. With both hands, I grabbed the front of his shirt and lifted him straight off the ground. "You ever steal from me again," I warned, slamming him back against the lockers and holding him there, his legs in the air, "and I'll be much tougher on you." He didn't say anything—he just looked at me with fear in his eyes, his breath sweet with chocolate.

I wasn't happy about my behavior. Aside from my childhood fights in the neighborhood, the only other person I'd ever put my hands on in a hostile way had been Dad, when he wouldn't let me out of the kitchen. And both then and now, I hated the feeling of seeing someone diminished by my actions, even if the other person was to blame. "Life isn't fair," I'd heard many times by then, but it didn't help. It didn't help when, later that summer, I watched from a distance as two kids rode off on my ten-speed Schwinn bike, which I had saved two hundred dollars to buy, or when, that fall, the middle guard on the opposing football team started spitting on my hands while I held the ball in place, knowing that I couldn't move until I hiked it (I was playing center now). And it didn't help when Ernie, who'd finally bought the shiny red Chevelle of his dreams with the money he'd saved working as a janitor for Mercy hospital, found his car sitting up on concrete blocks in the hospital parking lot, with all four of his mag wheels stolen. I don't know how many nights he dreamed aloud in the small space of our shared room—*cherry red*, he always called it, as if any other red were an entirely different color—but I do know that when I saw him come through the door that day, dejected, and lean on the counter like a wilting plant while he told Mom what happened, I was the one who started to cry. I retreated to our room and faced my Marys, but I didn't bother getting on my knees. Instead, I took aim at the bottom of the top bunk and launched a different kind of prayer at God. "We have it so hard already," I cried. "When someone like us finally gets something good, you take it away. Just like Taffy. Ernie worked so hard to get just this one thing, and you let it be ruined! Why would you do that?" Neither God nor a single Mary answered.

"You have to understand, Tom. God is mysterious."

I had just asked Father Gruden—an affable priest at St. Francis who had a tic that made him talk out of the right side of his mouth—why the church always says God is all-just when he allows injustices to happen all around us, and I'd cited Ernie's wheels as an example. "If God is so mysterious," I asked, "then how do you know for sure that he's all-just, or that he even exists at all? How do we know all these specific things about him on the one hand, yet the most simple and obvious questions have no answers?"

Father Gruden emitted a single knowing chuckle, as if my doubt was par for the Catholic course. "Everyone has questions, Tom. That's natural."

"So, you don't have an answer," I said, feeling both defiant and defeated.

This caused him to sit up tall. "Of course I have an answer. For one thing, you're assuming that justice must always happen on earth, but sometimes justice comes in Heaven."

The church had been good to me all those years. It had given me a stellar education and countless opportunities. It had given me hope. It had helped give my life a framework that I took comfort in. But suddenly, I needed that framework to make sense. "But what about people who endure so much injustice on earth that nothing could make up for it in Heaven? What happens to them?"

"Well, Heaven is for eternity, while our life on earth is but a speck in time. So, someone could have a wonderful eternity to make up for the short injustice they experienced on earth."

"What about a baby," I said, knowing I had to push the stakes if I was ever going to get an answer that made sense, "who is tortured and murdered? How could a caring and just God even allow that to happen in the first place? And are you saying that there are different levels in Heaven, depending on how much a person suffered on earth? Like one person gets a better Heaven than another to make it all even? I just want to understand."

Father Gruden sighed and gave me the look. By then, I'd received the look from enough priests to know: A) I'd exhausted Father Gruden's patience and B) the conversation was about to end. "The thing about faith, Tom, is that it's a gift from God," he said, keeping his hands flat on his desk as he stood. "Perhaps that's just not a gift you have yet."

I wanted to ask how it was all-just for God to give gifts only to some people and not to all, but instead I stepped out of his office and into the bright fall day. On the school bus home, I struggled with a knot of feelings I couldn't easily untangle. I didn't know whether I should be angry at God, at Father Gruden, or at myself for my lack of faith. I didn't know whether to gloat about my feeling that I'd outreasoned Father Gruden or succumb to the sadness of such a victory. As the city bus made its stops and people descended the stairs in moods from somber to silly, I mentally leafed through my reliable cast of heavenly characters—Jesus, Mary, my Guardian Angel, Grandma—but suddenly, I felt estranged from them, from God Himself, as if the once-open channels between us had dammed up, leaving me dry.

"You're being too serious about it all," said Father Fisher, a chummy, leprechaun-like priest who taught English and had taken our group of five friends under his wing. I'd just finished barraging him with my usual lineup of questions about God when he waved me away with his hand as if I were a fly. "You're one of the alive ones," he said, "the ones who are going to lap life up! So why are you wasting your energy trying to prove the unprovable instead of trusting that some things are just bigger than we are? Bigger than we can understand? Just have some fun, Tom!" Some might say Fisher, which is what the guys and I called him because he insisted on doing away with any semblance of priestly formality—a desire he emphasized by regularly supplying Barry, Joel, Gene, and Gary with six-packs of beer (while I stayed true to my promise to abstain)—went a little overboard in his overtures. For us, though, when it came to learning, in addition to his flourish in inspiring us to fall in love with the works of Sherwood Anderson and William Faulkner, he was the antidote to the staid aspects of our high school curriculum. He took us places—to the Toledo Opera and to Greek Town in Detroit for our first dinner of spanakopita, dolmades, and lamb— and those are the things I remember most about my high school education. "Personally," Fisher said, "I think God has a sense of humor. Why else did he make the Gloster Canary? Think about it," he said.

Though I had outgrown them in some ways, I still referred to our well-worn encyclopedias. I liked revisiting the places and artworks and bits of science that first captured my young mind, in part because time had brought a certain tenderness to those dog-eared pages. When I viewed them now, at sixteen, I found myself feeling a sense of nostalgia for the villages of Poland, India, and Morocco, as if I knew the women in the peasant skirts or the men bathing in a river, as if, in some ways, I was closer to them than I was to my own siblings. But when the volumes had no entry on the Gloster Canary, I turned to Mr. Barnette, a quick-moving, long-legged librarian whom I'd come to know at the downtown public library, for help. He spoke in a lofty manner that hinted at an English accent that gave him an air of erudition and formality. "Well, Thomas," he'd say in his deep voice, "let us have a look here, shall we?" and he'd always know just where to go, no matter which research project I was doing for school or which random questions I asked, such as the one about a comical bird with a bowl-cut crest, which, I soon saw, corroborated Fisher's notion of a God with a sense of humor.

Mr. Barnette was the only person I'd told about the new list I'd started: Steps to Success, which, despite its unoriginal title, had its own dedicated notebook, a navy blue, spiral-bound soon-to-be compendium of wisdom—a full and detailed roadmap to the glass tower of my dreams. "Given your interests, I know a book that might interest you," said Mr. Barnette, and he placed a copy of Eric Sevareid's *Not So Wild a Dream* in my hands.

In addition to going to the downtown public library on the weekends, I'd started going to the University of Toledo library, which was just down Bancroft Street from St. Francis, every day after football practice or lifting weights. I liked to do my homework there because it was quiet, it was spacious, and it kept me clear of Dad. I stayed until the last possible minute each night, doing as many extra math problems as I could before catching the last city bus and transferring downtown to the Stickney bus, which dropped me at the far end of Bronson Street. It would be nearly 11:00 by the time I got home, but without fail, Mom would be waiting up for me, ready to heat up leftovers or make me my favorite sandwich. Those rare moments with Mom—when many of the others were tucked away, when the pressures of life seemed to lift a little, and it was only the two of us, in the quiet, in the small talk, in the clinking of dishware—were when I felt closest to her.

It was Christmastime again on Bronson Street as I made my way home from where the Stickney bus had deposited me and passed by Mr. Chapman's animated front yard wonderland. On a street where, otherwise, there were only a few random strings of lights strewn over a window or a bush, Mr. Chapman's festive outdoor family continued to grow. A couple of new elves hammered in perpetuity on the same pieces of wood, while three new singing angels with mouths shaped into Os presided over the merrymaking. *Never stop adding elves and angels*, I thought. Then I stopped in the street and, in the light of Mr. Chapman's yard, quickly jotted it down in my Steps to Success notebook—a coded shorthand (in case someone stole my notebook) for me to remember to keep striving, to never allow complacency to wander into my life.

As I approached our house, one of the only houses on the street with its porch light still on, I noticed a large, dark lump in the snow on the side of our walk. When I got closer, I realized the lump was Dad. He was lying on his side, his face partially buried in the snow. I rushed over to him, fearing the worst, but as soon as I shook his arm and called out to him, he slurred. "Gettafuckoffa me."

"You'll freeze to death out here," I told him, sliding my arms under his limp body. "I can't believe you drove like this." I was surprised by how easy he was to lift and how frail his body felt—not supple like a baby, but as fragile as one. And under a gray-black sky that was pearly with the promise of more snow, I carried my father inside.

TWENTY-ONE

"Perhaps home is not a place but simply an irrevocable condition," says David in Baldwin's *Giovanni's Room*. I had learned in French class that the French have no exact translation for the emotion with which Americans imbue the word *home*, but Saint-Exupéry's *The Little Prince* shows us how home becomes *home* because of love. While my teenage sense of love hovered somewhere between the song "Wildfire," the memory of holding a girl's hand at a roller-skating rink in seventh grade, and Mom's homemade soup noodles, which she rolled out and cut with scissors, my relationship to home was shapeshifting. For one thing, I was almost never there. I continued to stay at the library until the last bus during the week, and when I wasn't working on the weekends, I was out with the guys—with the exception of Sunday evenings, when Uncle Dick and Harold came over and we piled in around our two uneven tables as if nothing had changed or would change, as if those dinners would go on forever in that small space on Bronson Street. Yet there was no denying that Uncle Dick moved a little more slowly now, and the hump on Uncle Harold's back had grown even more pronounced. We were all changing. I had a super new hairstyle, which I produced by placing a stocking cap over my long, wet hair and letting the ends curl up around it. I had also started reading *TIME* magazine from cover to cover, forcing myself to read every article—including those I had no interest in at first glance—because it seemed important to know the things some of the greatest minds had determined were worth knowing each week.

Susie had become so popular at her high school, Central Catholic (all but one of the seven siblings behind me would end up going to private Catholic high schools), that she was often inviting friends to our house—something I think the rest of us were too embarrassed to do—and had become so driven (a quality for which I had a soft spot) that when she bought my enormous paper route, she enlarged the territory even more. Ern let his curly hair grow into an afro the size of an extra head, and he took me to my first concert, Black Sabbath, at the Toledo Sports Arena. Marji started enjoying the attention she was getting from some of the more questionable guys in our neighborhood, in part, I think, because they gave her compliments—a commodity that didn't come easily in our house. Mary Jo and Beth were beginning to discover the joys of dance clubs; Jane and Judy started wearing their hair so differently that sometimes people didn't realize they were twins at first; and Rich, one year behind the twins, had a new favorite word: no. Exasperated by his stubbornness, Mom sometimes exclaimed, "I could wring your little neck!" while he stared back at her with his arms folded across his chest. Mom was changing, too, but in the way I'd grown up accustomed to seeing her change—her belly was now growing with her thirteenth child, a full six years after Barb.

Though it's true that change is often difficult to gauge when it's happening and that we tend to appreciate its profundity from the distance of time, there was one change that came suddenly and without warning to our little house on Bronson Street: Dad's surgery. In recent months, the drooping skin of his eyelids had become so lax that it had begun to interfere with his ability to see, so the VA hospital in Ann Arbor, Michigan, performed plastic surgery on him. When he came home, Barb, who was six at the time, took one look at his swollen face—deformed by two zigzag-stitched wounds that sprawled like a second set of eyebrows over the first, plus four more incisions along his upper and lower eyelids that gave the appearance of spectacles made of scabby millipedes—and she hid her face in her hands. "He's a monster!" she cried, peeking out from between her fingers. "He's scaring me!" Dad sat down in his usual corner as if we weren't even there. "I think they let the young residents practice on his face," Mom whispered, shaking her head.

The severity of his incisions called to my mind the horrific murder of his brother, and I wondered if Dad thought about him too. When I asked Dad if he needed anything, he told me to scram, and that familiar command gave me a strange sense of comfort, this one thing that hadn't changed.

As I read *The Little Prince*, a recommendation from Mr. Barnette at the library, I could see how it was possible to change from a child filled with wonder to an adult who mistakes a drawing of a boa constrictor, which had swallowed an elephant, for a hat. *Never mistake a snake digesting an elephant for a hat*, I wrote in my Steps to Success notebook, gloating at my cleverness, as if no one else in the world could decode my metaphor for the loss of wonder as we age. But despite all that was changing within me and around me, I could feel my natural reservoir of wonder expanding, not diminishing. I could feel, with each new experience, the eidolons of countless future experiences waiting for me, like the stars in the distances of the little prince's universe, laughing. There was wonder to be had even in the word for *star*, which I learned in French class and repeated in my mind like surf: *l'étoile*.

Wonder. *Merveille*. I felt wonder at my new job, managing the St. Francis gym on the weekends during the fall and winter when grade-school teams were dropped off to play basketball. For the task, I was outfitted with a giant ring of keys, which unlocked every door in the high school building and produced a bulge inside my front pocket that made me feel important. "Basically," I explained to Mom over a bowl of Count Chocula cereal, "I make it all happen. Without me, those little kids would be standing out in the cold without any basketballs." "That's nice, Tom," she said. "It's good to be reliable." *Always be reliable*, I wrote in my Steps to Success notebook. And each Saturday morning, as I reliably arrived at St. Francis at 7:00 a.m. on my new bike and unlocked the gym door and flipped on the lights, the familiar odor of sweat and paint and varnish elicited in me a prescient nostalgia, as if I could already feel the experience becoming a memory: the particular wonder of those early-morning moments of arrival when I was alone and the grass was sugared with frost; the cavernous space of the gym before the kids arrived; the experience of sawing and painting our school's mascot with Uncle Dick—a wooden knight mid-gallop on the gym wall.

I felt wonder at my other new job: mowing the parks of Toledo during the summer. As I chugged my way through the Toledo streets to the parks on a giant tractor, I waved to random people in their neighborhoods as if I were in a parade and they'd been waiting all day for me to release exhaust clouds in front of their houses. But the real show happened when I rolled onto the park's grass, shirt off, my hours of practice "benching the stack" on display as I nonchalantly flexed my pecs with each press and pull of the levers that unfolded the machine's six bladed legs. "It's an alien!" the little kids would yell, pointing. "It's a giant insect! It's going to eat me!"

And I'd smile and give the motor a little rev. Then I'd throw the tractor into first gear and mow those parks to perfection, making sure to keep my lines straight, to circle the trees without hitting them, and to avoid clipping any rocks.

I felt wonder as I traveled around Toledo in a sausage truck, donated by a meat market to Carty Finkbeiner, a local politician running for Congress. I'd met Carty when he'd come to St. Francis to speak about helping the poor—a key tenet of his campaign—and I'd raised my hand when he asked for volunteers. Unlike Saint-Exupéry's geographer who never goes anywhere, I knew that I would spend my life going everywhere I could—and in this case, it was to the front yards of hundreds of houses, where homeowners gave me permission to tap Carty's signs into the grass. Competitive as I was, I made a game of it—Who Can Place the Most Signs—and I usually won. "Well done, Tom," he'd say, flashing his infectious if slightly-too-ingratiating smile, "well done." He had a habit of repeating your name multiple times in any given conversation, which I noticed some people liked and some people didn't. "So, Tom, tell me why you always have a copy of *TIME* magazine folded in your back pocket?"

"I have to finish each one before the next one comes out."

"I see. Is that a school assignment, Tom?"

"No."

"You're just reading that on your own, in your spare time?"

"Yes," I nodded. "Right now, I'm in the middle of an article on the role of SWAPO in Southwest Africa," I said with a flush of pride in my voice. What I didn't tell him was that I was sick of reading articles about SWAPO but was incapable of breaking my self-imposed rule to read each issue from cover to cover, which meant reading every word of every article about Southwest Africa because, damn it, *TIME* had determined it was important.

"You're really going places, Tom," he said, which made me feel like he understood something fundamental about who I was. This was especially meaningful because Carty was the most successful person I'd ever known, and he, too, appeared to be brimming with wonder. "Oh, Tom," he'd exclaim when "Misty Blue" came on the radio, "here it is! My favorite song!" Then he'd sing as if he could never run out of energy or joy. *"Just the mention of your name turns the flicker to a flame...."*

Wonder, it seemed, was everywhere. When Carty's campaign manager tossed me the keys to his shiny blue Cordoba—a car I knew Ernie would appreciate—and sent me on an errand to pick up food for everyone at the McDonald's he owned, I could feel myself not walking as much as floating to his car. The truth was that I had more experience driving a tractor than a car, yet someone was trusting me with something costly, something important, and each time this happened—whether operating a floor buffer or an alien-mower, whether I held the keys to a school or to a car—it never failed to astound me. It was a trust that shimmered with potential and filled me with a humbling sense of awe and gratitude, because in many ways I felt branded by the projects, as if my place of origin were a birthmark anyone could see. Every time someone trusted me with something, I thought it was in *spite* of who I was, and not necessarily *because* of it. And now, as I drove down the road, windows down, music loud, as I leaned into the center of the car's front seat in that curious way I'd seen the guys in my neighborhood drive and that I assumed would convey to anyone bothering to notice that I was one cool cat, I couldn't believe how lucky I was. *This must be what it feels like to be rich,* I thought, as I loaded up that Cordoba with free bags of McDonald's.

Though Carty didn't end up winning, he would later go on to become a three-term mayor of Toledo. He would also become a mentor to me and the lead force behind most of my summer jobs in the years to come.

When I learned that Jimmy Carter was coming to speak at Woodward High, a public school that was only a short walk from Bronson Street, I couldn't help but wonder if he might need extra help from an expert placer of campaign lawn signs. Though my own presidential aspirations had waned since I was young, I was intrigued by Carter's running-the-plow-to-running-for-president trajectory; I was won over by his promises of honesty and his seemingly genuine goodness. He was an outsider, a bright hopeful entering the toxic stew of Washington on the heels of Watergate like a spring breeze no one saw coming, and he was coming to our neighborhood. I'd been reading about him in *TIME*, and though I wasn't as outspoken about politics as the rest of the guys, I mentioned an article I'd just read, "Jimmy Carter: Not Just Peanuts," while we were on our way to see, coincidentally, *All the President's Men.* "I like the way he says, 'If you don't want the government simplified, then don't vote for me.' It's like saying, 'If you don't like babies, then don't vote for me.'"

"But the details matter," said Gene. "If he just simplifies by putting agencies together the way he did in Georgia, then he's not doing anything to reduce costs and bureaucracy."

I was impressed that Gene knew what Carter had allegedly done in Georgia. "What I find interesting," I said, "is that so many people in his own party are against him. Some think he's not liberal enough. Others think he's an outsider, so they can't control him."

"People in politics are all about control," said Barry. "They don't always think about what's best for the country or even for their party. They think about what's best for them, even if it means taking down one of their own." I vowed to always vote for the person who I thought was best for the country and not best for me.

This was a new realization for me—that even those on your team can secretly wish for your failure. Had that ever happened to me on the football field? Had my schoolmates wanted to sabotage me? How naïve was I?

The stadium was packed, many of the seats filled with Black families who looked out at this Southern man—this easy-to-smile Southern Baptist who often started sentences with "When I'm president..." instead of *if*—with something alive in their eyes, a spark of something I was sure I recognized: hope. He told us he would work to ensure that everyone would have access to quality education, that he would always be honest, that he would lift up the poor. "Yes!" we called out, clapping. "Yes!" And even after Jimmy Carter was whisked away, people stuck around, talking and laughing in the bleachers as if it were a party.

Back on Bronson Street, a SWAT team had arrived. We watched from our windows as they surrounded the Bryants' house, guns drawn, the police lights making the steeple of the church across the street flash like a strobe light. One of the brothers was led out in handcuffs. His mother followed, wheeled out in a body bag. We knew it was her because she'd been obese—so much so that in recent years she'd struggled to walk—and now the bag that held her bulged out over the gurney. "She was so nice," cried Marji.

"She always wanted me to come over and sit with her." I couldn't remember having met her, and it occurred to me then, in the midst of this sudden tragedy, how different my siblings' lives were from mine, how we were, despite our close quarters, in some ways unknown to each other.

Some people claimed that the weapon Mrs. Bryant's son used to kill her was a tire iron. Others said it was a hammer or a trailer hitch, which seemed far-fetched. Some people named one brother as the murderer; some people named another. I wondered what would become of Terry, the soft-spoken older brother who'd once given Mom a ride home from the grocery store. What would happen to the rest of the family? Did Mrs. Bryant's son feel regret for killing her? Satisfaction? Fear of a life in prison? How was it possible for this kind of violence to be spawned in the first place? Are some people born with it? Or does it build over time, a perfect storm?

After the 1974 Super Outbreak of tornadoes traveled through Ohio, I'd been fascinated by those mysterious funnels that spill out of the sky, those soulless forces that travel along the earth and destroy things in their paths, and though I feared them, I secretly longed to see one. In the library, I learned that, in the late 1800s, tornado warnings had been banned from weather forecasts in an attempt to prevent mass panic, and the ban continued for four decades despite improved methods of prediction. Though the plan was misguided, I understood it. I wasn't afraid of most things—a gift, perhaps, from the same God who'd allegedly neglected to give me the gift of faith—but as I tried to grasp what had happened two doors away, when I imagined how I would have felt had it been my own mother on that gurney instead of Ms. Bryant, a fear unlike any I'd known tore through me, more powerful, I imagined, than a tornado.

❖   ❖   ❖

When Timothy, Mom's thirteenth baby, stopped moving inside her, she knew he had died. The doctors advised her to carry him to term anyway, so she went on with her days, rolling out crust for her apple pies, hanging the laundry on the line, tending to the countless needs of others, all while carrying the stillness of death. Then she went to the clinic that her obstetrician—who had delivered all twelve of us—recommended when he informed her that the family clinic would "fit her finances better," and she delivered her dead baby into the hands of a stranger.

Before she gave birth to Timothy, she'd delivered the rest of us without any medications, but at this new clinic, they gave her drugs, and when they took him out of the room before she could lay eyes on him, she was too woozy to ask anyone to bring him back, just for a minute, to say goodbye. Her sister took the unbaptized baby, which we were told would go not to Heaven or Hell but to a place called Limbo, and held a funeral for him. Mom didn't go. She never even learned where he was buried.

TWENTY-TWO

Even as a teenager, I was aware of how quickly time passes. Senior year arrived with the suddenness that comes with opening your eyes from a dream: in a blink, you're here, and all the days that came before curl like dissipating smoke, conjurable but intangible, around the concrete details of the current moment, which is, itself, in the process of change. Occasionally, our first days on Bronson Street would come rushing back to me— the penetrating quality of light, for instance, when I roamed the field behind our house on our first day there, carrying the treasures I'd found along with a word uttered by my father: *paradise*. Almost twelve years had gone by, and though the field hadn't changed, the passage of time had turned my perception of it into a scrappy patch of weeds filled with trash. When you're growing, some things just inevitably seem to shrink.

"I'd like to apply to the Ivy League schools," I informed Father Fisher, as we pulled into Owen's Tech, a junior college outside Toledo known for showing arthouse films like the one we were about to see—*Metropolis*, the 1927 silent film that Father Fisher called a "cultural must-see" and that none of the others in our moviegoing gang felt inspired to must-see that night. By then, I was aware that unlike my friends, whose parents engaged in deep conversations about things like art, politics, and the nature of existence, I had a deficit when it came to the elusive notion of culture. Though my hard work and success in school and on the football field had nourished in me a robust sense of confidence, I lived with a sense of belatedness, as if I were always a step behind, always trying to catch up to the things my friends knew—which is why whenever Father Fisher invited me someplace, I went. Maybe it was because the priesthood had prevented him from having children of his own that he seemed to delight in our cultural expeditions as much as I did. That year, he was my AP English teacher and college advisor, and I caught myself holding my breath in anticipation over how he would respond to my Ivy League aspirations. I don't know what I was expecting him to say—maybe something along the lines of, *Splendid idea! I'll drive you there myself!*—but I certainly wasn't expecting him to laugh. "Oh-ho-ho, Tom," he said, sounding a little too much like Santa Claus, "that seems like quite a stretch."

"Why?" I asked, trying to shake off the sting.

Father Fisher parked the car and looked at me. By the light of the parking lot streetlamps, I could see his eyes warm with the realization. "You're serious, Tom. Okay. Yes, yes, okay, we'll consider it," he said, tapping the top of the steering wheel with his fingertips. "We'll see if we can figure out a plan."

How did he do it, I wondered? How had Fritz Lang made a film that still captivated audiences fifty years later? The question of how others achieved their successes had become a constant point of curiosity and fascination for me. What secrets did they know? Did they keep lists like I did? Did they make rules for themselves? How did they choose their paths to success? How did a relative unknown like Jimmy Carter come to be governor and then president of the most powerful nation in the world? How did the famous authors of the books I read get from the first page to the last? How did Sylvester Stallone, the ultimate embodiment of the rags-to-riches

dream and an outsider like Jimmy Carter, write a screenplay for
Rocky in three days and become a Hollywood sensation practically
overnight? "Do you think he even slept?" I asked Mark, a fellow
student at St. Francis who had started hanging out with us in
junior year.

"Do I think who even slept?" He and I had just seen *Rocky* in
the movie theater, and he was driving me home, both of us stoked
and uplifted by the movie. Mark was a thoughtful and soft-spoken guy who was a champion swimmer. He had chlorine-sizzled
blond hair, delicate features, a light blue Chevette, and a family
membership to the famed Inverness Country Club in Ottawa Hills.
But despite the gulf between our zip codes, he, like the other guys,
never flinched when he came to the projects to pick me up or when
he met my father, who barely grunted a smoke-encased greeting
from his eternal corner of the couch.

"Sylvester Stallone. I read that he wrote *Rocky* in three days.
Three days! I can't even write a paper for Father Koelzer in three
days!" Father Koelzer was our AP history teacher—a brilliant but
irascible lover of constitutional law who smoked cigarettes during
class and who could as easily drop ashes on an inattentive student as he could trumpet praise for another student when he gave
the right answer. "I read that he based the movie on a real-life
fight between Muhammad Ali and an unknown fighter just like
Rocky," I said, feeling my childhood heavyweight championship
fantasies springing up like jumping beans. "Three days! He couldn't
have slept."

"Did you know that sleep deprivation is a form of torture? I
just learned that."

"To be successful like that, I'd be willing to be tortured for
three days," I said.

"Yeah," said Mark, "me too."

"What do you think it is?" I asked, watching the shadows of my fingers appear like long sticks on the dashboard in the headlights of a passing truck. "Is there some special ingredient successful people have?"

Mark shrugged. He was much better than the other guys at keeping his eyes on the road. "Talent, I suppose."

"Talent," I said, wondering if I had any. I knew I was smart, and I was pretty good on the football field, but was that enough? "Or maybe some people just want it more, so they're more driven than other people. It could be that, too, right?"

"Sure," he said, and I hoped it was true.

"Calculus is so beautiful in the way that it works," said Father Finn, a fun but strict teacher who always reminded us to show all our steps in solving homework problems because, as he liked to say, "Finn...is finnicky!" And though I'd never expected to hear a teacher describe math as beautiful, I could see exactly what he meant, which is maybe why I loved calculus so much. I could see how his calling it beautiful elevated our appreciation of it—redesigned it even—and also our understanding of it, and maybe even elevated us, not only as students but as people. "As the interval of time becomes smaller, we eventually reach the point beyond infinitesimal intervals, or the point of continuous change!" He scratched his chin, leaving a yellow chalk smudge on his face. "It boggles the mind, really, to think how Isaac Newton was able to just think this up so long ago, and how it works so perfectly." He paused to let his eyes fall upon each of us up and down the rows of school desks as he smiled like a kid with a secret. "I think," he finally said, "it's because there is a bit of God in calculus."

I don't remember what he said after that, but I remember the feeling of God in that moment—not as almighty or all-just, not as a scorekeeper or punisher, but simply as beautiful. "Moderation in all things but the love of God," the priests often reminded us, and here, in Father Finn's eyes, was that love.

Father Gussenbauer, a new-age priest who bore a striking resemblance to Jesus, was walking us through Kübler-Ross's five stages of grief when he lit up at the fifth: acceptance. "In some ways, every day is a lesson in acceptance," he said, cupping his hands into the shape of a chalice, as if the actual hand of Jesus might reach down and place manna into them. "There are any number of small daily losses, any number of life facts that miss the mark of our desires— that bullseye of happiness we tend to strive for. But what if we removed the bullseye and widened our expectations? What if we welcomed everything—delight *and* disappointment—just the same? Pretty soon, our disappointments wouldn't be so disappointing, would they? They would just be the flip side of a happy coin."

I wondered about Mom's happy coin. If it had a flip side, she didn't show it. In many ways, she gave us the ultimate gift in never burdening us with all she was carrying—it would be many decades, for instance, before she would admit that she cried herself to sleep more nights than not. But my seventeen-year-old, solipsistic self took her gift without fully understanding what it was. And if her gift were also a coin with a flip side, then one might argue that by shielding us from her reality, she was inadvertently implanting in us the notion that the role of mothers—or women even—is to sacrifice themselves for others. And the only way to do that while keeping a happy face is to be largely unknowable. Mom was a master at this, at being present without being present, and though

I loved her and wanted to know her, I also longed for her to know me. Yet, if someone had asked me to describe my mother in one word, it would have been *perfect*. Maybe we were more alike than I realized, both of us holding tightly to our lists—hers an interminable domestic to-do list; mine, an attempted roadmap to places far beyond the borders of Toledo.

"I don't know about that whole five stages of grief thing," I said to the guys at lunch. "I don't think my mom's gone through those stages since she lost the baby, though she seems distracted once in a while." Gene, Gary, Barry, and I were lording over our usual lunch table, hurrying to take our last bites so that we could play euchre. We'd started playing during junior year, and it had become something of an obsession, though only four of us could play at one time since the game required two sets of partners. Barry, who, like the rest of us, had become more confident over the years, no longer had to spit on his fries in order to usher them safely to the table, though he was still something of a spectacle, showering us and the table with food-specks as he talked. "Jesus, Hudgin, you need a food screen!" Gene liked to say as he held up his hands in front of his face. One thing Gene couldn't accuse me of anymore, however, was guarding my radishes as if they were a football. By then, I'd even gotten in on the daily food trade, exchanging the little bag of chocolate chips Mom packed in my lunch for some of Gary's fries.

Barry shrugged. "Maybe because she's had so many babies already."

"Maybe," I said, remembering how excited Gary was when his mother had recently gotten pregnant with his brother and how surprising it seemed to me to be excited about something that for me was so commonplace.

Despite Barry's reasoning, I couldn't shake my questions about Mom and what I perceived as her inadvertent failure of Kübler-Ross's grief stages, as if they were some sort of test, and on a night when Dad was out at the bar and I had Mom to myself for a few minutes, I followed her around the kitchen as she swept the floor. "Do you think you'll have any more babies?" I spoke quietly so that none of my siblings would hear.

Mom sucked in her breath as if I'd caught her by surprise, but she adjusted her glasses and responded in her usual unflappable way. "I don't know, Tom. It's up to God." She looked tired.

"Well, it's kind of up to you too. Isn't it?" I knew that the church forbade birth control, but I couldn't stop myself. "I mean, you could just tell Dad no."

Mom let the broom speak—steady *brush-brushes* over the checkerboard linoleum tiles.

"Or you could, you know, maybe leave him?" I shrugged, hoping that simple gesture might confer a casualness, a kind of take-it-or-leave-it backing off from what I'd said.

Mom stopped sweeping and looked me in the eyes. "And then what? Social Services would come take my kids away because I can't afford to take care of you on my own. I don't think that's what you want, Tom, is it?"

My throat burned with regret. "No."

"I didn't know it would be like this," she practically whispered. "When I married him, I didn't know. He was a good dancer. He was...." Her voice trailed off, and we left it there, until the broom swept it all away.

I was singing and holding a broom, standing in a place few football players ever dared to venture: the school cafeteria on audition day for the school musical. Because I was a big guy who could pass as a hulking farmhand, because my high school gang—by virtue of our years spent serenading the streets of Toledo to the thump and squeal of blaring car speakers—had instilled in me a haven of social confidence, and because I was in search of my own talent in the afterglow of Sylvester Stallone's success on the big screen, I was singing Jud's solo in my best, if somewhat shaky, tenor. In the two years prior, I'd sung in the chorus for the musicals, but this was my first time auditioning for a lead part. I'd never sung a solo in front of anyone, and I wasn't exactly sure what I should be doing with my hands, and when I remembered, I pressed them to my heart and furrowed my brow in my best attempt to convey the existential sadness of being "by myself in a lonely room." And when I looked out at the panel of four judges who were smiling as if they were pleased with my singing, I already felt like a star, so much so that I bowed at the end, which apparently wasn't customary for auditions, though it made our director, Mr. Stucker, laugh anyway. "Seeman, that was quite a rendition!" he said. "You seem like you might make a good Jud. We'll let you know."

True to his word, Father Fisher wasted no time in helping me with my Ivy League dreams. He coached me through several iterations of my college application essay, helping me spiff up my writing style and encouraging me to write openly about my background. He wrote a gleaming recommendation letter that sung of my hard work, A grades, prowess on the football field, and theatrical acumen, which he said showed "immense diversity." And he inspired my football coaches to reach out to the collegiate coaches, which is how I got invited to visit several Ivy League schools, including Dartmouth during its Winter Carnival.

Who can say what a dream is, besides a story you wake up from? Is it a future self? A shimmer of the past? A wish? A mirage? A place you've never been? A list you keep, like a mythic tree upon which you drape your iridescent visions? Is it those evanescent periods of change, like dawn or dusk, like any threshold you cross and, in the crossing, become new again? I think it's all of those things. And for me, Dartmouth was a dream: my first flight, the jet rumbling its power down the runway before lifting off; the road to the campus winding through the rocky faces of towering cliffs in central Vermont, so unlike the landscape in northern Ohio; a new experience of cold, underdressed in my thin varsity jacket, the world around me a frosty tale told in ice sculptures and ski slopes and rosy cheeks; the warmth of the dorm room where I would sleep on a couch in a room full of strangers who played Stevie Wonder's *Songs in the Key of Life* on full volume and beer pong in the basements of frat houses, everything smelling of beer, sweat, and shampoo; that moment at a party when I tried to talk to a girl but couldn't seem to assemble a series of words that added up to anything interesting or even fully coherent, the one year between our ages weighing in at more like ten; all the shapes and smiles and motion populating a world that was at once so foreign and so welcoming, a world that seemed to inhabit that metamorphic space of becoming—a place that whispered to the part of me that had come alive all those times I'd opened an encyclopedia and longed for distant lands, each one, like this one, a possible landmark in my future.

❖　❖　❖

"Today's the day," I said to Mark, still on my Dartmouth high as we entered the familiar warm mustiness of our school's tiny weight room. "I'm gonna bench the stack." Though the rest of the guys regularly attended the St. Francis football games, they never ventured into the weight room, so I appreciated the company.

Mark lit up. "Oh yeah? Oh yeah!" He gave the sides of my arms two good slaps, which made the three other guys populating the universal machine take notice.

"He's gonna do it," I heard one guy whisper to another as he scooted off the bench.

"Let's do this!" I said, flexing, putting on my terrycloth sweatband and growling a little.

Mark smiled, and one of the other guys grunted, our animal natures pumped up on teenage testosterone and, I can only assume, shared images of Rocky Balboa.

I put the pin at the very bottom of the stack of weights. Everyone looked on, the room dead quiet. As I lay back on the bench and gripped the bar, I could already feel the glory awaiting me, the clapping, the hooting, the kinglike status that only a few boys in the school enjoyed. Maybe Betty Caspar, one of the cheerleaders that came from one of the three local Catholic girls' schools, would make the many conversations I'd been having with her in my mind a reality once she heard the news that Tom Seeman benched the stack. I would be practically famous. But as I tightened my grip and pushed against the weight, the weight pushed back and won. I had only lifted it halfway before dropping it back on the rubber bumpers at the bottom of the stack. I considered trying again, but the moment was lost.

"Next time," said Mark, giving my arm a pat. "That was really close."

"Yeah," said one of the other guys, "next time!"

"That's okay," I said with an air of melodramatic defeat. "I'll live to fight another day."

One thing I enjoyed about rehearsals for the musical was getting to mingle with our female costars who, like the cheerleaders, came to St. Francis from the three nearby Catholic girls' schools. We all had a flush to our cheeks as we sang and promenaded around the stage, the hormone-soaked buzz and unusualness of proximity fueling our performances. I had won the role of Jud, the misunderstood farmhand in *Oklahoma!* And Gene, as expected, had been given the role of Jud's nemesis, Curly. My onstage love interest, Laurie, played by an excellent singer named Mary Ann, was captivating—her long white-blonde hair, clear porcelain skin, and cherry lips gave her the appearance of a real-life Disney princess—but my heart belonged to Betty Caspar, whom I had never officially "met," which is why, on a Saturday morning, I was crouched down in the hallway closet of our house, pinned between a tangle of bicycles, balancing the White Pages on my knees and holding a flashlight in one hand and the telephone on its long cord in the other. I didn't want anyone to hear my first call to a girl—a call I'd been rehearsing in my mind for months and which usually went something like, *Hi Betty, it's Tom Seeman from the St. Francis football team.... Yes, the one who totally took out the middle linebacker.... Yes, the one with the steely blue eyes. Anyway, I was wondering if you'd like to go to the prom with me?*

Betty wasn't the only one I'd been mentally conversing with; I'd also been having conversations with her father, a local doctor, inside the mansion I imagined they lived in. In my fantasy, he always put his arm around me in that chummy fatherly way father's do and said things like, *So, son*—he would always call me *son*—*I hear you've been visiting some Ivy League schools*. I would confirm, nodding in such a way that my chin stayed a little bit lifted the whole time, which is how I imagined rich people talked, and then I'd impress him with my knowledge about SWAPO.

There were two numbers in the phone book for the Caspar household, one for the main residence and a separate one labeled "Children's Phone." I chose that number, and while the phone rang, I felt my heart beating in my throat. I turned the flashlight off, and the darkness intensified my other senses, the thick odor of bicycle grease inside the closet filling my nose. When a girl's voice came on the other end of the line, I fell backward, which triggered a cymbal crash of toppling bikes. "Hi, hello," I said, "sorry about the noise."

"Hello?" the voice said.

I cleared my throat. "Yes, hi, this is Tom Seeman, from St. Francis. May I speak to Betty?"

The voice on the other end paused—a long, brutal pause. "Hold on, please," she finally said. There were several muffled sounds, followed by a whisper: "Who?"

"Tom *Seeman*," the voice whispered back. "From St. Francis."

"Tell him I'm not here!" whispered the second voice, the voice of my beloved.

The muffling gave way to the original voice. "She's not here. May I take a message?"

"Are you sure she's not there?" I asked with a hopeful lilt, hating myself for it.

"I'm sure."

"Okay, well, tell her Tom Seeman called."

I climbed out of the closet, pretending nothing had happened, and announced to no one, "The bikes are okay," feeling the flush in my cheeks as I returned the phone to the corner table near Dad and went back to my regular day.

In French class, I was falling more in love all the time, not only with the sound of the language but with the way the French structure their sentences. We had to memorize bits of dialogue, and for days, I walked around the house repeating two particular lines, while my family looked at me as if I were crazy.

In the book, there was a line drawing of two guys looking at a baby picture. "*Ce qu-il est laid, ce bebe,*" says the first guy. ("He is ugly, this baby.")

"*Eh, doucement, c'est moi!*" says the second. ("Hey, be careful, that's me!")

On the night of our third performance of *Oklahoma!*, my family, including Dad, sat in the audience, spanning an entire row. By then, I'd given up on Betty Caspar, and in our brief encounters on the football field, she never let on that she knew I'd called—she rarely even looked my way—though I suspected she knew who I was and, perhaps more importantly, where I lived. It wasn't a secret. It was my birthmark, part of the story that followed me wherever I went. "It's a strength, not a weakness," Father Fisher had told me, urging me to write about the projects and even my father in my college essay. "When people know where you came from and see where you are now, they'll know what you're made of." He told me to never forget where I came from, and I promised I wouldn't. I even added his advice to my Steps to Success list. And as I peeked out at the audience and saw my family, I realized that where you come from is less about the place and more about the people who inhabit it. Though I'd grown up with a natural distance between me and the rest of my family, seeing them there—Mom reading the program while my siblings fidgeted in their seats, chatting with each other, fussing with their hair, looking intently around the room, and even Dad, sitting at the end of the row, outside of his element, looking a little lost, as if he'd been walking along minding his business and someone had suddenly attached a giant family to him—was the feeling of *home*.

As I strut my hour upon the stage, to borrow from Shakespeare's *Macbeth*, which we'd been reading that year, I could feel poor Jud's plight as Gene delivered Curly's first lines of "Pore Jud Is Daid" in an attempt to convince me, poor Jud, to hang myself. Angered, I pulled a huge Noble knife from a leather sheath on my belt, and the audience gasped as I wielded it in the air.

Instead of adhering too closely to the original script, Mr. Stucker had decided to adapt it and thought it would be a good idea to give the audience a glimpse of the knife that would later be the cause of poor Jud's demise. "Foreshadowing! We're building the drama here, people!" he told us as we practiced our blocking in rehearsals. "Like Chekhov said, 'If you hang a pistol on the wall in the first act, someone better fire it in the second.'" But instead of putting a pistol on the wall, I was about to plunge my knife into it—or, more specifically, into one of the set's wooden beams—which I'd done without a hitch the two nights prior. Everyone had agreed that a real knife, and not the retractable blade I would fall on later, would only add to that drama, and they were right, because as I stabbed the wall, my hand slipped forward onto the blade.

"No matter what," Mr. Stucker had warned us, "don't break character," so, despite the shock and the blood that dripped from my hand onto the floor, I didn't miss a step or word. Instead, I delivered a Stallone-rivaling performance right up to my final harmony with Gene's baritone: "Pore Jud, Pore Jud!" When the applause quieted, I pulled a handkerchief from my pocket with my good hand and loudly blew my nose as I cried about my own imagined death, and the audience erupted into laughter, none the wiser.

Backstage between scenes, a flurry of girls tended to me. "You're so brave!" they cooed, bandaging my hand. "It's amazing how you stayed in character!" In the imaginary theater version of this scene, I would have leapt with my freshly swaddled hand and executed a series of tap-dance moves while singing heroically, but in reality's version I was motionless, smiling in an intoxicating haze of softness, beauty, and perfume—mute.

In the middle of April, I received three thick envelopes in the mail: one from Dartmouth, one from Brown, and one from Yale, all congratulating me on being accepted to their schools for the class of 1981. I carried this information around with me for days without telling anyone, secretly beaming as I processed what was happening. Someone—I don't remember who now—had given me a book back then, titled *Scaling the Ivy Wall*, and as I walked through the neighborhoods like old times, I realized that the wall I'd imagined so long ago, the one that threatened to keep me in the projects forever, was now in front of me, and I was going to scale it. I was going to step into the larger world, a world of extraordinary education, a world of mystery, of possibility, of wild animals, of wild places, of dreams. I would be joining my sister Mary Jo and my brother Ern as the first generation of our family to ever attend college. As I passed the houses I'd walked by thousands of times before, I remembered checking the box for St. Francis when I took my high school placement test, recalling that single mark as vividly as if I were still holding the pencil in my hand—that exact friction of lead against paper, a wish taking form before my eyes. What would have happened if I'd gone to a different school, I wondered? If I'd chosen different friends? If I hadn't kept my promises to myself? *Always keep the promises you make to yourself,* I wrote in my Steps to Success notebook that night, which, in itself, was another promise.

In a quiet moment with Mom, I told her. "Mom, I'm going to Yale next year."

In the midst of her spring window cleaning, she had taken all the screens out and was running a screwdriver along the tracks to get the dirt out. "Oh, that's great, Tom," she said, without stopping the screwdriver's path.

That night, I asked Dad to sign Yale's financial aid papers.

"I'm not signing anything," he said, folding his arms across his chest. It was his last grasp at control over me, and we both knew it.

"Do you realize what an incredible opportunity it is to go to Yale?" I asked, my voice cracking in the middle.

"Yale! Big shot here wants to go to Yale! Thinks his shit doesn't stink. Big lead in the musical, big football player, big—"

"Give me the papers," Mom interrupted, stepping in front of Dad. "And Harry, you go sit down."

I'd never heard Mom speak that way to Dad, and I think we were all surprised. Dad's head drooped forward a little, and, like a child who'd been sent to his room, he sulked off to his place on the coach, where I will always remember him as the strange fixture he was.

The next day, I got to school early and slipped into the weight room before anyone was there. I didn't growl. I didn't promise anything. I simply lay back on the bench-press, took a deep breath, and benched the stack. There would be time later for the public sweat, the flourish, the accolades, but for now, the satisfying sound of the full weight stack dropping back onto the rubber bumpers was enough.

"I don't get it," said Mark. "You don't even have your own tennis racket, and you're kicking my ass." It was prom day. He had loaned me a racket, and we were sitting in the grass between sets at Wilson Park, dripping sweat and guzzling cans of pop he'd brought.

"I'll tell you what I don't get," I said, holding up my drink as if I were about to make a toast. "Girls."

Mark half laughed, half sighed. "I think if either of us understood girls, we'd be going to prom tonight."

"Good point." There was no one at the tennis court that late spring day. The air was hot and still. A pair of robins hopped around plucking worms from the grass, which was speckled with dandelions and wild violets, then flew off to their nest and back again. "Did you know that male robins sing to the females and bring them food when they're courting?"

"Maybe that's what we've been doing wrong!" said Mark, thumping the ground with his hand. "No serenading!"

"And no breakfast in bed!"

We fell into an easy laughter, the kind that drifts off gently, like a memory of itself.

"You know," Mark said, dusting an ant off his white shorts. "I'd rather be here with you than at the prom."

"Yeah, me too," I said, realizing it was true.

TWENTY-THREE

We come full circle. We return again and again to our memories, which, like dreams, form an intricate and intangible architecture inseparable from the self: fluid, ever-changing. Once, on a sunny Saturday morning, two uncles took their nieces and nephews to a place called Pearson Park. Climbing rocks, reveling in the softness of pine duff underfoot, searching the forested distances for bears and bobcats, a boy was fearless with his wishes. His wishes made him hungry. They made him alive. They called to him, raw and exciting and tender. Inside his mind, his mother had built a chest to keep his wishes safe, though she thought all she was making were small details, like a vest for a stuffed bear. In the land of dreams, one thing becomes another. If magic is anything, it is that.

He arrives at a campground in Toronto. Not quite a boy anymore, he is still fearless with his wishes. He wishes for different things now, but he also wishes for the same things. He is fairly certain he has spotted the quick slip of a bobcat's tail among the pines. He breathes in the resinous sweetness of the conifers and remembers the place his uncles took him to, a different place but also the same, and he is moved by the same feelings of newness, wonder, and hope. The cushion of pine needles still delights, and as he walks upon it, he is walking with all his former selves. He is walking in a way no one else can ever walk because his experience is layered with his memories, his unmatched set of synapses and cells and stories. And though this precise combination of elements is unique, his condition is not. He wants to tell a story. In his mind, he is already telling his future children this story, about animals and pine trees, about wishes, because he wants to tell them that he believes in happy endings. Maybe he already knows that all stories with happy endings have love in them. If not, he will learn it. There will be time.

❖   ❖   ❖

We're crouched around a campfire. It is summer, and the guys and I have taken this four-and-a-half-hour drive to Toronto to celebrate our high school graduation. Paused in this transformative space between high school and college, between childhood and adulthood, we're laughing, poking marshmallows into the flames with sticks we collected. The Milky Way stretches in plumes across the sky like the frosty exhalation of a god. Once, I saw a meteor streak over our house on Bronson Street, a blazing flash that made the whole night light up. No one in my family remembers it, but for me, it still burns. Everywhere you look, there's an opportunity for enchantment. At eighteen, I've said yes to every opportunity, and on this night, as I look around the fire at my band of friends, I'm saying thank you.

We sleep in Gary's family's six-man tent, and this, too, feels like *home*. Someone speaks from inside a dream, or maybe it's a wolf. In the morning, the last embers of our fire meet the first moments of sunlight. We spend the day exploring Toronto, and that evening we come back to the tent and get dressed up in our jackets and ties. We go to a French restaurant, which is the fanciest place I've ever been, and we hold up menus written in thick, black calligraphy. We're growing up right then, in front of the other diners' eyes. The diners seem interested; they ask what the occasion is. Maybe they can tell by our still-boyish faces that we're on the cusp of something, of everything.

After dinner, we go to a bar because the legal drinking age in Toronto is eighteen. I drink 7 Up and remember the time Dad took me to a bar on our way home from my Saturday art class at the Toledo Museum of Art, on a day he remembered to pick me up. Mom didn't allow us to have soda pop, but as I climbed up onto the barstool, Dad ordered whiskey with a beer chaser and 7 Up with a cherry for me. At home, Dad had always been a stranger, and at the bar, he turned into a different person who was still a stranger. Gregarious, smiling, he talked to people with whom he had a shared history I knew nothing about. People liked him. "That's a good-looking boy you've got there, Harry," one man said in a gravelly voice. Dad nodded and clinked my glass with his. It was the only time I'd ever seen him look at me with pride.

The guys and I hold up our glasses and make a toast. "To college!" we say, and our glasses become windows, and bells.

TWENTY-FOUR

set down Grandma's old plaid suitcase, which Uncle Dick had
extracted from the recesses of their attic, along with my duffle bag
that had, years ago, fallen into a Michigan river during summer
camp, and I beheld the grounds of my new life. I had just passed
through the castle-like entrance of Phelps Gate and now stood on
Yale's Old Campus, home to the freshmen. The regal courtyard
was abuzz with activity, some students arriving wide-eyed and
effervescent, their parents carrying lamps and chairs and awkward
bundles, other students already settled in and flitting about the
grounds, playing Frisbee, tossing footballs, lying casually on the
lawns as if they'd been there all their lives. Music I'd never heard
before blasted into the courtyard from speakers in the windows
of dorm rooms: a song called "Scarlet Begonias" by the Grateful
Dead. Somehow these other students had arrived early enough to
set up their sound systems, and I marveled at the confidence it
took to DJ this public space. They say everything old is new again,
and as I stood surrounded by gargoyle-studded neo-gothic architecture and youth, I felt myself as part of a centuries-old lineage of
people pursuing "the kindling of a flame," as Socrates had once said
of education. Yale had arranged for my plane ticket and transpor-
tation to the campus, but once the taxi dropped me off and I stood
on my own, wondering which of those stone buildings was my
dorm, I felt strangely untethered from my family and friends—as if

a stork had just dropped me and my luggage from the sky into the middle of New Haven, Connecticut.

After asking someone for directions to Wright Hall, I arrived at my dorm room and was greeted by one of my roommates—a preppy and friendly sailor named John, who came from a wealthy Connecticut suburb—and his parents. "Oh, hello!" they all said, beaming and celebratory. John's mother stepped away from the common room's large bay window, which she was in the process of measuring with a bright orange measuring tape and came to shake my hand. "Are you okay, dear?" she asked, noticing the sweat dripping from multiple parts of me. "You seem a bit...toasty."

"I'm just wearing some extra clothes," I said, though I didn't specify that "extra" amounted to two pairs of shorts, a pair of sweatpants, and a pair of dress pants, all beneath a baggy pair of jeans. Nor did I tell her the reason for the layers: after I packed a thesaurus, a French dictionary, bed sheets, and towels, there was scant room left for clothing. I'd considered putting some of my clothes into grocery bags, but in the end, layering just seemed more efficient. Though I'd saved enough money from my jobs over the years to have easily afforded a new, larger suitcase, I hadn't even considered it. For me, Grandma's perfectly good, if slightly musty, suitcase worked just fine.

"I see," she said, bringing the tape measure to the love seat, which faced a sizable wood-paneled fireplace. "I'm going to have matching curtains and cushions made. Spruce this place up a bit."

As I saw it, our dorm room, which was really two bedrooms plus the common room, was already sprucier than I ever dreamed a dorm room could be. *I'm at Yale*, I kept thinking in a combination of jubilation and disbelief. *Yale*. Then I took off some layers of clothes.

The person I would sleep beneath in a bunkbed for the next year was a smiley Swede named Mats who was charmed by his own charm, while John and a humorous hockey goalie named Mark from Massachusetts would share the other bedroom. From the start, I think they were all a little amused by how out of my element I was. I was simply trying to figure out, for example, how the freshman dining hall—The Commons—worked. A grand room boasting towering brick walls adorned with ornate oak panels and enormous windows, eight elaborately gilded chandeliers, and a soaring vaulted ceiling latticed with carved timber trusses and crossbeams, the dining hall was equipped with a cafeteria-style line that featured a variety of fare including items I'd never encountered, such as moussaka, Chinese vegetables, and manicotti; an extravagant salad bar replete with several types of green and black olives, oversized loaves of bread with toothy knives for slicing, and artichoke hearts in an herb-specked brine; and an ice cream sundae bar stocked with every imaginable topping. "So, um," I said to John that evening, "do we just choose one thing?"

He gave me the kind of warm smile that could comfort a screaming infant. "You can have anything you like."

It wasn't computing. "You mean that huge salad bar *and* the hot food?" I asked, my voice hitting an unexpected high note. "Both?"

"Both."

Just this one simple thing—the freedom to have my radishes and moussaka too—readjusted my entire world view, and I found myself having to reconcile how Mom could be back home, figuring out how to stretch a cut of meat or going to the seconds store to buy damaged or expired goods at a discount, while I had more food available to me than I could ever eat. "I'll join you guys in a minute," I said. And as he walked away and I stood there, I imagined Mom in a different future. *Here*, I would say to her, filling her kitchen. *This is for you.*

The abundance at Yale, I would quickly learn, far exceeded its freshman dining hall and architecture. In addition to its rigorous academic programs, the university offered other educational opportunities as well: the Yale Repertory Theatre, for instance—a stone-trimmed, church-like building with bright red doors—featured plays starring professional and student actors; Woolsey Hall, an enormous, grandiose auditorium, hosted a variety of performers (I can still hear the gentle music of virtuoso classical guitarist Andrés Segovia with the wonder of hearing it for the first time) and presenters; and the Yale Film Society, which regularly showed old films the students curated according to theme in various classrooms scattered across the university. I went to every performance, presentation, and film I could, often studying at the library until the last possible minute before running to make it on time to the next new experience. Much of the time, I knew little or nothing beforehand about what I was going to see, and that made it more exciting.

Later, as I clomped to and fro upon the marble floors of Yale in my new navy-colored clogs (my roommates and I had each given twenty bucks to Mats so he could have wooden clogs like his shipped to us from Sweden, and we were the only guys on campus who wore them, as far as I could see), my mind swirled with all that was constantly rushing in. I contemplated the great minds we were studying in my philosophy class: How does the ancient Greeks' approach to living a life of fulfillment (*eudemonia*) pair with Sartre's tenets of existentialism? And the books we were reading in my French Literature class: At what point did Madame Bovary's reasonable desires turn into greed? And the performance of Moliere's 1660 play, *Sganarelle*: Is silliness a necessary reprieve in a happy life? And snippets from a talk by CIA director Stansfield Turner: "You have to think about how things will be not just in the short term but in the long run." And an impromptu breakfast alone with James Michener, who was visiting Yale to give a talk and happened to be sipping his coffee at the corner table in the dining hall one morning: "Writing a book will consume you, if you're doing it right." I thought about the protests on campus, particularly the anti-apartheid shantytown students built and would live in for months in an attempt to persuade Yale to divest itself of any companies that could benefit the regime in South Africa, and how different it was to see students engaged and taking action toward the same conflicts I'd been reading about in *TIME*.

Even my body was tasked with something new: rowing. Upon the urging of the freshman crew coach Mike Vespoli—who'd first spoken to me about the idea of rowing shortly after I arrived on campus and whose upbeat energy reminded me of my grade school football coach, Coach Gary—after the football season ended, I made the switch from football to rowing, a sport I'd never even seen before. I spent an hour each day lifting weights with the crew team and another hour each day in the "tanks," stationary concrete boats in the bowels of Payne Whitney Gymnasium, learning the rhythm and the glide of the oars against the rushing water, my legs and arms and lungs burning in ways I didn't know were possible.

There was so much to take in and so much to do, so naturally I organized my life with lists—daily short-term to-do lists, long-term to-do lists, longer long-term aspirational to-do lists that included the main goals of my life, and lists of movies I wanted to see and books I wanted to read and places I wanted to visit, in addition to my ongoing Steps to Success and Animals I Want to See One Day lists. The ancient Greeks also had a penchant for lists, I was learning—such as the five regimes, the four virtues, the four stages of knowledge development, the three parts of the soul, and the three social classes, for example—so I felt I was in good company. But my roommates weren't convinced, and one morning they made me a list of their own, which they tacked to the bulletin board above my desk:

TOM'S DAILY TO-DO LIST
1. Open eyes.
2. Pull covers off.
3. Breathe.
4. Sit up.
5. Put feet on floor.
6. Stretch.
7. Stand up.

Weighing in at fifteen steps, the list went on to see me through my morning ablutions, and as my roommates gathered around while I read aloud their detailed instructions for walking, we all had a good laugh.

Though my roommates and I shared not only a bond of proximity and footwear but also one of genuine affection, I missed the guys back home. I missed everything back home, where I'd always felt, in the simplest of terms, big. I'd walked the streets as if they were mine; I'd loved a dog; I'd officiated a funeral for a tortured cat; I'd faced down my father and his gun; I'd grown food in my own garden; I'd aced my papers and my tests; I'd supplied newspapers to a sizable swath of North Toledo; I'd benched the stack. But now, in this place that was at once a manifestation of my (carefully managed) childhood aspirations and an unfamiliar world filled with etiquette and accoutrements that were foreign to me, I felt small.

Forget for a moment that I didn't know that the difference between my roommates' jeans, which faded in the wash to the mottled blues of the sky, and my pair of jeans, which miraculously stayed the same deep navy no matter how many times I washed them, was the difference between cotton and polyester. Forget that I knew nothing about the coveted secret societies at Yale, about which I'd heard vague murmurs, or what an investment banker was (the career of the father of a kid on my crew team) or what Sandy Lane or St. Bart's was, aside from that it was where other students were planning to go with their families "on holiday." Even when it came to academia, one area where I'd always excelled, my studies were now demanding in a way that reminded me regularly that I wasn't in Toledo anymore.

When Thanksgiving came, I received a box in the mail from Mom. I looked at her handwriting where she'd addressed the box and at the assortment of stamps clustered in the corner, and it made me a little sad to think she'd spent the money to mail it to me. Inside the box was a Folger House coffee tin swaddled in pages of the *Toledo Blade*, and inside the coffee tin was an assortment of my favorite homemade cookies—pfeffernuesse, pinwheels, snicker-doodles, apricot kolaches, nut roll slices, and mint and cinnamon hard candies she'd boiled from scratch on the stove. I was grateful to be alone because as soon as the sweet jammy scent combined with the residue of coffee struck my senses, I broke down and cried. I put the tin down on my desk, where I sat and buried my face in my hands. Then I did something I hadn't done in a while. I prayed.

Or really, I complained. "Why?" I besieged God in a tear-ridden falsetto. "Why is it so difficult? I work so hard, and I still don't even really know what existentialism is! Can you help me?" I took a breath. "I just want to go home," I whispered, unsure if I was saying that part to God or to myself.

I wasn't so sure about God by then, or at least the Catholic version of God. The Catholic church had left me with a lot of unanswered questions, and even if everything the church taught was true, did I want to believe in a God who sent unbaptized children to Hell (but not unbaptized infants, who somehow magically go to "Limbo")? Yet the urge to press my hands together and whine up at the sky was an act of pure faith—maybe God had given me that gift after all—and when I finished, when I wiped the last tear from my cheek and reached into the tin, covering my fingertips in powdered sugar, I felt as if I'd been heard.

TWENTY-FIVE

When Christmastime came, I got a ride home with a few football players who were traveling on I-80, just south of Toledo, on their way to Chicago. As I handed them my portion of the gas money and stepped out of the car, I could feel our little Bronson Street house pulling on me like a magnet. I could already envision the scene: my stepping through the front door to smiles and squeals of joy, maybe even applause. I would be like a celebrity, a Yale man coming home to the family who missed him terribly.

"Oh hi, Tom," Mom said, when I opened the door and took my heroic pause. She was standing by the Christmas tree—the same artificial tree that had seen us through every Christmas in my memory—palming a wad of silver tinsel icicles that draped over her hand. "I'm just finishing off the tree a bit." She held the tinsel out toward me, and as I put my bag down and took some from her hand, she called out, "Hey kids, Tom's home."

Dad was sitting in his place, eyeing me with a surprising degree of contempt, even for him, but saying nothing. Jane and Judy came running down the stairs and wrapped their arms around me. Though I'd been gone only a few months, at twelve they seemed to have aged years, their faces slimmer, their figures softened by nascent curves. "We got your letters!" they said in tandem.

"I know," I reminded them. "Thanks for writing back."

"What the hell kind of shoes are those?" Dad finally spoke.

I looked down at my feet. "They're clogs," I said, "from Sweden."

"They look like girls' shoes."

"They're popular at Yale," I lied.

He took a pull on a cigar, and a piece of tobacco stuck to his lip as he spoke. "He's not in the door for five minutes and already has to remind us he's a bigshot at Yale."

"Be quiet, Dad," said Susie, coming down the stairs. She gave me a one-armed hug. "Your shoes look great."

Soon the rest of the family flooded into the living room—with Barb, the youngest, now in second grade, there were no babies anymore—and we talked about everything and nothing, and no one asked me about my new life or my studies or even about how I came to own clogs from Sweden, and though it was a happy occasion, one I'd been looking forward to for months, what I felt instead was a discordant feeling of disappointment. This was the place I'd missed, the place I cried to God to come back to? This tiny, dingy cave of a house that reeked of cigar smoke, which, now that I'd been away, struck my senses with a vengeance? This living room that harbored a mean couch-dwelling sentinel who blew out insults like fire from a dragon's mouth? I had the strange urge to turn back around and chase down the car that had dropped me off, but then Ernie said it was good to have me home; Rich, who was now in sixth grade, flicked the lights on and off several times to show me how he was making a light show for his friends' rock band, and Dad groaned; Marji, who was three months pregnant with a neighborhood boy's baby, did a momentary Isadora Duncan-like dance; Joe, now in fourth grade, showed me a house with a crooked roof that he was making on an old Etch-a-Sketch; and I draped the tinsel I was holding onto some plastic branches, and the urge passed. I was learning the importance of being able to hold two seemingly conflicting ideas or feelings in one's mind at the same time, and as I stood among my siblings, whom I loved and from whom I'd also always felt somewhat separate from, and my parents—one who conjured heaven, the other hell—I saw how it was possible to love a place and hate it at the same time. It's in the space between, I was realizing, that life happens, and it's up to us to choose how we live it.

That night, I went for a run. Coach Vespoli had been clear: "Don't let the break take away all the hard work you've done to get in shape for the spring rowing season." It was already snowing—fat flakes that fell so slowly it seemed they might never land. No one was out, the neighborhood shut like an old suitcase, and time was doing that weird thing it does when it feels as though not even a minute has passed or will ever pass—the minutes suspended like the snow. What was different though, as I breezed through the neighborhood, was the freedom I felt in coming back from the other side of the wall. I had returned home not only to my family but to the boy I once was and, in some ways, still was and always would be.

I was so caught up in my thoughts that when I came upon Mr. Chapman's house, his front yard took me by surprise. I stopped and faced the lighted angels singing, the grazing deer wearing blankets of fresh snow, the elves in their eternal grind of present-making. Somehow, the scene looked smaller than I'd remembered it, and a nostalgic feeling buzzed through me, a warm ache. I'd recently learned that *nostalgia*, translated from the Greek, means literally, *homecoming pain*, and I wondered if maybe all joy is laced with a little bit of sadness because every arrival carries within it a departure. The words of Socrates chimed through my thoughts—*An unexamined life isn't worth living*—and that called to mind his teaching that wisdom can only be achieved when one becomes aware of one's own ignorance. And as I stood in the falling snow, pondering the meaning of life as I had done countless times before, I realized that though I still wrestled with my understanding of existentialism, I was learning something after all.

The snow began to fall more rapidly, with small gusts whisking shapes in the air—the wings of snowbirds, dancing ghosts, the flutter of a page—and I picked up my run. I looked back once at the glowing tableau, and then, for several streets, I let my mind go as blank as the color white, my footprints marking time in the snow.

❖ ❖ ❖

Back in my dorm room, I was writing Mark a letter. (While I was home, the guys and I renewed our tradition of listening to Styx while driving to the movie theater.) The football players I'd arranged my ride back to campus with had to return to Yale before winter break was over, and when we got back, the campus was still deserted. Though we had a phone in our room, I never used it for fear of the charges. Instead, I regularly sent letters to my friends and family—lackluster accounts of the minutiae of my days that somehow felt vital to share. Mark was my most regular pen pal and also the one I confided in the most:

> *I think I need a boost in the "social" area. I might take*
> *a girl or two out. I mean, we've been out with girls a lot,*
> *but I haven't specifically taken out a girl all alone yet.*
> *So maybe I will.*
>
> *Something that gets me down once in a while is the*
> *ergometer (a machine to test rowing strength). The*
> *guys on the team reached a consensus that the ergome-*

ter was the machine to be most terrified of. It is one of the worst feelings. It totally exhausts you. People have thrown up and fainted many a time. Some guys even lose concentration and stop right in the middle of a piece (crew jargon). They say that their mind talked them out of finishing.

The ergometer has a dial and a counter. They keep track of how well you do. And you must do well to have any chance at racing in the spring. In other words, kill yourself on the machine.

Yesterday I had another erg piece to do. The coach told me to go off the line at a pretty good speed but not to kill it right at the beginning. In other words, he was pacing me. Well, the method worked great. My score went up 150 points, and improvement possibilities are unlimited, for I now have confidence on the machine. This is the end of my cutesy (but true) little story.

When I finished my letter, I went outside. It was a clear night, the stars flickering so wildly I could almost hear them. I immediately spotted the Big Dipper and followed it to the end of the Little Dipper's handle, where Polaris, the North Star, pulsed, a fixed compass that for eons has led travelers to new lands and new lives.

Out of the corner of my eye, I saw the lithe movement of a cat trace the shadows. It might have had stripes. It might have been hunting. It might have been loosed from a story told long ago. But then, in a flash, it was gone.

TWENTY-SIX

I t's summer on Bronson Street, 1979, and I'm home until late August. My youngest brother Joe and I are playing doubles on the basketball court with a couple of guys I've never seen before. They both have arms like cranes, and they're fast on their feet. This is my first time on the court with Joe, and I'm surprised by how practiced he is, matching these older kids with apparent ease. But he looks concerned because I've just missed a skyhook and my guy got the rebound and threw it out front. I understand. Our neighborhood belongs to the younger kids now, and Joe wants to shine in it.

Though I'm out of practice, it feels good to move after spending another day on the banks of the Maumee River, shut inside the sweltering grain cars I clean for Nabisco at the trainyard next to the massive cylindrical grain elevators. Each day, I grow a gritty second skin of wheat or corn dust, then come home and contort myself under the bathtub faucet, trying to get it all off. It's a new job since last summer, when I started paying UAW dues and rode my bike in the dark to work nights in the foundry of a GM transmission factory, pulling hot metal pieces from a giant press that emitted fumes so noxious they made the guy next to me throw up. I'd come home each morning smelling of chemicals, my clothes covered in the milky white coolant that dripped from the steaming car parts, and after cleaning myself up, I'd lie in my childhood bed, trying unsuccessfully to sleep during the day in a crowded house that was loudly awake. I kept remembering the mindless drudgery of the factory workers from the film *Metropolis* and feeling grateful for Yale—grateful that I wouldn't have to stand for years in front of a loud machine belching gasses and liquids and heat.

Apparently, I have a penchant for dirty jobs, or maybe it's just that I'm one of a few willing to do them. I'm saving money for Paris, where I'm going in the fall as part of a Junior Year Abroad program. I plan to speak only French when I'm there, and I've already started a list of some of my favorite words: *pantoufle* (slipper), *mante religeuse* (praying mantis), *brindille* (twig), *libellule* (dragonfly), *coquelicot* (poppy), *tristesse* (sadness).

But for now, it's summer as it ever was. At night, the guys and I drive around with the windows down and sing more fervently than we did in high school: our current favorite is Supertramp's "The Logical Song." Some nights we go to Music Under the Stars and listen to the Toledo Symphony Orchestra at the Toledo Zoo amphitheater. We share the stars and the music with strangers in the balmy air stoked by fluttering zephyrs that remind us we're alive. We're becoming something, though we're still not sure what.

The basketball court on Bronson Street is cracked, the edges strewn with broken glass. There's no net left on the basket except for a single strand of chain hanging down from the rim. But there is no less thrill to the game. Joe's guy is dribbling toward the basket, and Joe is following step for step. I can still hear Donald Quinton when I'd first braved the court years earlier, overconfident in my cut-off jean shorts: *Let him play*. Today, his kindness is part of a history of kindnesses that trail behind me like the tail of a kite.

The guy with the ball attempts an inside pass to my guy, but it goes off his fingertips and out of bounds. It's our ball now, and Joe locks eyes with me, so I pass it to him at the top of the key. He dribbles hard down the lane toward the right side of the basket. The defender thinks he's driving for a layup and bodies him away from the basket. But Joe scoops the ball underhanded straight from his dribble and, with one hand, releases the ball upward toward the basket before the defender even realizes it's a shot. I've never seen a shot like this before, and because I don't think it's going in, I start positioning for the rebound. But then the ball just kisses the upper right-hand corner of the backboard and deflects straight through the rim. "What the hell kind of shot is that?" my defender says. "That shit shouldn't even count!" says Joe's defender. "Oh, but it does," Joe says, proud in his cutoff sweatpants-shorts. "That's my special shot. No one ever blocks it."

Later, as we walk home, I tussle Joe's hair in the manner of big brothers everywhere. I have not always been the most attentive older brother, but I'm trying. "That's a weird shot you've got," I say.

"Yeah," he says, "but it goes in."

TWENTY-SEVEN

If asked, I would have guessed that Parisians play basketball differently from Americans, judging from the other cultural differences I've been enjoying since I arrived in France—espressos at outdoor cafes with small round tables and wicker chairs; baguette sandwiches filled with chocolate; beds topped with fluffy duvets free of tucked-in top sheets that trap your legs while you sleep; little specialized shops for everything, with shop owners who greet you by singing their salutations (*"Bon-jour-eu!" "Mer-ci-eu!"*); cinemas all over the city, including tiny ones tucked away where I watch old French films and every Fred Astaire dance film ever made; and a gleaming metro that sprawls out into every corner. But here, on this court in *le gymnase*, the entertainment value of a moving ball defies cultural differences, and we speak the same language without saying a word. I've been trying to make Parisian friends, not only because the American friends I've made in the program sometimes get annoyed by my insistence on speaking French when they continue to speak English—*Pourquoi continuez-vous à parler en anglais quand nous sommes à Paris?*—but also because I've always wanted to learn how people live in other parts of the world, and this is my first opportunity. I find sports to be the easiest way to make friends, so I also row with a Parisian crew team on weekends.

When I first arrive in France, I live with a family in Tours, a town in the Loire Valley known for its classic French accent. The father is a high school English teacher who speaks English with a

British accent. The mother makes me crepes for breakfast, but she is understandably uneasy about strangers living in her house. After a month, I move to Paris, where I live in the 16th Arrondissement with two other students in an apartment building with wide marble stairs and a madame, *La Comtesse de Lasteyrie*, a passionate cook who takes us to her family's countryside chateau and serves us coq au vin in the courtyard. Some days I feel I'm living in a story—an illuminated text with paintings of trellises and teakettles bedecked with decadent flowers edged in gold leaf—and not in a real life.

I have a thick, pocket-sized booklet called the *Plan de Paris*, which is an exhaustive map of Paris, including a layout of the metro that looks as if someone created it with a Spirograph *moderne*. I love this book as much as I have loved any book because it is a key, and it never fails me as I tour the city in my clogs.

I often go to museums with my new friend James, an art history student, and I'm called back to my first days inside the Toledo Museum of Art, when I built a city inside a cigar box. James explains the painting method *en plein air* to me, and I think that must be the best way to paint—outside in the open air, in all nuances of light, with birds and storms and other wild things—*les choses sauvages*—rushing into view. When I tell him I like Renoir best, he wants to know why. I say it's because his paintings give me a particular kind of access to another time, and because I like going to his parties. "I like having a sense of what was important in people's lives then," I tell him. "Even what they wore feels important. Especially the hats," I add. *"Le chapeau important!"* he says, and we laugh in front of the soft colors.

In *Breathless*, a film we're studying in my French Cinema class, Patricia hangs a poster of Renoir's *The Portrait of Irène Cahen d'Anvers* on her bathroom wall, telling Michel in her English-accented

French that "Renoir's a really great painter." Later, Michel pulls her close and gazes into her eyes. It appears they're going to kiss, but instead he pulls back and tells her she looks like a Martian up close. I live countless lives from my safe side of the movie screen.

The Renoir painting Patricia hangs on her bathroom wall is a portrait of the daughter of a wealthy French Jewish banker. It was stolen by the Nazis and later resurfaced, one of France's treasures. I don't know yet that I will one day see the painting up close at a museum in Zurich. I don't know yet that I will one day marry a Jewish woman more enchanting to me than any painting.

We don't know yet, as my friends and I huddle around a radio and listen to updates on the Iran Hostage Crisis—each of us encapsulated in our own silent bubble of angst and helplessness as we learn that Operation Eagle Claw has failed—that the hostages will be freed. We don't know so many things, and that's what makes dancing at a party to Michael Jackson's *Off the Wall* so potent—we're not weighed down yet with knowledge. We're still new, even to ourselves.

It's a sunny day on the Seine, the cumulonimbus clouds billowing against an azure so saturated it could be a painting of the sky. There are few boats on the river, and the water feels smooth against my oar.

"Take it up two beats in two...one, two," the coxswain commands.

I'm the Stroke of our Eight, and I do as she says and pick up my pace. I'm breathing hard now, giving it my all as we row from Neuilly toward Paris. It's a casual row, so after a few minutes, she lets us take it back down, and for a time, the eight of us move as if we're all arms on a single body.

This is the feeling I've always loved best—the wind ruffling against me, as it is now against my back, a sensation so complete that it washes everything else away. As we glide through time along an ongoing story on the shores—the greenery of the Bois de Boulogne giving way to the straight lines of city architecture—we are a body of rhythm, of beating hearts, of breathing, of circadian clockwork that ferries us each night into dreams.

A few nights ago, some friends and I thought it would be fun to get our fortunes told. We entered a small room in the back of a shop filled with incense and tarot decks and let a woman in blood-red lipstick examine our palms. She said we could ask her three questions, but I asked her only one, in my best French: "*Am I on the right path for success?*" I held my breath, a little afraid of the answer. How would I change my life if she said no? With one ruby-painted fingernail, she traced a line on my hand. "*Mais oui,*" she said. I exhaled and relaxed into the answer I hadn't realized I'd long been needing to hear. She went on to predict other things, much of which I will soon forget, though it's thrilling in the moment to believe in a spyglass to the future. I can't know yet that she is right about one detail—I will have four children—just as I can't know yet the things she doesn't predict: that I will one day work in the glass tower of my dreams, that I will live in three other countries and travel to over one hundred and take Mom with me to six of them, that I will eventually own the company that makes the shoes I'm wearing, that I will follow through on a deal I made with a kind police officer who once helped me get home and I will help other kids climb out of poverty, that I will break down sobbing when Dad dies of cancer, that I won't buy Mom the dryer I promised, but instead I'll buy her a house of her own.

"Eeeasy all," the coxswain says, "Let it run."

We stop rowing, and the boat coasts along in the sunshine while our oars drag on the water beside us. The water is a steely color, small ripples throwing light. Since I've been in France, I've seen several Impressionist paintings of the Seine, pastel reflections of bucolic scenes that could well be the dwelling places of angels. Joan of Arc's first vision was of the archangel Michael, one of many premonitory visions that would help her lead the French army to victory. A martyr and heroine, she was nearly my age when she was burned at the stake, her ashes thrown into the Seine. I haven't painted in years, but for a moment, I feel the desire to paint the river as a woman with a hundred hands, keeping us all afloat.

"Ready all, row," the coxswain says. We dip our oars back into the water and quickly pick up speed, while the river changes colors in the light.

LATER

The mahout stands in the headlights, wearing a loin cloth. Deep in the forest, in Madhya Pradesh, India, you are very far from home. You have always dreamed of seeing a tiger, but yesterday, a driver ferried you around the park for hours searching for tigers with no luck. In Khajuraho the day before, a boy had approached you with an offer to be your translator, and you paid him handsomely to tell the driver that you doubted he would ever find a tiger by driving on the roads this way. "You are right," he said, as translated by the boy. "If you want to see a tiger, you have to see the elephant man."

Because tigers are easiest to spot at dawn, after they've finished hunting and are looking for a cool place to rest, you arrive at the mahout's encampment in the darkness of 4:00 a.m. Your driver leaves the Jeep headlights on so you can see, but you smell the elephants before you see them—an overpowering combination of musk and excrement that somehow invites you closer.

Because it's important you understand what the mahout tells you, you bring the boy from Khajuraho with you to translate what the mahout says. The boy is around twelve years old, ebullient and smart. "Here are the elephants," he says, and he leads you to them. Though you have seen elephants at zoos, you think the one that now stands beside you is much, much larger than a zoo elephant. "What if he steps on my feet?" you ask the boy, but the elephant has already reached for you, the thousands of muscles in his trunk moving in such a way as to precisely deliver the tip of it to your pocket, where he is now crinkling the plastic on the crackers you have stashed there in case you get hungry. "Here," you say, opening them, giving him some, as if you have a choice. He does not step on your feet. He appears to be smiling.

The mahout leads you to a rickety wooden ladder, which you climb up to mount the elephant. The seat on top is tiny in comparison to the breadth of the elephant's back, and it is angled so your legs stick straight out in front of you. The boy translates the mahout's instructions: "Tap with your right foot to go right. Tap with your left foot to go left. Tap both feet to go forward." What you will be tapping is the top of the elephant's head, which you do as gently as if it were a baby.

In the half-light, you move deeper into the forest, the mahout leading astride his own elephant, the boy following behind you on the smallest elephant in the herd. The flora is dense, dry, and shrubby, and you can already feel the heat burning off the night like a furnace suddenly turned on. You are swaying with the elephant's strides, telling him that he is good and that you will give him more crackers when you get back to the camp. "Shhh," says the mahout, and the boy translates what he says next: "We must be quiet to not scare off the tigers."

You pass a slender waterway, and the mahout starts speaking rapidly but softly, pointing. You wonder if he has, at last, found a tiger, but the boy does not know the name for what you see as your elephant catches up: a chital, thickly dotted with white spots. Your elephant sees the chital, too, but marches forward undeterred. You are beginning to think you might never see a tiger.

The world has brightened, and the heat has risen many degrees, when the mahout stops and gets off his elephant to point again, this time at fresh tiger tracks in the dirt. He speaks in a whisper, and the boy translates in a whisper: "We are close."

How close, you wonder, but then you see him—a shock of orange and black stripes partially hidden in the brush in a small stream: the Royal Bengal tiger. He is stretched out and languid, the heat settling around him like gold. You can hear him panting, his canines flashing like a promise, the delicate pink tip of his tongue belying the fierceness upon which you know his life depends. You tap both of your feet on your elephant's head to ask him to move closer, but your elephant instead backs up, an instinct upon which his life also depends. What you don't know is that in seven years, all the wild tigers of Panna will be killed by poachers. But for now, this wild tiger is alive, and you have met his eyes, and you feel as if you have just been told a secret—about the earth, about yourself—and you already know it is a secret you will never attempt to translate.

AFTERWORD

As I stood at my mailbox with the envelope in my hand, I hesitated to open it. What was inside would determine my future as a law student: my score on the Law School Admission Test. By then, I knew well how a life can perch on the wobbly unknown of a test score. What would have happened, I still sometimes wonder, if I hadn't done well on the high school admission test that opened the door to St. Francis? In one version of the story, I don't go to Yale but still end up where I am now, living a good life with my wife and four kids. But in another version of the story, I'm a failure in my own eyes, or even a criminal, hardened by the loss of my dreams. This is not an uncommon fate for those who grow up in poverty. For many, dreams don't come true, no matter how hard they work or how faithfully they believe in the American Dream that promises to swing open the Door of Opportunity if only they knock.

Though I worked hard for the success I have, I wonder if the same doors would have opened for me if I'd been Black, like most of the other kids in my neighborhood. It's always been an unfair system, but of all the promises I've made to myself over the years, of all the lists and notebooks I've kept, of all I've been taught in the highest institutions of education, the most important lesson I've learned is that every act of kindness, no matter how small, makes a difference.

At Yale, as I held my still unopened test scores, I wasn't thinking about any of that yet. Still a virgin to so many things—including to more sophisticated ways of thinking—I was single-minded: *succeed, succeed, succeed.* I hung onto the labels I'd achieved at Yale—*summa cum laude,* Phi Beta Kappa—as if they were trophies placed under a spotlight, gleaming reminders that I'd kept my promises to myself, starting with the one I'd made in the fourth grade: I would not be like my father. And now my A-grades and honor society were my rewards—proof that we can shape our lives, proof that every kind person who had ever helped me had invested wisely.

For a long time, I'd been surprised every time someone trusted me, maybe because when I was growing up, trust was a rare and precarious thing. When a police officer gave me bus money after my father left me stranded at the Toledo Museum of Art, he was trusting I'd use the money as he intended to find my way home. When the head janitor at my grade school gave me the task of running the floor buffer, he was betting I wouldn't run the machine through a wall. Whether it was the free ride to sleepaway camp, the keys to my high school, the keys to an expensive city tractor, the extra time Coach Gary spent with me, the statue Mrs. Noble across the street purchased from me even though I'm quite certain she hadn't woken up that day hoping for a slightly misshapen glass rendering of Mother Mary, the chance Father McMenamin took in inviting me to attend St. Francis, the trips to museums and films and festivals that Father Fisher shared with me, the hours Mr. Barnette spent guiding me at the Toledo Public Library, the array of jobs Carty helped me find, and so much more, every gift made it possible for me to be ripping open an envelope in a small enclave of the Yale Station Post Office.

At first, I didn't see my test score on the paper. All I saw was the 800, which I knew was the perfect score against which mine would be measured. I kept scanning for my number, turning the page over and back again, until finally I realized what I was looking at: I'd earned a perfect 800 on my LSAT. An overwhelming sense of gratitude rose up in me then, a resounding voice I can still hear: *Thank you for believing in me.*

Remarkably, all my siblings went on to find their own versions of education, fulfillment, and happiness. And though we've landed in five different states, all twelve of us get together with Mom in Toledo every Thanksgiving, most of us bringing families of our own (last year there were sixty-two of us). We still gather in a local park to play touch football, and our kids join us. We laugh as we remember our hotly contested kickball games that stretched into nighttime on Bronson Street. We tell our kids about the legendary Uncle Dick and Harold (they died before our children had a chance to know them and before any of us thought to fully express our gratitude for all they did for us)—Dick's unsung role as our secret Santa, Harold's indestructible joy, their loving commitment to our family—stringing together old stories like Christmas lights. Mom no longer cooks; at ninety-two, she now lets others cook for her. And though we're not an emotionally effusive family, one thing I learned while I was writing this book is that every one of us sees Mom as a hero. Several of my siblings have said the same thing: "Because of Mom, I didn't even know we were poor."

I don't make many rules for myself anymore, though I have kept my promises, including to never take a drink of alcohol. And there's a newer rule I try to honor every day: Do something kind for a stranger. Some days it's something small, like letting someone into my lane in traffic, and some days it's something sizable, like creating a scholarship for underserved kids in Toledo's low-income communities to attend St. Francis, the school that gave me a scholarship and changed my life. Most days, my promise falls somewhere in between.

I serve on the Board of Directors of the Boys and Girls Clubs of Boston, and I'm actively involved in fundraising, which is crucial when it comes to providing as much help to as many children as possible. But one of my most meaningful experiences with the organization happened on a smaller scale, with a single child, when I donated a little of my time. Early in my involvement with the Clubs, I'd come to observe an art class, and the assignment was to make a drawing for Halloween. I was paired up with a six-year-old girl from Mexico named Olivia. She wanted to draw a jack-o'-lantern, so I showed her how to make her circle more pumpkin-shaped and helped her add a stem. She beamed at the attention, smiling and looking into my eyes. When I asked her what kind of expression she wanted her jack-o'-lantern to have, she gave me a puzzled look. "I mean, how do you want your jack-o'-lantern to feel?" I asked. I gave her some examples, trying my best to look happy, angry, sad. She laughed as she mirrored me, and then she added her own expressions: scared and surprised. I wondered then how many times she'd been scared in her young life and about the sorts of things that surprised her. And as I wondered these things, she surprised *me*.

"Loved," she said. "I want my jack-o'-lantern to feel loved."

So we gave her jack-o'-lantern heart-shaped eyes and a toothy smile, and I silently wished the same for her.

ACKNOWLEDGMENTS

I owe a debt of gratitude to President Bill Clinton for lighting the spark that set this book in motion. His encouragement motivated me to do the hard work of getting my story on paper.

Without my mother, who, as these pages show, gave everything to her children, this book and my life as I know it likely wouldn't exist. To her I am eternally grateful. And to my siblings, who provided memories and insights while I was writing this book and who have all worked to keep our family together through the years, thank you.

One person spent three years helping me write this book: Rita Zoey Chin. The same story can be told in many different ways, and Zoey forced me to make the many decisions necessary to tell this story in the best way. From the first day I worked with her, she understood my goals and my story—thanks, in part, to her own childhood hardships, chronicled in her memoir, *Let The Tornado Come*. Without her, this book would not have happened. I offer my greatest gratitude to you, Zoey.

My deep appreciation goes to Anthony Ziccardi of Post Hill Press, not only for publishing my book, but also for believing in it from the start and giving freely of his energy and expertise. Thank you also to the amazing Post Hill Press team, especially my fabulous managing editor, Maddie Sturgeon; Jim Villaflores, who designed a beautiful cover; and D.J. Schuette, whose keen edits made this book better.

Thank you to my brilliant publicist, Carisa Hays, for her warmth, wisdom, and steadfast commitment to this book; and to my phenomenal marketing director, Nancy Sheppard, for her energy, enthusiasm, and ingenuity.

I have immense gratitude for the following people who went out of their way to help me usher this book into the world: Sanjiv Chopra, Deepak Chopra, Michael Whouley, Doug MacKinnon, Bryan Rafanelli, Maura Phelan, David Ambroz, Tom Greene, Keith Gilbert, Alice Finn, and Toby Faber.

Thank you to St. Francis de Sales High School, the Toledo Museum of Art, the University of Toledo Library, and the downtown Toledo Lucas County Public Library—and especially my favorite librarian, Don Barnette, may he rest in peace—for giving me space and inspiration to learn and grow.

To my high school crew, Mark Bevington, Joel Harrington, Barry Hudgin, Gary Morsches, and Gene Zmuda, thank you for taking a trip down memory lane with me. I'm honored to still be able to call you my close friends.

I am the luckiest to have been blessed with an extraordinarily kind and loving family. Thank you with all my heart to my four wonderful children, Addy, Isabelle, Tate, and Lulu—especially Isabelle, who came up with so many dazzling cover ideas—and to Barbara and Ted Alfond for their many expressions of support.

I reserve my greatest praise for my beloved wife, Jenny Seeman. You inspire me every day with your boundless generosity, talent, and commitment to our family. You were my first and best reader, and this book benefited immeasurably not only from your sharp insights and patience but also from the way you always put your whole heart into everything you do. Fortunately, you didn't seem to mind learning about some of the naughty things I did as a boy.